The Meaning of Blindness

Attitudes Toward Blindness and Blind People

Michael E. Monbeck

The
Meaning of Blindness

Attitudes Toward
Blindness and
Blind People

INDIANA UNIVERSITY
PRESS
Bloomington and London

Contents

For Diana,
a princess

Acknowledgments

In the course of writing this book and preparing it for publication, I had the good fortune of receiving many kinds of assistance from friends and colleagues. I would like, therefore, to express my gratitude to the following individuals: Ron O'Reilly of Goddard College for helping me in the planning stages; Mary Maie Richardson, Chief Librarian, Migel Memorial Library, American Foundation for the Blind, for her assistance in the research phase; Zofja Jastrzembska of the American Foundation for the Blind, William Matthews of Cornell University, Dr. John Romig Johnson, Jr., of General Theological Seminary, and Frances A. Koestler for their comments on and criticism of the completed manuscript and for encouraging me to submit it for publication.

I would especially like to thank M. Robert Barnett, Executive Director of the American Foundation for the Blind, Patricia Scherf Smith, Director of AFB's Information Department, and Mary Ellen Mulholland, AFB Publications Director, for taking a personal interest in this book and for arranging for the partial subsidization by AFB of its publication.

Most of all, I wish to acknowledge my indebtedness to my wife, without whom I could not have written this book and to whom I have therefore dedicated it.

NEW YORK CITY   MICHAEL E. MONBECK

Introduction

HAVING WORKED FOR THE American Foundation for the Blind for more than ten years,[1] I have encountered quite a number of different attitudes toward blindness and blind people. Among these are many that I myself had before learning more about the subject and before meeting and getting to know many blind people. Most of these attitudes are similar to those held toward other physical handicaps or toward people who vary in some way from the norm. Occasionally, however, some rather unexpected attitudes are met. For example, when I mention my place of employment to some individuals, they respond by saying, "How can you stand to work with blind people? That must really be creepy." Basically, this kind of response at first struck me as a perfectly natural curiosity about involvement with blind people, but the way in which it is phrased does seem to indicate a particularly affect-laden attitude toward blind people. It is almost as though they were saying that there must be something odd about anyone who is involved with blind people, that one in such work must have some morbid interest in blindness or has become hardened in some way to the fact of blindness.[2]

The question of attitudes, of course, arises in almost every phase of work with blind people and must be dealt with in the adjustment process of newly blinded individuals, in education, and in rehabilitation. It is a decided influence whenever blind people come into contact with sighted people, including not only members of the general public but also those in work for the blind. Workers for the blind, in other words, must be concerned both with the attitudes of society and with the attitudes that they themselves bring to their task and to their clients or students.

The first thing one notices about attitudes toward blindness and blind people is that although there have always been only a comparatively small number of blind persons (in the United States only a fraction of one percent of the total population), they attract more attention and have more agencies serving them than any other handicapped group, including those with handicaps that are more widespread and more disabling.[3] In the report of a recent investigation of attitudes toward the disabled, it is observed that ". . . blindness appears to have a unique position with respect to other kinds of physical disabilities. There is a personal relevance and immediacy to blindness that is much stronger than is true for other conditions." Deafness, for example, is a most serious handicap, but, "The sense of profound loss associated with blindness was rarely noted with deafness." [4] Indeed, despite the fact that various kinds of sensory deficits and physical handicaps have much in common,[5] it is reportedly very difficult to predict what an individual's attitude toward blindness will be from his attitudes toward other physical handicaps.[6] These experiences and observations, then, have led me to the present investigation of the origins of attitudes toward blindness and blind people.

Before proceeding, however, a few remarks on attitudes in general would perhaps be in order. We will consider the specific nature of attitudes in greater detail in the third chapter, but for the present we must try to set forth some definitions to guide our investigation until we reach that point. For our purposes, it would seem that the simple, "dictionary" definition of "attitude" is the most suitable: "manner, disposition, feeling, position, etc., with regard to a person or thing; tendency or orientation, esp. of the mind." [7] More complex definitions, for example those given by sociologists or psychologists, are

more scientifically precise and exclusive, but they have a tendency to place attitudes within the dimension of a single disci-
pline. That is, there is in such definitions an inherent bias toward viewing attitudes in only one way and limiting the possible origins of attitudes to one particular source. To utilize any
specialized definition of "attitude" at the beginning would,
therefore, tend to limit our investigation. Even though we will
at a later point reduce the sources of attitudes to only a few
basic ones, it is our intention to begin with a presentation of
the attitudes toward blindness and blind people that have been
reported in the literature, without regard to their origins. Once
this is accomplished we can then consider the explanations,
hypotheses, and theories regarding the origins of these attitudes.

Another factor involved in choosing this approach is the
extreme complexity of the subject: attitudes are anything but
simple, a fact clearly supported by the literature. Siller and his
associates classified attitudes toward disability into 17 components and warned specifically against attempting a one-sided
emphasis in explaining them.[8] In the matter of the variety of
attitudes, too, Lukoff and Whiteman conclude that ". . . public attitudes toward blindness do not comprise a homogeneous
entity . . ." and, they go on, "A second aspect of this differentiated view of blindness is the stress upon attitudinal components as contrasted with a stress upon a single overall attitude toward blindness. . . ."[9] Finally, even though it is commonly assumed that there is a single stereotype of the blind
person, an assumption often shared by the blind themselves,
studies nevertheless indicate that attitudes do vary widely.[10]

1 Attitudes Toward Blindness and Blind People

ONE OF THE MOST COMmon reactions of sighted people to even the most superficial contact with a blind person is a feeling of pity and sympathy, a feeling often expressed in highly sentimental terms.[1] Perhaps because pity is the socially accepted reaction not only to blind people but also to most other kinds of physically disabled people,[2] we find it as an underlying factor in most of the attitudes toward blindness recorded in the literature. Pity, also, is understandable as a spontaneous, empathic reaction of a normal, that is, nondisabled, person toward one who is handicapped. On the other hand, the pity lavished on blind people often is rather out of proportion to the *actual* limitations imposed on an individual by blindness. Unfortunately, the actual limitations, the real problems of being blind are generally not known or understood by the average person.[3] The facts about what it is like to live without sight are neglected in favor of many, very widespread misconceptions. As will be evident from the balance of our discussion, such misconceptions play a role in most attitudes toward blindness.

The fear of blindness, for example, is extremely strong in many individuals. It is not uncommon to hear such statements as "I would rather be dead than blind" or "It's worse than being dead."[4] Undoubtedly blindness is a serious handicap, but to consider it as the worst possible handicap or as one so overwhelming that no one could endure it is overstating the situation.[5] Naturally, anyone who does view blindness in this light will feel great pity toward blind people. Without denying the difficulties of being blind, however, blind people themselves do not consider it the worst possible disability. In a survey of attitudes toward blindness, the blind respondents frequently mentioned that they thought deafness, paralysis, double amputation, mental disorders, epilepsy, invalidism, and crippling conditions would be worse than blindness.[6]

Although one survey did indicate that extreme fear of blindness may not be as prevalent as it sometimes seems,[7] it is nevertheless encountered, not only in its direct, overt forms, but through its indirect manifestations. Specifically, a very common phenomenon is the avoidance by sighted people of any contact with blind people.[8] One observer has noted that the sighted often ". . . behave as though blindness is a contagious disease that will jump from one person to another like microbes or germs." To some, blindness is so frightful that they cannot even discuss it; sometimes "they even shun the use of the word 'blind,' and instead they use words such as 'sightless,' 'non-seeing,' and 'visually handicapped.' "[9]

The desire to avoid contact with blind people often becomes a general rejection of them in many areas of daily life. For example, in a survey which asked educators to rank categories of exceptional children according to those they would most prefer to teach and those they most understood, it was found that "The great majority of the respondents . . . not only placed the visually handicapped child on the rejection end of the continuum, but also signified that they knew very little about these children in comparison to those having other types of disability."[10] In another survey, 197 elementary and secondary school principals were queried about whether they would accept certain kinds of disabled individuals as student-teachers and as full-time teachers in their schools. Of the five categories of disability listed on the questionnaire, those in the category "blind" were the most often rejected, although those in the "deafness" category were rejected nearly as often.[11]

Another area of misconceptions about blindness includes a number of ideas and feelings about the specific nature of blindness itself and its effect on the blind person as an individual. These common beliefs also contribute their share to the avoidance and rejection of blind people by the sighted.

It is believed, for example, that because of the overwhelming seriousness of the loss of sight, blind people must be utterly miserable and unhappy and their lives quite tragic.[12] It is thought that they are always somber, that to be in their company would be depressing, and, therefore, that it is better to avoid close contact with them. Further, a display of humor or playfulness by a blind person is seldom accepted at face value, but is, rather, interpreted as an example of his extreme fortitude or an attempt to hide his sorrow.[13] As Cutsforth has so pointedly put it, this idea is so fixed in the mind of the sighted public that "it is something from which the blind are utterly unable to escape." [14] To deny that any blind person did not occasionally feel unhappy about his loss or depressed or even miserable would be absurd. It is an entirely different matter, however, to characterize blind people as a group as being melancholic or as constantly longing for the return of their sight. Few, if any, other groups of handicapped people are viewed in this way. Chevigny and Braverman note, "One of the remarkable facts connected with this entire situation is that the pain man believes must be caused by the absence of sight he does not also feel to be caused by the absence of hearing." [15]

This misconception is continually being reinforced in people's minds when blind people are described metaphorically as living in a "world of darkness." [16] "The implication," writes Cutsforth, "is that the blind who so desperately desire to see are confronted, by their inability, with a world of experiential darkness filled with all the horrors of gloom, fear, loneliness, and whatever else the timorous seeing experience in the dark." [17] The emotional appeal of this idea has allowed it to creep even into the writings of otherwise careful and thoughtful authors. R. S. French, the principal of a school for the blind and the author of a major study of the social and educational implications of blindness, begins his treatment of the problem of inactivity by calling it "the worst curse of the world of darkness. . . ." [18] Bernard Seeman, in his very objective and informative book on the sense of sight, reinforces the notion that a world without sight is like a cavern or an abyss that is inhabitable only by primitive forms of life.

> What is sight to us? Admittedly, life is possible without sight. There are creatures that have evolved in lightless caverns and in the depths of the ocean abysses, certain fish and lizards that need no sight because theirs is a world of darkness. They must depend upon other senses, as do the blind among us.[19]

Agencies for the blind, supposedly one of the primary forces in changing the sighted public's attitudes toward blindness, have not escaped the attractions of the analogy of light-darkness, sight-blindness. There are "lighthouses" that guide those on their "dark" pilgrimages. Those with "darkened" lives are saved from sitting in "darkness." Publications about blindness or blind people have such titles as *Lookout, Illuminator, Light, Beacon, Insight,* and *Outlook.*[20]

Despite the obviously great appeal of the "world of darkness" as an image, it is a false idea. On the physical level, darkness can only exist by contrast with light. Tests have demonstrated that in an environment totally without light, even those with normal vision will, after "dark adaptation," experience a neutral gray sensation or one of lightlessness, but not of darkness.[21] Furthermore, this conclusion is supported by the reports of the experience of blindness made by blind persons.[22] On the psychological level, the idea of a "world of darkness" is also inaccurate. According to blind people, being blind just does not include the ramifications of gloom and fear. As one blind individual puts it, "It is fortunate that it is not blackness. That, it seems to me, would be depressing." [23] Another writes that ". . . blind people themselves, to the best of my knowledge, are unaware [of any sense] of 'walking in darkness.' " [24]

Another common belief about the effect of blindness on the individual is that he becomes nearly helpless. The burden of tragedy and misery is thought to be so overwhelming that the ordinary individual must inevitably be completely paralyzed and incapacitated.[25] The sighted are, as one observer has written, "thoroughly convinced that life in perpetual darkness is impossible." [26] A less extreme version of this belief holds that while blind people may perhaps be able to do some things for themselves, they are for the most part rather useless. It is admitted, for example, that a blind person might be able to learn to dress himself and to get around his own house, but not that he could hold a job, head a family, or in any way lead a "normal" life.[27]

It hardly seems necessary to refute such beliefs, for clearly there is nothing in the loss of sight itself that prevents an individual from doing anything but seeing. Through the public education efforts of hundreds of agencies for the blind, the usefulness and self-sufficiency of all but a very small minority of blind people (usually those with other handicapping conditions) has been more than adequately demonstrated. In spite of these efforts, however, and in spite of the thousands of blind people throughout the country who are living "normal," productive lives, these beliefs do persist. Lukoff and Whiteman found that 80 percent of the blind people in their survey agreed that "sighted people are generally surprised if a blind person can do something." [28]

One of the reasons for the persistence of this belief is the highly visible presence of blind beggars on the streets of most large American cities.[29] Although the number of blind beggars is rather small, it is the image of the beggar that is most commonly called to mind by the words "blind man." It is not surprising that the blind beggar is so conspicuous, for it is his business to be noticed and to be instantly recognized as useless, unable to work, and worthy only of pity. The ordinary, average blind person on his way to work or out shopping is only rarely noticed and almost never remembered.

While agencies for the blind and blind persons themselves continue to campaign vigorously for the recognition of the abilities of the blind, another of their activities tends to cloud the issue. Certain highly protective legislation, legislation which gives the impression of assuming that blind persons are helpless, is regularly suggested by agencies and supported by blind people.[30] Whatever the merits of such legislation or the real problems it is intended to solve, its existence to many does confirm the idea that blind people need special assistance and protection or otherwise they would not be able to function at all.

So entrenched has the idea of the uselessness of blind people become that it is believed that there is really no point in giving them a chance. The prediction of failure, therefore, becomes self-fulfilling, for without the opportunities to demonstrate their abilities blind people do seem to be useless. "Believed incapable of socially useful activity, they are assigned to a privileged sanctuary or role at the boundaries of the game." [31] Not only are they denied the benefits of activity for its own sake, but also the social and personal rewards of competition and achievement.[32] Hector Chevigny has described this situation as follows:

> Toward the blind the world presents a face it turns to no other group on earth. Everyone else must struggle for his survival. The blind, however, need not want. Society, profoundly convinced of the utter helplessness of the man who has lost his sight, stands ever ready to help him. ... .[33]

Such exclusion, though a great injustice in itself, also contains a serious pitfall for the individual blind person.

Salvation for one who loses his sight consists of avoidance of a vicious cycle in which the world's fixed notion of the helplessness of the blind creates that helplessness, and their consequent exhibition of helplessness confirms the world in its fixed notion.[34]

In other words, there is a constant danger that the blind person will succumb to being treated as helpless by believing that he is indeed helpless and by slowly becoming helpless. This erosion of self-confidence and of the ability to function leads some blind people to count themselves out, to exclude themselves from socially useful activity. In one survey of blind people, for example, nearly 10 percent did not believe that, if they were employed in a competitive job, their work should be as good as that of a sighted person; 36 percent of those surveyed thought that away from their own house they should have a sighted guide.[35]

To the blind person who believes in his own abilities and usefulness, the problem of not truly being given a chance to do things for himself is particularly galling and offensive when it is claimed that such treatment is "for his own good." [36] Here there is not only the assumption that he is helpless and useless but that it is better for him not to experience the failure that must inevitably result from his attempts to do things. There is also the implication that the blind person should know better than to think that he can accomplish anything useful; that, therefore, he is not really able to look out for himself; and that without others to look out for him he would be easily led astray or deceived in some way. These feelings could perhaps be characterized by the following: "I have no confidence in your ability to function and, therefore, I will protect you from your own false assumption that you can function." Although this is a hypothetical statement, the suggestion of one very concerned sighted person that blind people "be taken off the streets of New York, traffic being so hazardous" was seriously made.[37]

We come now to three beliefs that seem curiously out of place in the twentieth century, beliefs that are based less on misconceptions or the overemphasis of various aspects of being blind than on superstitious feelings and ideas. First, there is the notion that blindness is a punishment for some past sin, a sign of some moral failing.[38] The unfortunate conclusion drawn from this idea is that the blind person is, in some unspecified way, responsible for his own blindness. The reaction of many individuals when a tragedy has overtaken someone is to ask, perhaps only half-consciously, "What did he do to deserve that?" Apparently this is a somewhat normal reaction, for the idea of punishment and responsibility preys on the minds of many otherwise well-adjusted blind persons. Chevigny recounts his experience with this feeling:

> I was fighting as hard as I could fight against the notion that I had been marked out in some way, against the suspicion that it might be a personal visitation after all. I was beating down the inevitable question *but why should it happen to me?* and trying to keep it from rising again with the answer that surely God had meant nothing personal by it.[39]

The belief that blindness is a punishment has its most tragic results in blind children when their parents become convinced that they are being punished for their sins through the child.[40] Finally, this belief is reinforced whenever blindness is called an "affliction," for as Father Carroll has pointed out, "the word of its nature, and by its derivation, suggests punishment." [41]

That blindness is a punishment for sexual transgressions is borne out by a second anachronistic belief, the association of blindness with venereal disease. This association is due less to the fact that gonorrhea is a cause of both congenital and adventitious blindness than to the suspicion that it might be the cause. Indeed, the fear that others think venereal disease is the cause of blindness produces much of the guilt, shame, and disgrace reportedly felt by many blind people and by some of the parents of blind children, because these reactions are produced even when venereal disease is decidedly not the cause of blindness.[42] The avoidance reaction of those who ". . . behave as though blindness is a contagious disease . . ." (noted above) may very well be grounded in the suspicion that venereal disease was the cause of an individual's blindness.[43]

Finally, from both of these two beliefs comes the more general idea that a blind person carries some sort of social stigma. It is felt that for some unknown reason he has been singled out and marked with the "sign" of blindness. He is different, atypical. The blind person himself may feel that he is an outcast, that he and his problems are misunderstood by sighted people.[44] The implication of stigma is that the individual is not only abnormal, but that he is physically, psychologically, morally, and emotionally inferior. The carrier of the stigma is to be avoided, not primarily because he is inferior but because the stigma itself makes those who associate with him inferior too.[45] In other words, there is a "fear of social stigma resulting from association with such a person," a fear also commonly found in reactions to conditions such as hunchback and cerebral palsy.[46] The idea that blindness is a stigmatizing condition is evident in the reported cases of blind persons being disallowed as blood donors, regardless of the cause of their blindness, or of the great social pressure exerted in discouraging marriage between blind and sighted persons.[47]

From all the various attitudes toward blindness and blind people discussed so far, there emerges one idea that is common to them all: that blindness has the same effect on all individuals and, therefore, regardless of what differences there may be among blind people, their blindness makes them more like each other than they would be if they were sighted. In other words, people who are blind are thought to form a homogeneous group rather than a set of individuals who share only the fact of blindness.[48] To be thought of and treated only as a member of the group causes many blind people to lose their sense of individual identity.[49] In one survey of blind people, 23 percent seemingly agreed that they do indeed belong primarily with other blind people for they expressed a preference for their company rather than the sighted.[50] The identification of the blind as a group also leads quite easily to the idea that that group is by nature separate and distinct from the general population. The goal of integrating blind people and sighted people in most areas of life, therefore, is likely to be rejected in favor of a pattern of segregated facilities and programs.[51] (It must be pointed out that although the treatment of blind persons does in some respects resemble that of ethnic and racial minority groups, segregation in the sense used here has a somewhat different meaning than it would in that context. The difference in such attitudes will be discussed in a later chapter.) A final example of the devaluation of the individuality of blind people is the belief of many sighted people that they may pry into the private affairs of a blind person or ask him any questions they wish.[52]

Another observation that can be made about the attitudes discussed so far is that in each of them there is an overemphasis on loss, not just the loss of sight but the belief in other nonsensory losses. If we examine, for example, the seven factors suggested by Siller and his associates as characteristics of attitudes toward blindness, we find that four seem to emphasize loss: "rejection of intimacy" (loss of qualities that attract others), "generalized rejection" (loss of most positive personality traits), "inferred emotional consequences" (a loss of independence and psychological normality), and "imputed functional limitations" (loss of the ability to function in general). A fifth factor, "authoritarian virtuousness," implies that blind people have gained desirable traits, while the two remaining factors, "interaction strain" and "distressed identification," are concerned with problems in the nondisabled person when in contact with a disabled person.[53] The emphasis on loss is evident, too, in discussions of the implications of blindness which dwell on all the things that blind people cannot see: paintings, cathedrals, sunsets, the faces of loved ones, etc.[54]

The attitudes and beliefs considered thus far in our discussion constitute what might be called a "primary" set of ideas about blindness and blind people. These are attitudes which are usually elicited by simple questions or that are spontaneously offered when the topic of conversation touches on blindness or when a blind person is in some way encountered. The beliefs are expressed under similar circumstances, often as an explanation for an attitude or in support of some observation about blindness or blind people. Having discussed these, we can now consider a "secondary" set of attitudes and beliefs which, though they stem from ideas in the primary group, can be characterized as being "thoughtful." That is, the ideas to be discussed in the following pages usually only emerge when a sighted person reflects on blindness and its effect on the individual. This is not to say that such attitudes are any fairer to blind people as individuals or that the beliefs are closer to the facts of blindness, for they are not. Because of the considered, reflective, and thoughtful nature of these ideas, it will be seen that they are for the most part concerned with the personality and other personal qualities of the individual blind person.

As noted earlier in this chapter, no one denies the fact that blind people have problems. Judi Sorter, a young blind woman, writes, "I have problems, but so do you. I have learned to deal with my problems, as well as I can, just as everyone should. I want you to understand that I'm not so different, really." [55] It might be added that blind people organize their lives and deal with their problems in ways that, as Miss Sorter implies, are very similar to those of sighted people. The commonly held view, however, is somewhat different. Typical comments, gathered in a survey of attitudes, include, ". . . they view the world differently. Because they can't see, they think differently . . ." and "How do they think? How can they organize things?" [56] Blind people are thought to be more contemplative and inner-directed than average people, to be given to abnormal ways of thinking and behaving, and therefore, to be to some degree maladjusted.[57] In other words, it is thought that blindness adversely affects the way a person thinks and, in turn, the way he behaves.

In what specific ways are blind people believed to be maladjusted? There seems to be quite a number of assumed problems of varying degrees of severity. Some feel that blind people are unfriendly and aloof, or self-pitying, or hypersensitive and prone to anger. Though minor enough as occasional moods, these problems, when thought of as general characteristics, would indicate a belief that blindness causes psychological warping of the individual.[58] That such negative emotions are occasionally to be encountered in blind people is not to be denied and, indeed, one blind man writes that because blind people must constantly cope with the negative attitudes of others, ". . . perhaps we are to be pardoned if we are slow to react positively when meeting a person free from . . . prejudices." [59] On the other hand, there is no reason to assume that because a person is blind he is psychologically warped.[60]

Another belief, one mentioned in passing earlier in this chapter, is that blind people are consumed with envy of sighted people, that they can do nothing but yearn for the return of their sight.[61] This belief does have some basis in fact, at least insofar as it has been established that those who lose their sight in later life often do have such a preoccupation.[62] Even among these individuals, however, the problem does not seem to be of quite the proportion implied by the term "consuming." Among those blinded earlier in life, there is no evidence that this feeling is any more than a passing phenomenon, a normal and short-lived problem of the adjustment to blindness. For the congenitally blind individual, sight, of course, is unknown, has no meaning, and, therefore, is not an object of envy.

Beyond these moderate problems, blind people are thought to suffer from great physical and intellectual lassitude.[63] This condition is considered a natural consequence of the above-mentioned beliefs in the helplessness of blind people and the great misery thought to characterize their lives. E. E. Allen, a leading educator of the blind in the early part of the present century, is quoted as saying, "Blindness borrows trouble; its victims are overcome by self-pity. Too frequently there follows a sinking of the fires of life, a flagging of energy resulting in idleness, morbidity, and ennui. Any people so oppressed in mind tend to deteriorate in every way—even morally." [64] We have, then, a very interesting progression of ideas: the assumption of helplessness and misery leads to the assumption of idleness and boredom which, in turn, leads to a belief in a tendency to immorality. As French so succinctly puts it, "On the whole, the changed mental and physical states due to blindness may lead to a lowered moral tone." Sexual immorality and the "solitary vice" (masturbation) are, of course, what they are getting at. Their point is not that blindness causes immorality, but that ". . . it is simply a correlate with blindness and as much a physiological defect as the blindness itself." [65] The implication that a blind person is doubly defective, however, remains despite the attempted disclaimer. Moral defect is also held responsible for the alleged cruelty and viciousness of some blind people,[66] for, because they cannot see the victims of their inhumanity, they are not constrained in their actions.

As has been noted, the "primary" set of attitudes toward blindness emphasizes various kinds and degrees of loss. The "secondary" set emphasizes the effects of these losses on the individual blind person, effects that are largely negative or in some way undesirable. There are, in addition, a number of misconceptions about the effects of blindness on the individual that are believed to be quite positive, namely, that the loss of sight brings with it certain compensations. These ideas are probably grounded in the belief (noted earlier) that blindness is overwhelmingly catastrophic and, therefore, that there must certainly be some kind of compensation or existence without sight would be absolutely impossible. Two kinds of compensation are thought to follow almost automatically with the onset of blindness, sensory compensation and certain advantageous personal qualities or orientations.

The sensory compensations that are believed to accrue to blind persons are a superacuity of the remaining senses or the sudden acquisition of some additional sense, for example, "facial vision" or "eyes" in the skin.[67] Because of these supposed changes in the senses, it is thought that blind people can detect certain kinds of obstacles in their path without touching them, that they can tell colors or the denominations of paper currency through the sense of touch, or that the acuity of their hearing is increased and its range extended.[68] These compensatory mechanisms do not exist. "Blindness does not lead to any refinement of the senses of touch, hearing, or smell, but to a greater keenness in the interpretation of the information furnished by these senses." [69] It might be noted also, however, that certain common activities of blind people could, when not closely observed, give rise to this belief in sensory compensation. Two examples should suffice. Blind people often arrange their paper currency in their purse or wallet so that each denomination is folded in a certain way and placed in a certain position. Although the bills are originally separated with the aid of some sighted person, the later correct identification of the bills by the blind person could easily confound the passing observer and lead him to conclude that the blind person could "feel" the different kinds of bills. In developing his ability to travel independently, the blind person learns to concentrate on very faint auditory clues to his immediate environment. These clues include echoes from nearby objects and structures, echoes which anyone can detect if he listens closely, but which if never noticed would lead to the belief that there is some sixth sense that enables blind people to avoid obstacles.

Blindness is also thought to be compensated by certain special gifts and desirable personal characteristics, qualities that the individual would probably not have if he had not lost his sight. Blind people, for example, are thought generally to have a spiritual temperament, to be religious, and to like music and to be gifted at it.[70] Blindness is sometimes thought to be a blessing in some ways and to improve a person's character by bringing him "probably closer to the really important things of life." [71] The negative beliefs mentioned earlier notwithstanding, blind people are considered by some to be very friendly, cheerful, docile, and tractable, and to "create a wholesome and courageous atmosphere about them." [72] Lukoff and Whiteman note the following examples of "positive" responses to blind people: "Blind people have a greater ability to understand other people's suffering"; "Blind people tend to be more understanding than sighted people"; "The blind tend to get a more accurate first impression of others than most people do." [73]

Throughout this chapter we have largely dealt with more or less negative attitudes toward blindness and blind people. These attitudes would seem to be the most destructive to the acceptance and self-realization of blind people and, consequently, they very properly receive the greatest attention in the literature. The idea that certain compensatory mechanisms accompany blindness, while seemingly a positive kind of belief, nevertheless, is also negative in its effect, for it is a generalization (quite as inaccurate as the patently negative generalizations) and it tends to set blind people apart from "normal" people, to emphasize differences without regard to the larger number of characteristics shared by blind and non-blind people. It must sorely try the patience of blind people to be always explaining the simple fact of blindness. We can detect a slight note of such annoyance in the following statement by young Judi Sorter:

> I am totally blind. That means I cannot see light, people, shadows, or objects. It *does not* mean that I cannot hear, or conversely, that

I have extraordinary hearing; that I am terribly stupid, or extremely bright; completely helpless, or totally independent. It means that I cannot see. That my eyes do not work.[74]

It is difficult to characterize the attitudes toward blindness and blind people that have been discussed in this chapter. Their division into "negative" and "positive" attitudes or into misconceptions and superstitions does not lend itself to useful conclusions. As Blank puts it, "Society is strongly ambivalent toward the blind, about whom the seeing have contradictory and paradoxical beliefs. . . . The blind are both saints and sinners, pariahs and prophets." [75] The use of such words as saint, sinner, pariah, and prophet, however, does point up the emotionality of attitudes toward blind people. Much of the literature on attitudes is concerned with improving the attitudes of the public and it is often suggested that more rational and informed opinions could be promoted through de-emotionalizing the old attitudes.[76] For example, the idea of sensory compensation was exhaustively investigated by scientists from about the turn of the century to the 1920's. The results, showing that there was no verifiable basis for this idea, have greatly strengthened the public education efforts of agencies over the last 50 years. Has it helped? Not really. Even 20 years ago it was observed, "For some . . . this left the manner of functioning by the blind an even more mysterious thing than it was before. Seemingly the only contribution has been negative." [77] In other words, there appears to be some heretofore undervalued irrational element in attitudes toward blindness and blind people, a feeling-tone that persists in spite of rational arguments and demonstrated facts. The mysteriousness of functioning by blind people, just noted, is one example of this. Father Carroll notes that some "set blind persons apart in some magic supersensory area." [78] Beyond the idea of sensory compensation, other similar attitudes have been noted: blind people are sometimes thought to have magical powers for heal-

ing, luck, psychic influence, or foresight (prophecy). They
are sometimes thought to be in a state closely related to that
of the dead, one which, of course, is fraught with mystery and
powerful emotional associations. Or, they are believed to dwell
in a rich, inner world of imagination, also a mysterious realm
to most people.[79] In short, blind people have a somewhat be-
witching or spellbinding effect on the average person; they are,
in the original sense of the word, fascinating. Schauer had described three different types of reactions which seem to involve
this fascinating aspect of blind people:

> 1. A very primitive attitude of "blind," unfeeling curiosity
> devoid of restraint, as can be seen in children and mental defec-
> tives.
> 2. An attitude of fear to look at the strange sight because it
> is "not right" to look, as it might hurt the person looked at, re-
> sulting in avoidance.
> 3. An attitude to feel one with the blind person; to lose one's
> identity; to become about blind oneself [sic], out of uncritical
> empathy, resulting in overindulgence.[80]

Perhaps it is this idea, that blind people are mysterious
and that blindness has certain magical or "secret" aspects, that
forms the cornerstone of all the other attitudes toward blindness. In other words, the ideas, feelings, and beliefs discussed
in this chapter might, for example, be a result of rationalization (a conscious attempt to explain away irrational reactions
or perceptions) or perhaps projection (a psychological process
in which material from the unconscious is seemingly encountered in other persons) with mythology supplying the imaginal
potency necessary to sustain and renew such a constellation
of impressions. Before we can address ourselves to this hypothesis, however, we must look into a number of other theories regarding the origins of attitudes. First, in chapter two, we
will consider the possibility that attitudes are transmitted to
us from the past through literature and fairy tales. Following

that, in chapter three, we will investigate the social and psychological dynamics of the ways in which people perceive and react to other people. Most of the speculation about the origins of attitudes toward blindness and blind people fall within these two general frames of reference. Once we have determined the explanatory power of these two approaches, we will, in chapter four, consider the symbolic significance of blindness for mankind in general and the way in which this meaning influences the individual's perception of and attitude toward actual physical blindness and real blind persons.

2 Attitudes Toward Blindness
and Blind People in the Past

IT IS GENERALLY AGREED that attitudes are, in one way or another, "acquired through the principles of learning."[1] One source of attitudes, therefore, would clearly lie in our cultural heritage, in the attitudes of both our recent and more distant ancestors which are transmitted to us as part of the general process of socialization. Several observers in the field of work for the blind have looked specifically to this area both for sources of present-day attitudes and for factors that tend to reinforce those attitudes. Lukoff and Whiteman, for example, write:

> Many observers have identified a series of stereotypes that have been associated with blindness. Some of this traces back to ancient folklore; many of these stereotypes are also found in the literature of the western world, including many of the great literary classics.[2]

M. Robert Barnett, in a speech given at the 1970 convention of the National Federation of the Blind, said, ". . . many present-day attitudes toward the blind had their origin in the literature of ancient times, or in mythological tales, or in biblical literature, both the Old Testament and the New Testament."[3] Lowenfeld, Imamura, and Twersky have also expressed similar ideas.[4]

Evidence of interest in blindness and in blind people can be found in almost every historical period and in every culture.

The earliest representation of blind people is apparently the blind harpers portrayed in tomb carvings at Sakkara, Egypt, which date from the IIIrd Dynasty (c.2900 B.C.). In the New World, blind people are portrayed in Chimu pottery made in Peru about A.D. 600.[5] Although the number of blind people has never been large, as was noted in the introductory chapter, blindness was somewhat more common in the ancient world than it is today, at least as it is in the United States and Western Europe. In the Near East, the center of the ancient world, blindness is thought to have been the major type of disability from the earliest times to well into the modern era. The Ebers papyrus, an Egyptian medical "textbook" dating from the XVIIIth Dynasty (c. 1500 B.C.), has an entire chapter devoted to eye diseases.[6] Herodotus, traveling in Egypt in the fifth century B.C., reports that there were physicians that specialized in diseases of the eye.[7] Hippocrates, Celsus, Dioscorides, and Galen, to mention only the most prominent of ancient physicians, all devoted much of their writings to blinding diseases.[8] Finally, as will be seen in the balance of this chapter, blind people are portrayed throughout the religious, traditional, and artistic literature of the world.

Before beginning our discussion of particular attitudes toward blindness and blind people in the past, we can note that the general treatment (to be distinguished from portrayal) of blind people in the Western world falls into three historical phases: treatment as liabilities, as wards, and as members of society.[9] On the other hand, as we have seen in the preceding chapter, present-day attitudes certainly point to the fact that blind people are cast in all three roles today and that the third phase is an ideal toward which only a small shift has been effected in very recent times. By the same token, most students of the depiction of blindness and blind people in the past agree that there were no historical periods in which blind people were uniformly portrayed as either liabilities, wards, or members of society, but that all of these, plus many other social

roles, do emerge.[10] The point is that while the treatment of
blind people has historically changed somewhat, beliefs about
blindness and blind people have shown very little significant
alteration over the last several thousand years.

To illustrate this last point, it is well known that, in primitive or economically marginal societies, blind infants were
usually not permitted to survive. This practice was, of course,
not limited to blindness but was a routine response to mal-
formed or otherwise visibly imperfect infants around the
world.[11] In ancient Greece, infanticide was provided for in
both the law codes of Lycurgus of Sparta and of Solon of
Athens. Plato and Aristotle gave ethical approval to the practice.[12] Clearly, it was assumed that a blind infant would always
be a liability and that such a liability could not be tolerated.
With greater prosperity, most societies stop the practice of
infanticide, but continue to consider blind people as liabilities;
the choice is merely made to tolerate the liability. Aged blind
people in such primitive societies are often treated well (for
example, in the Five Tribes of the Upper Mississippi and Mis-
souri rivers and the Wogeo of New Guinea). They are considered liabilities, but, in recognition of their having made
their contribution before losing their sight, an effort is made
to care for them. In other societies, aged blind people are
treated with scorn and are neglected (the Ainu of Japan, in
the Marquesas, and the Crow Indians of the Platte and Yellow-
stone rivers).[13]

Another point of agreement about blind people in the
past is that they have always been of interest to writers, seemingly out of proportion to their numbers. One observer, writing in 1912, claims, "Blindness allows of more artistic treatment than other afflictions, and is the one most frequently selected for portrayal."[14] Twersky, author of one of the best
studies of blindness in literature, declares that the interest in
blind people "in itself is significant, indicating that they have

been found especially interesting or curious, stimulating to the imagination and the emotions." [15]

In the following pages, we will take, in turn, each of the attitudes and beliefs discussed in the first chapter and explore its antecedents in literature, historical records, mythology, and folklore. By combining a number of those attitudes and beliefs, we have selected 15 basic ideas for this survey. They are that blind people, because of their blindness, are:

1. Deserving of pity and sympathy.
2. Miserable.
3. In a world of darkness.
4. Helpless.
5. Fools.
6. Useless.
7. Beggars.
8. Able to function.
9. Compensated for their lack of sight.
10. Being punished for some past sin.
11. To be feared, avoided, and rejected.
12. Maladjusted.
13. Immoral and evil.
14. Better than sighted people (idealized).
15. Mysterious.

It will be noted that items eight and 14 were not discussed separately in the first chapter. The idea that blind people are not helpless and useless has been included to show that the negative beliefs regarding the abilities of blind people were not universal in the past and that the modern attempt to integrate blind people into sighted society is not without some historical precedence. The idea that blind people are better than sighted people has been included for the simple reason that the tendency to extreme idealization, though not evident in a pure form today, was extremely popular in the past and does shed some light on several modern attitudes and beliefs.

Although the following 15 surveys are by no means exhaustive, an effort has been made to represent as wide a range of material as possible in each of them. Both primary and secondary sources have been utilized throughout.

1. Pity and Sympathy

The idea that blind people are particularly deserving of pity and sympathy is, in its earliest manifestations, always connected with religious feelings and beliefs. Showing pity toward blind people was one of the marks of being religiously devout. For example, Job, in his reflections on his past conduct, says, "I was eyes to the blind and feet to the lame . . ." (Job 29 : 15).[16] As Best has observed, pity was historically about the most that blind people could expect.[17] It was, nevertheless, an improvement over the kind of attitude that condoned the infanticide noted earlier. The Buddha taught that mercy should be extended to the weak and deformed.[18] The reputation of Jesus, in his own time, for mercy and pity especially for blind people is shown in the Gospels. On several occasions, blind men upon encountering Jesus specifically ask for his pity (Matthew 9 : 27–29 and 20 : 30–34, Mark 8 : 22–25). Blind people are also given special consideration in the Koran and are mentioned several different times.[19]

Because of the Christian ideals of charity and pity, ideals which were so important in the appeal of the early church to the poor, oppressed, and enslaved multitudes of the Roman Empire, blind people came to be considered the special wards of the church.[20] Beginning as early as the fourth century, innumerable hospices and cloisters were established for the relief of blind people and other unfortunates. St. Basil set up the earliest "haven" at Caesarea in Cappadocia. Others were founded by the Hermit of St. Lymnaeus in Syria (fifth century), by St. Bertrand, Bishop of Le Mans, in northwest France (seventh century), by William the Conqueror at four different sites in France (11th century), and by Duke Welf VII at Memmingen, Bavaria (1178). St. Louis of France placed an already existing institution under his royal protection in 1260.[21] With the spread of Protestantism, much of the charity formerly provided through the church was replaced by secular intervention, for example, in the Poor Law of Queen Elizabeth (1601).[22]

A most outstanding example of unselfish kindness to a blind person is that of Dr. Samuel Johnson toward one Anna Williams. Boswell says:

> Though Johnson's circumstances were at this time far from being easy, his humane and charitable disposition was constantly exerting itself. Mrs. [used alternatively with Miss, a custom of the times, for she was never married] Anna Williams, daughter of a very ingenious Welsh physician, and a woman of more than ordinary talents and literature, having come to London in hopes of being cured of a cataract in both her eyes, which afterwards ended in total blindness, was kindly received as a constant visitor at his house while Mrs. Johnson lived; and after her [Mrs. Johnson's] death, having come under his roof in order to have an operation upon her eyes performed with more comfort to her than in lodgings, she had an apartment from him during the rest of her life, at all times when he had a house.[23]

Johnson, as is well known from Boswell's *Life,* was an extremely devout Christian and his treatment of Miss Williams is certainly a testament to the sincerity of his beliefs. Boswell too, for that matter, was similarly Christian in his portrayal of Miss Williams. In 74 references to her in his biography, only five contain any mention of her blindness and it is clear that his perception of her was one of a person, not of a "blind person." On the other hand, Denis Diderot, the eighteenth-century French philosopher and encyclopedist, attempts to write dispassionately about blind people, but the result often reveals that his true attitude was one of extreme pity.[24]

2. Misery

The belief that blind people are incomparably miserable and that their disability produces a sense of utter hopelessness can easily be shown to have been quite widespread in the past by simply noting that blindness and blind people have very seldom been treated humorously. In classical literature, such humor is rare ". . . though there is much humor in classical literature, and though there were sightless buffoons in nearby Egypt and probably also in Greece itself as well as Italy." [25] There is a bawdy tale in the medieval *Les Cent Nouvelles Nouvelles* involving the blinding of a monk that is told quite humorously,[26] and a Spanish folktale involving an amusing encounter between a blind man and a bull.[27] In modern literature, Theodore Dreiser includes a comical beggar in his *My Brother Paul*.[28] Seemingly, serious visual handicaps are not considered a joking matter, although less serious eye problems are often portrayed quite humorously. Seeing double, having a squint, or having only one eye are motifs treated with amusement in folk literature.[29] The myopic cartoon character Mr. Magoo is a good modern example.

Past depictions of blind people as being miserable, on the other hand, can be found in abundance. The Greeks considered blindness the worst of misfortunes, one which could easily overwhelm an individual.[30] The idea that blindness is worse than death, one of the common themes in past depictions, is expressed by the chorus in Sophocles' *Oedipus the King*, ". . . for thou wert better dead than living and blind." [31] In ancient Jewish literature, similar sentiments are expressed. In a story in the Apocrypha, Tobit is asked if all is well with him and he replies:

> How can anything be well with me now? I am a blind man; I cannot see the light of heaven, but lie in darkness like the dead who cannot see the light. Though still alive, I am as good as dead. . . .
>
> (Tobit 5 : 9)

Blindness was commonly among the misfortunes (along with madness) included in Sinaitic and Arboth-Moabite curses; it was considered the worst of infirmities (more so than deafness,

dumbness, and lameness) throughout the Bible, Talmud, and
Midrash where it is often said, "The blind man is as one
dead." [32] In the New Testament, this traditional attitude was
given support, for example, when Jesus read a passage from
Isaiah in which blind people are grouped with those especially
deserving of release from their misfortunes (Luke 4 : 17–19).

The lack of humor in the depiction of blind people in
classical and Biblical literature may be connected with this
equating of blindness with death; in other words, it may be a
part of the taboo against mocking the dead.[33] Teiresias casti-
gates Oedipus for having taunted him with his blindness.[34] In
Leviticus (19 : 14), it is written, "You shall not . . . put an
obstruction in the way of the blind," and, similarly, in Deuteronomy (27 : 18), "A curse upon him who misdirects a blind
man." To cause the blindness of another, as in the case of
Odysseus putting out the single eye of Polyphemus, the Cyclops, brings a curse down upon the evildoer. Odysseus, it will
be remembered, was doubly cursed by Poseidon, the father of
Polyphemus, for not only did he blind the giant but during his
escape he mocked him for being blind.[35]

In modern times, we have Diderot writing ". . . certainly death to [a blind person] is a much less disagreeable
affair" than for the sighted.[36] Schiller, in his *William Tell*
(1805), has the son of Henry of the Halden say of his father's
blinding at the hands of a tyrant, "To die—is nothing—nothing! but to live,/ And not to see—is misery indeed!" [37] Charlotte Brontë, in her portrayal of Edward Rochester, the heroine's beloved in *Jane Eyre* (1847), makes several references
to the great misery of one who loses his sight. For example:

> Entering the room very softly, I had a view of him before he
> discovered my presence. It was mournful, indeed, to witness the
> subjugation of that vigorous spirit to a corporeal infirmity. He sat
> in his chair,—still, but not at rest: expectant evidently; the lines of
> habitual sadness marking his strong features.[38]

It is interesting to note, however, that in the scene in which
Jane is being told that a great personal misfortune has befallen
Edward, his ex-butler says, " '. . . he is alive; but many think
he had better be dead. . . . He is stone-blind,' he said at last.
'Yes—he is stone-blind—is Mr. Edward.' I had dreaded worse.
I had dreaded he was mad." [39] This certainly indicates a slight
shift in the assessment of blindness as compared to other misfortunes. Unfortunately, except for a folk story involving a
starving man who lets himself be blinded in return for food
(blindness *rather* than death),[40] this new perspective is only
rarely encountered until very recently.

Gwynplaine, the facially deformed protagonist of Victor
Hugo's *The Man Who Laughs,* and Dea, his blind companion,
are both characterized as being exceedingly miserable:

> The isolation of Dea was funereal, she saw nothing; that of
> Gwynplaine sinister, he saw all things. . . . They were beyond
> the pale of hope, and had reached the depth of possible calamity;
> they had sunk into it, both of them. An observer who had watched
> [performing in a side show morality play] would have felt his
> reverie melt into immeasurable pity. What must they not have
> suffered! [41]

Levy, in his study *Blindness and the Blind* (1872), calls
blindness "one of the greatest evils to which the human race is
liable" and "so heavy a calamity." Later on he asks, "What
can be done to remedy the exceedingly heavy sufferings that
now press so grievously upon the greater number of blind fe-
males?" pointing to the fact that being a woman in that era
merely compounded the misery of being blind.[42]

In the fiction of the recent past, misery is often the most
outstanding quality of blind characters. Pew, the villainous
blind ex-pirate in Stevenson's *Treasure Island,* at one point
cries out, "Oh, shiver my soul . . . if I had eyes!" [43] Kipling,
in his *The Light That Failed,* has blind Dick Heldar swearing
at his best friend ". . . because he was alive, and all the world

because it was alive and could see, while he, Dick, was dead in the death of the blind, who, at best, are only burdens upon their associates." The final line of the book, expressing Kipling's idea of a "happy" solution to blindness, is "His luck held to the last, even to the crowning mercy of a kindly bullet through his head." [44] In *The End of the Tether* (1903) by Joseph Conrad, blind Captain Whalley drowns, but as Twersky says, ". . . he really wants to die anyway, because he is blind." Twersky also cites war-blinded Maurice, the subject of D. H. Lawrence's *The Blind Man,* as an example of an individual who is portrayed as being depressed and wretched because of his blindness.[45] Finally, George S. Wilson wrote in 1906 that blind people are portrayed in general as "outwardly happy, yet in many cases, inwardly wretched. Frequently they are subject to moods which often become melancholy." [46]

3. Darkness

As was seen in our discussion in the first chapter, a large measure of the misery that is thought to accompany blindness is derived from the belief that blind people live in a "world of darkness." This association of blindness with the fearful idea of darkness is a common one throughout literature. The meaning of darkness, which will be discussed more fully in a later chapter, is vividly presented in Ecclesiastes (11 : 7–8):

> The light of day is sweet, and pleasant to the eye is the sight of the sun; if a man lives for many years, he should rejoice in all of them. But let him remember that the days of darkness will be many. Everything that is to come will be emptiness.

In Isaiah (29 : 18 and 35 : 5), we read of the blind and their world of impenetrable darkness. Blind Oedipus says, "O thou horror of darkness that enfoldest me, visitant unspeakable, resistless, sped by a wind too fair!" [47] The image of darkness is used by Milton throughout his "Samson Agonistes" (1671) to express the effect of blindness on the Israelite hero.

Samson: O dark, dark, dark, amid the blaze of noon,
         Irrecoverably dark, total eclipse
         Without all hope of day!

.   .   .   .

Samson: Then had I not been thus exil'd from light;
         As in the land of darkness yet in light. . . .

.   .   .   .

Chorus: Which shall I first bewail,
         Thy Bondage or lost sight,
         Prison within Prison
         Inseparably dark? [48]

It is interesting to note that, in spite of this use of the image of darkness, Milton describes the experiential quality of his own blindness in quite other terms.

> . . . on the gradual failure of my powers of vision, colours proportionally dim and faint seemed to rush out with a degree of vehemence and a kind of noise. These have now faded into uniform blackness, such as ensues on the extinction of a candle; or blankness, only varied and intermingled with dimmish grey. The constant darkness, however, in which I live day and night, inclines more to a whitish than a blackish tinge. . . .[49]

Sebastian Guillié, an early teacher of the blind in France, alludes to blind people as ". . . condemned to live in profound darkness. . . ." [50] Dickens, who visited the Perkins Institution and Massachusetts Asylum for the Blind in 1842 and saw the famed deaf-blind Laura Bridgman, quotes from a report by Samuel Gridley Howe about the young girl: "But what a situation was hers! The darkness and the silence of the tomb were around her. . . ." [51]

Darkness figures heavily in Hugo's descriptions of Dea and Gwynplaine, two characters discussed briefly above: "From the depth of her incurable darkness, from behind the black wall called blindness, she flung her rays." "Their existences were shadowed by two different kinds of darkness, taken from the two formidable sides of night. Dea had that shadow

in her, Gwynplaine had it on him." "Dea had a veil over her,
the night. . . ." [52] Finally, in 1917, Frank Spindler interpreted a painting of a just blinded soldier kneeling on a
World War I battlefield:

> The picture excites a throb of pity in the hardest heart. The artist
> has well depicted the greatest misfortune imaginable. In an instant
> to be plunged into life-long darkness—never to see the glorious
> day again.[53]

4. Helplessness

The idea that blind people are helpless, that they can do
very little for themselves, was expressed by Sophocles in *Oedipus the King*. Oedipus, in searching for the murderer of
Laius, wants to accuse Teiresias of the deed, but, as he says,

> Know that thou seemest to me e'en to have helped in plotting
> the deed, and to have done it, short of slaying with thy hands.
> Hadst thou eyesight, I would have said that the doing, also, of this
> thing was thine alone.[54]

And when Teiresias warns Oedipus of his downfall, Oedipus
replies, "Night, endless night hath thee in her deeping, so that
thou canst never hurt me. . . ." This powerlessness that
Oedipus attributes to the blind seer is also assumed to affect
him after he becomes blind, for he says, "Ah, friend, thou still
art steadfast in thy tendance of me, thou still has patience to
care for the blind man." [55]

In the Bible, blind people are often characterized as
groping, stumbling, or unable to find their way. In Deuteronomy (28 : 28–29) we read:

> May the Lord strike you with madness, blindness, and bewilder-
> ment; so that you will grope about in broad daylight, just as a
> blind man gropes in darkness, and you will fail to find your way.

Similarly, in Isaiah (59 : 10):

We grope like blind men along a wall,
feeling our way like blind men without eyes;
we stumble at noon as if it were twilight,
like dead men in the ghostly underworld.

In the Apocrypha, too, "Tobit rose to his feet and came stumbling out through the courtyard door" (Tobit 11 : 10). After Tobit's sight is miraculously restored, it is written, "At the sight of him passing through the city in full vigor and walking without a guide, the people of Nineveh were astonished" (11 : 16). In the New Testament, we find the parable "Can one blind man be a guide to another? Will they not both fall into the ditch?" (Luke 6 : 39; cf. Matthew 15 : 13–14), a motif which is also present in folk literature.[56]

Eli, who counseled the young Samuel in how to respond to a direct call from God (1 Samuel 3 : 1–9), is pictured as old and blind when a great battle between the Hebrews and the Philistines occurs. After the battle, a messenger comes to report the outcome to Eli. He is found sitting by a gate, "staring with sightless eyes," and, when he is told that his two sons have been killed and the Ark of God captured, he falls from his seat and fatally breaks his neck (1 Samuel 4 : 15–18). The implication is that part of his inability to cope with these tragedies, in addition to his extreme age, is that his blindness has weakened his will and resistance.

Milton was perhaps considering his usefulness as a blind man when he wrote his famous 16th sonnet. It begins:

When I consider how my light is spent,
Ere half my days, in this dark world and wide,
And that one Talent which is death to hide,
Lodg'd with me useless. . . .

Despite the often quoted last line—"They also serve who only stand and wait."—Milton was, of course, quite active after losing his sight and wrote much of his greatest poetry while blind.

Guillié discusses the prevalence in the early nineteenth century of the belief that blind people are helpless and useless.[57] Brontë describes the blind Edward Rochester as a "caged eagle," who can only move gropingly. He feels that he is not even capable of talking Jane out of wanting to marry him because he is nothing but "a sightless block." A large measure of Jane's love for Edward, in fact, is that he is helpless and she can finally be of service to him (before his blindness, Rochester was quite self-sufficient).[58] Hugo's Dea is pictured as always being passive and defenseless.[59] Levy notes that ". . . excessive mental and bodily toil are more injurious to the blind than to the sighted." [60] Kipling's Dick Heldar is shown as quite helpless. On one occasion he admits that he can't dress himself because he is blind. When his friend, Torpenhow, asks if there is anything he can do for him, Dick replies, "No! Leave me alone. How often must I remind you that I'm blind." Later in the story it is said that if Dick asserts himself, "Then the meanest menial can see that he is blind and, therefore, of no consequence." Dick's friends also believe that he is "out of the race,—down,—*gastados,* expended, finished, done for." [61] Maeterlinck, in his 1890 play *The Blind,* uses blind people as symbols of mankind's ignorance and shows them confused, groping, lost, and utterly helpless.[62] There is, finally, a motif in folk literature in which blind men are trying to kill a pig, or some other farm animal, but end up accidentally hurting each other.[63]

5. Fools

The idea that blind people are helpless has often been equated with the idea that they are fools, that they can easily be tricked, manipulated, or exploited by others in ways usually detrimental to themselves. For example, in Jewish mythology Cain was slain by a blind archer, Lamech, whose aim was directed by his son who mistook Cain for a wild animal (God, it is said, had put a horn on Cain's forehead to mark him; thus

Lamech's son's mistaken identification).[64] This same motif is also encountered in Norse mythology. The evil giant Loki discovers that mistletoe will kill the otherwise indestructible Balder. He fashions an arrow from mistletoe and when all of Balder's friends are playfully attacking him to see the weapons glance off of his body, Loki fools Höd (also Hodur, Hoder, Hödhr), the blind brother of Balder, into shooting the deadly arrow which kills Balder.[65]

Returning to Biblical times, there is the incident in Genesis (27 : 1–27) when Jacob fools his old and blind father, Isaac, into blessing him rather than his elder brother, Esau. It is interesting to note that part of the ruse involves Isaac's desire for a particularly spicy food which he asks Esau to prepare for him as a kind of inducement to his giving the blessing. Jacob, of course, prepares the tidbit first (an angel was delaying Esau) and fools Isaac. Isaac's predilection for a spicy dish is explained in an extra-Biblical Jewish legend that says that because he cannot see his food, he cannot enjoy it with full relish and therefore his appetite must be tempted with special dishes.[66] Kipling writes that, for his blind hero, ". . . tobacco would not taste in the darkness." [67] This belief is still encountered today, but only rarely, and would seem to be a part of the larger belief that the helplessness of blind people even extends to their use of their other senses. Getting back to Jacob and Isaac, it is also written that the fooling of Isaac was necessary and beneficial. Because of his spiritual blindness, Isaac was not able to discern the wickedness of Esau and, if he had had unimpaired eyesight, he would not have blessed Jacob.[68]

Another Jewish legend recounts the story of Moses being pursued by the Pharaoh's troops after he has escaped from the executioner's block. The soldiers are struck blind and Moses easily eludes them.[69] In 2 Kings (6 : 18), an enemy army attacks Elisha, but when God strikes them blind, Elisha fools them and leads them away. An army of Amorites were, according to yet another Jewish legend, struck blind by the angel Gethel (or Ingethel). Each soldier mistook his neighbor for an adversary and they slew one another.[70] In Muslim folklore, old and blind Abu Quhafa is worried about the welfare of his grandchildren. To ease his mind, his family places stones in a money chest and fools him into believing it is gold.[71]

The medieval German folktale, first given literary form by Hans Sach in his *Der Eulenspiegel mit den Blinden* (1553), shows numerous incidents of a trickster making fools of three blind men.[72] It was also around this time that the words *hoodwink* and *blindfold* came to be synonymous. In his book *Phrase and Word Origins,* Alfred H. Holt gives the following under the entry for *hoodwink:*

> As long ago as 1560, this meant "to blindfold," as in the game of "blindmanbluf" or "hoodman blind"—both very old names for our Blind Man's Bluff. From "blindfold," the transition to "cheat, deceive" was easy.[73]

Perhaps the most famous incident in literature of a blind man being deceived, and also one of the most unbelievable, is to be found in Shakespeare's *King Lear.* The Earl of Gloucester, after being blinded by Regan and the Duke of Cornwall, is taken in hand by his son Edgar, who is in disguise, and led through an elaborate deception that is seemingly intended to let Gloucester come to terms with his grief and suicidal impulses without hurting himself.

Glou. When shall we come to the top of that same hill?
Edg.   You do climb up it now. Look how we labor.
Glou. Methinks the ground is even.
Edg.   Horrible steep.
       Hark, do you hear the sea?
Glou.   No, truly.
Edg.   Why, then, your other sense grow imperfect
       By your eyes' anguish.
Glou.   So may it be, indeed.

> Methinks thy voice is alter'd; and thou speak'st
> In better phrase and matter that thou didst.
> Edg.   You're much deceived. In nothing am I changed
> But in my garments.

He is then told that he is standing at the edge of a precipice. He falls forward and Edgar, by changing his voice, convinces Gloucester that he (Edgar) is another person at the bottom of the cliff and that miraculously Gloucester has survived the fall. In all this, Gloucester is completely taken in.[74]

Milton's Samson says, ". . . I dark in light expos'd/To daily fraud, contempt, abuse and wrong,/Within doors, or without, still as a fool,/In power of others, never in my own. . . ." To Dalila, he says, "How wouldst thou use me now, blind, and thereby/Deceivable, in most things as a child/Helpless, thence easily contemn'd, and scorned,/and last neglected?" [75]

Valentin Haüy first became interested in the possibility of educating blind children (he was the founder of the first school for the blind—in Paris, 1784) after seeing an example of the cruel exploitation of a group of blind people in a Parisian café. He writes:

> Eight or ten poor blind persons, with spectacles on their noses, placed along a desk with sustained [i.e., provided] instruments of music, where they executed a discordant symphony, seemed to give delight to the audience.[76]

Another elaborate deception perpetrated on a blind person is to be found in *The Cricket on the Hearth* by Dickens. In this instance, Caleb, the father of the blind girl Bertha, succeeds for some time in convincing her that their miserable existence is really quite splendid.[77] In *The Light That Failed,* we read, "Dick had been sent to bed,—blind men are ever under the orders of those who can see. . . ." [78]

The deception of blind people in folk literature is quite

common. There is a North American Indian tale of a blind
hunter whose aim is guided by his mother or wife who then
deceives him into thinking that he has missed the target and
eats the game herself. Another motif (found in Europe,
Africa, and among the North American Indians) involves a
group of blind men being duped into fighting with each other.
In the South Pacific, there are tales involving thefts from
blind people and the deception of blind guards. In Indonesia,
there is a fable of a dwarf-deer pasting the other animals' eyes
shut and then causing a panic when it pretends that hunters are
coming. And there is a European story about a physician who
bandages his patient's eyes and then proceeds to steal her be-
longings.[79]

6. Uselessness

The idea that blind people are useless is, of course, closely
related to the idea of helplessness, discussed above. In that discussion, however, the emphasis was on the personal quality of
self-sufficiency, while in this section our examples will be
drawn from the area of social worth and usefulness to others.
For example, Twersky cites Oedipus, as he is represented in
Oedipus at Colonus, as one who is not only helpless (Antigone
is still leading him), but useless as well. In the 20 years that
have elapsed since his self-blinding, Oedipus has done nothing
but wander around and ". . . seems to have no contact at all
with the world, save through Antigone." [80] French, in his
study, points out that the supposed social uselessness of blind
people was the determining factor in their being destroyed as
infants.[81]

In the Bible, blind people are among those disqualified
from the priesthood (Leviticus 21 : 16–23). Jesus is quoted
in Luke (14 : 13–14) as saying, ". . . but when you give a
party, ask the poor, the crippled, the lame, and the blind; and
so find happiness. For they have no means of repaying

you. . . ." Among the early Muslims, an individual could be disqualified from appointment as caliph if he were blind.[82]

Milton's despairing Samson says:

> Now blind, disheartn'd, sham'd, dishonour'd, quell'd,
> To what can I be useful, wherein serve
> My Nation, and the work from Heav'n impos'd,
> But to sit idle on the household hearth,
> A burdensome drone. . . .[83]

And Samson's father, Manoa, agrees: "Better at home lie bed-rid, not only idle,/Inglorious, unimploy'd, with age out-worn." [84] Haüy, writing in 1786, says that before his efforts proved the educability of blind people, only a few very exceptional individuals were able on their own to do anything use-ful, ". . . whilst the rest of their brethren appeared consigned by destiny to idleness, languor, and dependence, without a pos-sibility of escaping from a durance so horrible in its nature, and so permanent in its continuance." [85] In more recent litera-ture, W. S. Gilbert's *Pygmalion and Galatea* (1871) shows Pygmalion completely reduced following the onset of blind-ness.[86] In *The Professor's Daughter* (1899), Anna Farquhar has her blind heroine humbling her pride and allowing her ad-mirer to burden himself with a blind wife, one who will be of little use to him.[87]

7. Beggars

"Blindness and begging," writes Levy, "appear so inti-mately connected with each other that in the minds of many persons the existence of the former seems to indicate the pres-ence of the latter." [88] During most of recorded history, in fact, the role of beggar has been the one most frequently assigned to blind people.[89] In the ancient world, in both Egyptian and Hebrew cultures, most blind people were beggars.[90] Teiresias, in *Oedipus the King,* warns Oedipus: ". . . a blind man, he who now hath sight, a beggar, who now is rich, he shall make his way to a strange land, feeling the ground before him with his staff." [91] Of the several blind men encountered by Jesus, all appear to be beggars (Mark 10 : 46–52, John 9 : 6–8).

Michael Anagnos, head of the Perkins Institution for the Blind in Massachusetts, is quoted as saying in 1882, "From Bartimaeus [one of the blind beggars encountered by Jesus] to Lesueur—the first pupil of Haüy—the blind were left to procure a precarious subsistence begging at the entrance of temples, in the churchyards, or by the wayside." [92] Gowman reports that in medieval Europe, "The blind were given sole rights for the sale of various amulets and the chanting of certain prayers. As beggars, they were stationed at cathedral doors and many wore distinctive dress symbolizing their blindness." [93] There were even guild-like brotherhoods of blind beggars in thirteenth-century France which were "sanctioned by religious approval, legal privilege, and the customs of feudalism . . ." and which had the effect of "gathering about mendicancy a cloak of religious acceptance and pointing up the idleness to which the blind had long been condemned." Sixteenth-century England experienced a "golden era" of beggary such that ". . . swarms of beggars reached such proportions that a shift in attitudes took place, investing the blind beggar with an aura of evil and rascality." [94] Similarly, on the Continent, the eighteenth century was nicknamed "the century of beggars." Beggars were seemingly getting out of hand, but the reaction of the public was not to alleviate their poverty. Instead, they were packed into asylums and hidden from public view.[95] It is not surprising then that when blind people were seen in public it was still as a beggar.[96] Even in modern times, when in most of the United States mendicancy has been legally banned, Best reports that, in 1934, 14 states specifically exempted blind people from the law.[97] And, of course, in most areas such laws are not enforced against blind people anyway.

To survey the literary and traditional representation of blind beggars would be impossible to do adequately and, it would seem, such a survey is not really necessary. We will, therefore, cite only two examples, both of which have some added interest. The first is Gervais in *The Blind Man of Argenteuil,* a sixteenth-century Norman tale. Although Gervais is a beggar, and therefore one usually counted among the lowest of the low, his identification of a murderer by the sound of his voice is accepted in court and the culprit is convicted. A confession, however, is thrown in just in case the blind beggar's identification of the villain is thought to be too unbelievable.[98] Secondly, in *The Redemption of David Corson,* a nineteenth-century novel by Charles Frederick Goss, we find what seems today a most startling transformation. A roving quack doctor, a kind of modern-day buccaneer who is noted for his self-sufficiency and ability, is blinded in a fist fight. Later in the story, it is discovered that, as a result of his having lost his sight, he is now a poor, squalid beggar with a tin cup.[99]

8. Usefulness

As noted in the introductory section of this chapter, the following survey is included to show that throughout recorded history blind people have been portrayed as able to function and to be useful. It is strange that these portrayals and historical facts have from the earliest times to the present existed side by side with those outlined in the last few sections. In the following section, we will explore some of the beliefs about how blind people are able to function, and so this discussion will only include examples of "uncompensated" blindness; in other words, people who, except for their blindness, are quite ordinarily endowed and without special powers.

Herodotus tells of Anysis, a blind Egyptian king who, though driven off his throne by invaders, returned after their departure and resumed the government.[100] The Cyclops Polyphemus, after being blinded by Odysseus, is deceived and the hero and his men escape. When he is taunted, however, he twice very nearly destroys Odysseus' ship by throwing huge rocks at it.[101] Historically, in the ancient world, blind people were occasionally employed as prostitutes, rowers, seers, operators of hand-mills, and scholars specializing in the memorization of law codes or sacred texts.[102] There is a story in the Talmud of one Rabbi Sheisheth who, though blind, continues his studies, reasons well, and gets about by himself with a cane.[103] One of the individuals included by Plutarch in his *Lives* is a Corinthian general named Timoleon. Although he resigned as sole commander of the army when his sight failed, Timoleon was often called by the legislature to decide important or difficult questions. His rulings were always accepted and after his death he was given many honors.[104]

In the sixteenth century, it is told, there lived a blind girl named Joan West, who maintained herself by knitting stockings. She was later martyred.[105] In *The Blind Beggar's Daughter of Bednall-Green* (Elizabethan?), the blind beggar is really blind, but is only disguised as a beggar. In actuality he is the son of the rebel lord, Simon de Montfort, blinded in battle and disguised to escape his enemies.[106]

In the Far East, the fate of blind people was much the same as in the West, but for a small minority at least, there has been a formal social and occupational niche. In Japan, since the ninth century, blind people have been given a virtual monopoly in massaging, shampooing, chanting, and treating illnesses with counter-irritants.[107] Notable blind Japanese include Hokiichi Hanawa (1746–1821), a great historian, literary authority, and intellectual; and Michio Miyagi, a composer who died in 1956.[108] In China, many blind people were soothsayers and, in India, transmitters of oral tradition.[109] A blind Chinese Buddhist priest, Ganjin, made many important contributions to Japanese culture in the eighth century.[110]

Boswell, as was noted above, rarely refers to the fact that Dr. Johnson's friend, Anna Williams, was blind. One of those references, however, is quite interesting and a fine illustration of the topic of this section.

We went to [Dr. Johnson's] house for tea. Mrs. Williams made it with sufficient dexterity, notwithstanding her blindness, though her manner of satisfying herself that the cups were full enough appeared to me a little awkward; for I fancied she put her finger down a certain way, till she felt the tea touch it.

In a footnote, he adds the following:

I have since had reason to think that I was mistaken; for I have been informed by a lady, who was long intimate with her, and likely to be a more accurate observer of such matters, that she had acquired such a niceness of touch, as to know, by the feeling on the outside of the cup, how near it was to being full.[111]

The establishment of the first school for the blind by Haüy was a confirmation of the belief that with proper education blind people could be socially useful. He had found a few individuals who were self-educated and, learning from them he felt confident that most blind people were educable.[112] Guillié, who succeeded Haüy as head of the Paris school, writes, ". . . no longer, as formerly, will you be repulsed by your fellow-creatures, and considered as a degraded species. . . ."[113] In a sense, this school, as Gowman notes, marks "the beginning of the asylum period in its secular form."[114] In other words, the school in Paris and the other schools for the blind established soon thereafter throughout Europe, in Britain, and in the United States were supported partly because they were an expression of Christian charity, but also because they took at least a few blind children out of public view and off the streets. That few people really believed that the schools had any practical use is clearly seen in the experiences of those establishing schools for the blind in the Midwest in the mid-nineteenth century. As Best reports:

. . . there was, despite ardent assurance to the contrary, not a little doubt expressed in certain quarters as to the feasibility of the movement. . . . More than one school experienced something other than an easy task in overcoming the objections to their work and in dissipating the conceptions regarding them. . . . In other instances, uncertainty was expressed as to whether the blind could actually be instructed. . . .[115]

In the 1860's, Levy made an informal survey of organized services for blind people throughout the world. He found that, except for Western Europe, America, and a few other countries, almost nothing was being done to help blind people and in most countries there were not even estimates of the number of blind people who lived there.[116] Finally, Graham and Clark observe that when Sir Arthur Pearson began his work in rehabilitating the war-blind after World War I, ". . . the concept that, given help, these men could lead near-normal lives was a startling, new idea." [117]

Returning to literary depictions of blind people as other than totally useless, we find Elizabeth Maclure, an active, self-assured blind character in Sir Walter Scott's *Old Mortality* (1816); Margaret, the blind grandmother of the title character in Charles Lamb's *Rosamund Gray,* who spins, sews, and manages her household; and the blind, semi-paralyzed beekeeping widow, Old Alice, in Scott's *The Bride of Lammermoor*.[118] Despite the general sentimentality of his depiction of Dea, Hugo does occasionally show that she does care for herself and moves about her limited environment with ease and grace.[119] Bardo, in George Eliot's *Romola* (1863), is a scholar who, though his sight fails him late in life, continues with his work.[120] Wolf Larsen, in Jack London's *The Sea Wolf* (1904), is still feared after he becomes blind. At one point, it is written ". . . he stepped on deck and started forward, walking with a swiftness and confidence which surprised me." It is quickly added, however, "And still there was that hint of the feebleness of the blind in his walk." [121] Wilson, in his 1906 survey of blind characters in recent fiction, finds many authors who, though recognizing the serious problems faced by blind persons, show that ". . . this obstacle is not regarded as insurmountable." [122] H. Rider Haggard created an outstanding example of a quite believable blind character who is neither helpless nor overly idealized (a theme to be discussed shortly). He is Olaf, the hero of *The Wanderer's Necklace* (1914). A Northman, or Viking, in the service of Irene, Empress of Constantinople, Olaf falls from favor and is blinded by Irene. Soon after losing his sight, he says:

> I had sunk to misery's lowest deep, who did not know that even then its tide was turning, who could not dream of all the blessed years that lay before me, the years of love and of such peaceful joy as even the blind may win.[123]

He is rescued from prison and shows himself still to be competent, resourceful, and courageous. He is made governor of Lesbos, leads his army in defeating an invading Muslim army, and travels disguised as a harper through hostile Muslim Egypt to rescue his beloved.

Finally, in folk literature there is a motif in which a blind man carries a lame man and thus, through their combined efforts, they are able to get along. This motif is found in tales from Europe, Ireland, the Philippines, and the Navaho Indians.[124]

9. Compensation

The idea that blind people could be useful, in spite of their blindness, was often explained by reference to the idea that loss of sight was compensated by other gifts. Among the Ancient Greeks such compensations were believed to be from the gods, and, therefore, of a special divine nature.[125] Traditionally, Homer's gift of poetry was considered to be of divine origin and, if the blind poets in the works attributed to the allegedly blind Homer are any indication, he himself considered it so. There is a seemingly autobiographical passage in the Homeric "Hymn to Delian Apollo" and, of course, Demodocus, the blind bard in *The Odyssey,* is described as having received his gift of song directly from the Muse. Both poets are shown as being greatly honored.[126] Teiresias' gift of prophecy was from the gods,[127] as was his magic staff which guided his steps.[128] Similar beliefs were held in Korea, Turkey, and Russia.[129]

In the seventeenth and eighteenth centuries, a number of philosophers became interested in the abilities, real and potential, of blind people.[130] This speculation, which will be reviewed in a later chapter, was relatively free of ideas involving compensation, although there was some hint that the general "psychology" of blind people was different as a result of their blindness. From this time on, therefore, the belief in compensatory abilities, for the most part, lost its divine connotations and was expressed within a framework known as the "vicariate of the senses." Guillié, for example, in his essay on the instruction of the blind (1819), writes that blind people have added powers of concentration, analysis, memory, imagination, and judgment and a great thirst for knowledge. "They have no need," he goes on, "like us, to guard themselves against the illusions of the senses, since they cannot be seduced by the senses. . . . How much more certain must their judgment be, in this respect, than ours." [131]

Writing in 1872, Levy observes:

> It has often been remarked that the loss of one sense is made up for by increased power in the remaining senses. This is an adage frequently repeated and popularly believed, but its truth has been more or less denied by those immediately occupied in matters connected with the blind.[132]

Two pages later, however, Levy, who was blind himself, writes that he can "perceive objects through the skin of my face," a power he calls "Facial Perception." Jack London in *The Sea Wolf* (1904), mentions this "fabled sixth sense," but seems to reject it in favor of a more plausible explanation. In this instance, blind Wolf Larsen is aware of a shadow crossing his face in bright sunshine and London writes, ". . . the only conclusion I could reach was that the sensitive skin recognized the difference of temperature between shadow and sunshine." [133] Nevertheless, in later depictions, compensatory powers continue to appear. In *La Symphonie Pastorale* (1925), André Gide creates the blind character Gertrude, who, before being educated, is portrayed as an outright idiot and, after, concentrates better, learns more, and thinks more clearly than most sighted people.[134] Langworthy, in her 1930 survey of the representation of blindness in literature, remarks that the abilities of blind people are both over-estimated and under-estimated. She also notes that some authors include many curious and strange devices that they think would be of practical use to blind people; most are very amusing and quite useless (for example, colored strings running from a blind person's chair to objects around the room or furniture that moves on rails hidden in the floor).[135] Barker and his colleagues note that there have long been newspaper accounts pointing to accomplishments of blind people and implying some extraordinary power or skill on their part. Unfortunately, their feats are usually quite ordinary: employment, graduating from school, traveling without a guide, doing simple carpentry, etc.[136] In folk literature, not counting such common motifs as blind prophets and seers, we find a North American Indian tale of a blind trickster figure who finds his way by asking trees their names and determining where he is from their answers; and an English tale in which a blind man is shown as very bold: he crosses a narrow bridge which his guide is afraid to attempt.[137]

10. Sin and Punishment

Hector Chevigny, in his autobiographical *My Eyes Have a Cold Nose,* writes:

> With variations in circumstances and time . . . , every man who suffers a calamity of the objectively tragic quality of blindness

finds himself, like Job, surrounded by people who, in effect, debate with him on the nature of the evil which has befallen him.[138]

In ancient times, as well as in the present, it was often decided that the individual must have done something to deserve his loss of sight, that his blindness was a punishment for some past sin of his. In India, for example, organized work for the blind has been resisted in many areas because "blindness is considered punishment for particularly bad sins committed during an earlier existence." [139]

There are numerous examples of blindness inflicted as a punishment in classical literature. In several instances, the gods take pity on their victim and, as noted in the preceding section, grant him certain powers in compensation for his blindness. The most famous instance of this is in the case of Teiresias. Blindness without compensation was thought to be one of the most extreme kinds of divine punishment. Oedipus, though his blindness is self-inflicted, was nevertheless being punished by the gods in a manner commensurate with the heinous crimes of patricide and incest.[140] In *Oedipus the King,* the chorus asks:

> Man of dread deeds, how couldst thou
> in such wise quench thy vision?
> What more than human power urged thee?

And Oedipus answers:

> Apollo, friends, Apollo was he that
> brought these woes to pass, these my
> sore, sore woes. . . .[141]

In *Oedipus at Colonus,* it is clear that his many years of blindness had in no way been compensated—he is broken and utterly wretched.[142] Plutarch, when his story reaches the point when Timoleon goes blind, is careful to point out that failing eyesight was hereditary in Timoleon's family and "Not that he had done anything himself which might occasion this defect, or was deprived of his sight by any outrage of fortune. . . ." [143] Seemingly, blindness implied punishment for sin unless otherwise explained.

In ancient Hebrew culture, as represented in the Old Testament and in extra-Biblical legends, blindness was decidedly associated with the power of God. Whether a story involves a clear-cut case of punishment for sins or not, divine intervention was usually assumed and the possibility of unrealized sins thus sustained. For example, in Genesis (19 : 9–11), the Sodomites who come to arrest Lot are blinded by two angels and Lot escapes. It is difficult to say whether they were blinded because they were Sodomites, and therefore evil, or because they were an obstruction to Lot's escape from the city. In Exodus (4 : 12), God makes this point very clear when he says to Moses, ". . . Who makes [man] clear-sighted or blind? Is it not I, the Lord?" In Leviticus (26 : 14–16), when Moses is given the injunction to obey the commandments, he is warned that dimming sight is one of the prices of transgression; Moses repeats this warning when he gives his concluding charge to the people (Deuteronomy 28 : 65). In Jewish legend, Balaam is blinded for an impure thought, and when Moses and the Israelites are doing battle with the giants Sihon and Og and the army of Amorites, God sends hornets to blind all the Amorites to insure the victory of the Israelites. Samson, blinded by the Philistines ostensibly to reduce his threat to them (Judges 16 : 21), was, according to legend, being punished for his lust. It is written, "he who went astray after his eyes, lost his eyes." [144] Blindness as a punishment for sin is mentioned at least twice in the Book of Job, once by Zohar, one of Job's comforters (11 : 20) and by Job himself (17 : 4–5). Other moral injunctions backed by a threat of blindness are found at Psalm 69 : 23, Proverb 30 : 17, and Zephaniah 1 : 17. In the Apocrypha, when one of Tobit's kinsmen learns that Tobit has lost his sight, he says, ". . . But what grievous news that so good and charitable a man has gone blind," that is, one who had done nothing to deserve blindness (Tobit 7 : 7). In the New Testament, Jesus, on one occasion, denies that a certain man's blindness is due to sin, either his own or his parents, but that "he was born so that God's power might be displayed in curing him" (John 9 : 1–5). On the other hand, Paul calls down a heavenly curse of blindness on the evil sorcerer Elymas to demonstrate God's power and Elymas' false ways (Acts 13 : 8–11).

In Shakespeare's depiction of Gloucester in *King Lear,* Twersky observes that ". . . blindness for whatever other reason it is inflicted on Gloucester is fundamentally retribution from on high for his adultery. . . ." And Milton, when he himself was losing his sight, was forced to defend himself from his political enemies who were pointing to his blindness as a sign of punishment from on high. Despite this personal experience with the injustice of such a view, he seldom makes an effort in his writing to refute the blindness-as-punishment idea.[145] In "Samson Agonistes," for example, he appears to emphasize this side of Samson's blinding.

> . . . tell me Friends,
> Am I not sung and proverbed for a Fool
> In every street, do they not say, how well
> Are come upon him his deserts? . . .

.   .   .   .

> . . . of what now I suffer
> She [Dalila] was not the prime cause, but I my self,
> Who vanquisht with a peal of words (O weakness!)
> Gave up my fort of silence to a Woman.

.   .   .   .

> Appoint not heavenly disposition, Father,
> Nothing of all these evils hath befall'n me
> But justly; I myself have brought them on,
> Sole Author I, sole cause: if aught seem vile . . .[146]

Indeed, as Twersky points out, the poem "fills in, elaborates, clarifies all the attitudes toward the blind pointed to in the

Biblical account and more besides the same unfavorable kind." [147]

In more recent fiction, we find two evil and sinful characters who are purified through divine intervention in the form of blindness caused by lightning. There is the criminal and scoundrel Edward Jackson in Frederick Marryat's *The Little Savage,* and the swashbuckling Elizabethan gentleman-adventurer Amyas Leigh in Charles Kingsley's *Westward Ho!* [148] Victor Hugo felt compelled, in the same way Plutarch had been in regard to Timoleon, to say that Dea, the blind girl in *The Man Who Laughs,* had done nothing to deserve her fate, that though she was blind, punishment for sin was in this case not to be admitted. [149]

Another aspect of blindness viewed as a punishment that must be considered as historically pertinent to the origins of present-day attitudes is the practice of blinding political enemies and criminals convicted of certain crimes. Physical punishment and sin, as Gowman points out, are closely interwoven, particularly in the Old Testament, and "the two strands remain tangled in the minds of men. . . ." [150] Many of the examples already cited in this section, therefore, could also be listed as instances of blindness induced by man for secular crimes rather than by God for sins. For example, Oedipus, Samson, and Gloucester could be included in both categories.

As a physical punishment, blinding has always been considered worse than death because, as Chevigny and Braverman say, "it was held to deprive a man of enjoyment in living even as it preserved his life." [151] In antiquity, we find that the king of Babylon, after conquering Zedekiah, king of the Israelites, kills his sons before his eyes and then blinds him (2 Kings 25 : 6–7). Fareed Haj, throughout his book *Disability in Antiquity,* shows that blinding and other physical mutilations were common forms of punishment during the Arab caliphate in the Near East. The motif of blinding for certain crimes is found in the folk-literature of Sweden and Finland,

Greece, Spain, Brittany, and the Indians of North America.[152] In an article entitled "The Gloucester Treatment," Margaret Robertson recounts instances of both punitive and political blinding in the British Isles from the time of Canute (in an entry from 1014 in the *Anglo-Saxon Chronicle*) and William the Conqueror (*c.* 1070) to more recent times.[153] Graham and Clark note that punitive blinding was still used for thieves in Tibet and Afghanistan and by the Herero of South Africa for their enemies, the Bushmen, until very recently.[154] There is also a folklore motif showing blinding used for personal vengeance on an enemy. It usually runs something like this: A can have one wish, but his enemy B will get twice the wish. A, therefore, wishes that he may lose one eye; B thus loses both his eyes.[155]

11. Fear, Avoidance, and Rejection

Rejection of those who are blind is most completely expressed in the practice of infanticide noted earlier. Even for those blinded later in life, there would seem to be an almost universal reaction of fear and dread, an immediate emotional reaction that has taken a variety of forms in its expression.[156] In some cultures, blind people have been merely shunned, while in others they have been actively persecuted. As we shall see in a later section, they have sometimes been worshipped, but this is really only the other side of the same coin. One who is thought to have been "touched by God," possessed by evil spirits, or marked by the stigma of sin or disease is psychologically or socially set apart from normal human beings.[157] The position of blind people in the past was, on the whole, such that

> . . . any suggestion of a return to the past can fill a blind person only with horror. He thinks of the centuries of misery and degradation to which he was relegated, of the fact that for 3,000 years of European culture he was socially ostracized, condemned to form a class without rank or status, able to live only as a beggar.[158]

In ancient Hebrew culture, blindness disqualified men from serving as priests (Leviticus 21 : 16–23) and animals from serving as sacrifices (Leviticus 22 : 22). According to legend, all blindness and lameness was divinely cured among the Israelites after the exodus from Egypt, so that the revelation on Mount Sinai could be given to a sound and healthy people.[159] At 2 Samuel 5 : 8, it is written that "No blind or lame man shall come into the Lord's house." Reportedly, the Talmud commands that the benediction normally given on the death of a near relative be pronounced whenever a blind person is encountered.[160]

One of the functions of the traditional occupations assigned to blind people in Japan, Korea, Africa, and the Middle East (as noted in section eight, above) was to set blind people apart, to segregate them from "normal society." [161] Even the early schools for blind children were actually more like asylums than educational institutions.[162] Dickens, after his visit to the Perkins Institution and Massachusetts *Asylum* for the Blind, reports that all the blind "inmates" had a green ribbon bound around their heads covering their eyes, apparently as some kind of identification or mark.[163] Guillié remarks in 1819 that it is difficult for qualified blind people to find work because of the repugnance felt by many potential employers.[164] Levy, in 1872, reports "a strong and widely diffused prejudice . . . against blind organists." [165] In *The Outsider,* a novel by Ernesto Sabato published in 1950, the artist-protagonist says:

> I said that I have a poor opinion of mankind; I must now confess that I do not like blind people at all and that in their presence I feel something of the same sensation that cold, damp, and silent animals, such as snakes, give me.[166]

Graham and Clark have found that among primitive peoples, "The most common reaction to blind people . . . is derision . . . ," found among the Navaho, the Lau (Fiji), the Tupinamba (Maragnan Island), and the Baganda

(Africa). Other social constraints reported by them include: blind girls not permitted to marry (Turkey and East Africa) and blind men not permitted to be chief (Twi-Ashanti and Wolof in West Africa).[167] An interesting motif in folk literature is one in which a blind fiancée tries to conceal her blindness in order to hold her man and fails to do so by mistaking some object for another.[168]

12. Maladjustment

Of all the attitudes under consideration in this chapter, the idea that blind people, because of their blindness, are maladjusted has the shortest history. This is undoubtedly due to the fact that the concept of maladjustment itself is a rather recent idea. Before the eighteenth century, it was rather rare to look upon minor social deviations in terms of adjustment or maladjustment; there were a plethora of other explanations, including folk "psychology" and superstitions, that would have readily come to mind first. Diderot is among the first to conclude, for example, that because sympathy is a product of our having seen others in misery or pain, blind people are therefore without sympathy. In fact, he goes on, their entire moral code is different from the one followed by sighted people.[169] Guillié echoes Diderot's judgment and throughout his essay he enumerates blind people's differences: their thoughts are distorted; their sensibilities are deficient; they are ungrateful, without conscience or piety, incapable of acting in their own best interests, and victims of self-love.[170] Kipling portrays Dick Heldar as losing all self-respect after losing his sight. In another place, he writes, "His imagination, the keener for the dark background it worked against, spared him no single detail that might send him raging up and down the studio. . . ."[171] G. S. Wilson, writing in 1906, accuses blind people of rebelliousness, of having "a marked tendency toward the musical [?], the weird and fantastical," and of being deceitful.[172]

13. Immoral and Evil

Although the portrayal of blind people as immoral and evil is not completely confined to the modern era, it is true that it is only recently that such portrayals have become common. Before the nineteenth century we can only cite a few examples. In Jewish legend, Satan is sometimes called Sammael, "the blind one." [173] In the medieval Spanish tale *The Pleasaunt Historie of Lazarillo de Tormes,* translated into English in 1586 by David Rouland of Anglesey, the protagonist, Lazarillo, at one point becomes the servant and guide of a deceitful, crafty, wretched, niggardly blind beggar-confidence man.[174] Schiller, in his play *Don Carlos* (1787), portrays the extremely cruel and merciless grand inquisitor as blind. His cruelty is at least partly due to his blindness, for as one of the characters says, "The world has one less access to your heart—your eyes are sunken night." [175]

Beginning in the nineteenth century, however, there are quite a few such depictions. The most outstanding of these include the ruthless, greedy, and cynical Stagg in Dickens' *Barnaby Rudge* (1841)[176] and the cruel and vicious Pew in Stevenson's *Treasure Island.* Of the two, Pew has probably had the greater influence on modern attitudes by virtue of the great popularity of *Treasure Island.* Despite the fact that Pew only appears briefly in the story, his impression on the reader, as on Jim Hawkins, is powerful. On first seeing Pew, Jim says, "I never saw in my life a more dreadful looking figure." Shortly thereafter, Pew feigns helplessness, gets a hold on Jim, and orders him to lead him to the captain, to which Jim says to himself, ". . . I never heard a voice so cruel, and cold, and ugly as that blind man's." [177] In *Kidnapped,* another very popular novel by Stevenson, there is a blind character named Duncan Mackiegh. Young David Balfour's first reaction upon encountering Mackiegh, even after being told by him that he is a catechist, is one of suspicion, for ". . . his face went against me; it seemed dark and dangerous and secret." His suspicion is soon borne out by Mackiegh's attempt to rob him and the innkeeper's later identification of Mackiegh as a notorious robber and murderer.[178] As Twersky points out, Stevenson obviously considers Mackiegh's evil to have been caused by the fact of his blindness.[179]

Wolf Larsen, the brutal sea captain in London's *The Sea Wolf,* loses his sight late in the story. The hero, Humphrey Van Weyden, and the heroine, Maud Brewster, in discussing their situation, say:

> "But there can be no danger now? from a blind man?" she queried. "I shall never be able to trust him," I [Humphrey] averred, "and far less now that he is blind. The liability is that his part helplessness will make him more malignant than ever. . . ."[180]

John Buchan, in his 1924 novel *The Three Hostages,* portrays the old and blind Mrs. Medina as filled with hatred and evil and as the inspiration behind her son's criminal activities.[181]

The appearance of evil and immoral blind characters in modern literature is in one sense an improvement over many of the other, age-old negative portrayals. As Twersky puts it, "The blind when shown as immoral cannot be made out as completely helpless. They must at least be able to do some immoral things."[182] Pew, for example, after his interview with the captain at the inn, ". . . suddenly left hold of me [Jim Hawkins narrates the story], and, with incredible accuracy and nimbleness, skipped out of the parlor and into the road. . . ." Later he is shown at the head of a gang of cutthroats.[183] Duncan Mackiegh is reportedly a deadly shot, aiming his pistol by sound, and quite capable of moving through the trackless Scottish wilds by himself.[184] When Humphrey in *The Sea Wolf* calls Captain Larsen blind and helpless, Maud reminds him of Larsen's undiminished strength and agility.[185] In folk literature, when blind people do evil, they are often shown to be quite clever and capable. For example, in the Scottish story of the Lochmaben harper, a blind itinerant musician successfully carries out an intricate plot to fool the English king and his entire court in order to steal the king's favorite horse.[186] Other motifs feature blind people as thieves and victims of blinding taking revenge on those responsible for their condition.[187] An interesting explanation of the use of blind villains by some authors is suggested by Patterson in her 1912 article "The Blind in Fiction." She writes:

> It is, perhaps, because the readers expect the characters to be weaker or less capable than their sighted fellows that make Stagg . . . and Blind Pew . . . seem so abhorrent and shocking. These characters would be despicable under any circumstances, but being blind they are horrible.[188]

14. Idealization

The depictions to be discussed in this section, like those in the section on the maladjustment of blind people, are found largely in the literature of the past 200 years. The idealization of blind people is, of course, related to the idea of compensation and in many ways overlaps with it. On the other hand, it can be distinguished from the older notion that blind people are endowed with extraordinary abilities, skills, or talents. The idea under consideration here involves the spiritual nature of blind people, their sensibilities, their personal orientation to the world and to other people. An early personification of this idea of past attitudes toward blind people can be found in Billy Blind, an Elizabethan fairy who may be connected with the figures of Auld Hoodie and Robin Hood. He was, writes Briggs, "A friendly domestic spirit of the Border Country, chiefly mentioned in ballads. . . . Billy Blind's chief function seems to be to give good advice." [189]

The idealization of blind people was particularly popular in nineteenth-century novels. Bulwer-Lytton, in *The Last Days of Pompeii* (1854), creates the blind character Nydia, who is unbelievably sweet, pure, noble, and self-sacrificing.[190] Muriel, in Dinah Maria Craik's *John Halifax, Gentleman* (1857), is pure, sweet, other-worldly, extremely devout, and ". . . carries such an atmosphere of good with her that all are influenced by it. . . ."[191] Hugo's blind girl, Dea, in *The Man Who Laughs,* is similarly characterized.

> A captive of shadow, [Dea] lighted up the dull place she inhabited. From the depth of her incurable darkness . . . , she flung her rays. She saw not the sun without, but her soul was perceptible from within.[192]

Wilkie Collins, who was influenced by Diderot, creates a very believable blind character in his *Poor Miss Finch* (1872), although Leonard Frankland, a blind character in his *The Dead Secret* (1873), is a bit too noble and self-sacrificing.[193] Unbelievably clever blind detectives appear in mystery stories by Isabel Ostrander (*At 1:30*—1916) and Clinton H. Stagg (*Thornley Colton, Blind Detective*—1923) and a similarly endowed blind lawyer in *The Blind Man's Eyes* by W. McHarg and E. Balmer (1916).[194]

Langworthy suggests that perhaps these authors made their blind characters ideally good because they could not conceive of them having the opportunity to be otherwise.[195] Wilson, on the other hand, attributed such characterizations to imagination run riot, especially in the cases of Bulwer-Lytton, Hugo, and Craik. Their imagination, he writes, "was neither restrained nor its creations within the control of reason. All [of their characters—Nydia, Dea, and Muriel] were dreamy, emotional, and visionary."[196]

15. Mysteriousness

As we have seen in several of the preceding sections (particularly in those on darkness; compensation; sin and punishment; fear, avoidance, and rejection; and idealization), blindness and blind people have long been associated with mystery, magic, and the supernatural. The widespread belief that blind people are especially suited to the occupation of soothsayer and seer, to cite but one example, clearly places blind people in the realm of the extraordinary.[197] Oedipus says of Teiresias, his "soul grasps all things, the lore that may be told and the unspeakable, the secrets of heaven and the low things of earth. . . ."[198] In *Oedipus at Colonus,* we find that Oedipus, though without divine compensation throughout most of his days as a blind man, is suddenly possessed and able to lead his companions.

> My children, follow me—thus—for I now have in strange wise been made your guide. . . . This way—hither, this way!—for this way doth Guiding Hermes lead me, and the goddess of the dead! [199]

The strength of the association between the occupation of soothsayer and blind people is clearly shown in modern productions of Shakespeare's *Julius Caesar.* In the play, the soothsayer who warns Caesar "Beware the Ides of March" is never identified as being blind, but, for example, in the 1953 motion picture version, directed by Joseph L. Mankiewicz, he is portrayed as a blind man.

From some of the examples cited in our discussion of sin and punishment, it can be seen that blindness is often connected with miracles, as when God blinded the Sodomites and the Amorites. In Jewish legend, several miracles, including all blind people regaining their sight, occurred at the birth of Isaac. Isaac's own failing eyesight was originally caused by the tears of angels falling into his eyes while he lay bound upon the sacrificial altar.[200] The whole question of Jacob's "mistaken" blessing of his grandchildren (Genesis 48 : 8–20) appears to be an example of prophecy, for he claims that he blessed Ephraim first, instead of Manasseh because Ephraim would be the greater of the two. Ahijah, a blind prophet, correctly predicts the death of Jeroboam's son and the end of his reign (I Kings 14 : 1–18).

John Milton, because of his profound religious faith, was able to accept the fact of his blindness completely and to reject the notion that it was God's curse.[201] Although he did not view his blindness as a blessing or as giving him any magical insight, his acquiescence to the will of God might easily be misconstrued. This acquiescent spirit is expressed in a letter from Milton to his friend Cyriak Skinner:

> Yet I argue not, against heaven's hand
> Or will, nor bate a
> Jot of heart or hope; but still bear up
> And steer right onwards.[202]

When we read, therefore, in "Paradise Lost," after a description of the state of being blind,

> So much the rather thou celestial light
> Shine inward, and the mind through all her powers
> Irradiate, there plant eyes, all mist from thence
> Purge and disperse, that I may see and tell
> Of things invisible to mortal sight.[203]

it is clear that he is speaking of a religious experience and not of the prophetic spirit. In other words, the reason one loses one's sight may be for one's personal redemption (perhaps through mystical revelation), but not for some social purpose —whether as prophet or savior. This religious view of blindness is also expressed by Milton in two works discovered after his death, one written in prose ("The Sacredness of the Blind") and one in verse (called "Lines by Milton in His Old Age").[204] Similar sentiments are expressed by Richard Standfast in a group of poems called "The Blind Man's Meditations" written in 1684.[205] The blindness of Edward Rochester in *Jane Eyre* leads him also to a religious experience.[206] Even without misconstruing such experiences, however, the role played by blindness in them is undoubtedly partly responsible for the association of blindness and blind people with deep religious feelings and, by extension, with such mysterious phenomena as foresight, unusual insight, and supernatural or magical powers. Victor Hugo's Dea is a case in point.

> The audience regarded Dea with a sort of mysterious anxiety. She had in her aspect the dignity of a virgin and of a priestess, not knowing man and knowing God. They saw that she was blind, and felt that she could see. She seemed to stand on the threshold of the supernatural. The light that beamed on her seemed half earthly and half heavenly.

And again, later on:

> . . . Dea was silent, and absorbed by that kind of ecstasy peculiar to the blind. . . . Blindness is a cavern, to which reaches the deep harmony of the Eternal.[207]

Other examples of idealized, divinely compensated, and almost saintly blind people are to be found in *The Blind Girl of Wittenberg* by John G. Morris, *Melody* by Laura Richards, and *Sir Nigel* by A. Conan Doyle.[208] In 1906, Wilson writes that blind people "are secretive, mysterious, and self-contained. . . ."[209]

Blind people are also believed to have magical powers in South Vietnam, Korea, and among the Nuer tribes of Africa and the North American Indians.[210] There is an Aesopian fable in which a blind man feels a young wolf and recognizes its savage nature.[211] Blindness itself is explained in various parts of the world in such magico-religious terms as retribution for sins committed in a past life (Buddhists), misconduct in this life (the Highland Chinantecos of Mexico), the work of sorcerers (Burma), walking in the shadow of an impure woman (Gujarati—India), and a curse by off-islanders (Truk Island).[212] In folklore, too, both magic sight and blindness are most decidedly connected with magical objects (including fairies, hempseed, spikes, salves, powders, ointments, and the Virgin Mary's shift used as a banner). There are many interesting motifs in folklore related to blindness in animals, and magical cures for blindness using such items as herbs, spittle, feathers, honey, water, a bird's tears, dew, ointments, wands, the sun's rays, and blood.[213] Although it is claimed that more advanced peoples are more objective in their assessment of blindness,[214] the mystery of blindness still seems to exercise some influence over modern man. The effectiveness of emotional appeals on behalf of blind people is well attested [215] and Zarlock reports that many blind people "placed unusual confidence in the efficacy of medicine and religion to restore health and strongly believed they would regain their vision through a miraculous cure." [216]

In conclusion, it is clear that there is ample evidence to support the hypothesis that the present-day attitudes toward blindness and blind people discussed in chapter one have long been a part of our cultural heritage. Indeed, many attitudes have been shown to be cross-cultural in nature, indicating some commonality in man's experiences with and reactions to blindness and blind people. The exact part played by past attitudes in the formation of the attitudes of today is difficult to say. In some instances, it may be that a past attitude is learned directly and taken on with little modification. Attitudes from the past may also play some role in reinforcing present-day experiences with and reactions to blindness and blind people or even in predisposing individuals to certain reactions.

Before we leave our discussion of past attitudes toward blindness and blind people, there are two authors who have dealt with blindness and whose stories we should consider. Their unusual treatment, however, has prevented their being included within the context of this chapter. Both can tell us a great deal about the relationship between people with a full set of senses and people without one of those senses.

The first of these is H. G. Wells, whose short story "The Country of the Blind" was first published in 1904. Very briefly, the story is about a completely isolated and idyllic Peruvian mountain valley in which all of the inhabitants have, through the action of some mysterious mutation or disease, been without sight for nearly 20 generations. Wells admirably demonstrates that man can and does adapt his existence to whatever conditions he must face. The inhabitants of this "world of blindness" are shown as completely self-sufficient and, because of the fortunate circumstances of their valley, reasonably well off. Into this little world, Pedro, a more or less illiterate native mountain-climbing guide, is accidentally thrust. Assuming that "in the land of the blind, the one-eyed man is king," Pedro learns to his utter dismay that his having sight is of no particular advantage in a world organized completely on the basis of four senses. The daily routine of the inhabitants is supported by a "four-sense" theology and cosmogony; they have no remembrance or even a conception of sight and so count it a harmful deviation or mutation. Wells, therefore, indicates the true nature both of normality and deviation and of the relationship between a majority and a minority.

Secondly, we have Edward Bellamy making a similar point in his short story "The Blindman's World," which was first published in book form in 1898. In this story, the world of the blind men is Earth as viewed by the inhabitants of Mars whose complement of senses includes foresight. Speaking to a "blind" earthling, who has been mysteriously transported to Mars while in a dream state, a Martian says:

> The slowness of your progress is not so remarkable to us as that you make any at all, burdened as you are by a disability so crushing that if we were in your place I fear we should sit down in utter despair.

He goes on to point out that in their exploration of outer space they have found that all other intelligent beings normally possess six senses. He then says:

> . . . it is conceivable that the remoter parts of the universe may harbor other blind races like your own; but it certainly seems unlikely that so strange and lamentable a spectacle should be duplicated. One such illustration of the extraordinary deprivations under which a rational existence may still be possible ought to suffice for the universe.[217]

The parallels between these attitudes and those of the "five-sense" majority toward the blind, "four-sense" minority in our society are certainly very striking.

3 Psychosocial Origins of Attitudes Toward Blindness and Blind People

W^{E HAVE, UNTIL NOW,} been using the term "attitude" in its general, commonly accepted sense—"manner, disposition, feeling, position, etc., with regard to a person or thing; tendency or orientation, esp. of the mind." Using this definition, we have discussed the particular attitudes of sighted people toward blindness and blind people. In the preceding chapter, we began our investigation of the sources of these attitudes with the idea that, since attitudes are in some way learned, past attitudes could be transmitted directly to the individual. In this chapter, our emphasis will be upon the fact that attitudes are held by individuals, as were attitudes in the past, and that they are related in some way to the experiences and reactions of the individual. In fact, it can be noted that both past and present attitudes are derived ultimately from this personal and interpersonal sphere, the psychosocial nexus of daily life.

While it is true that there are numerous social mechanisms influencing the way in which an individual relates to himself and to others, these so-called "pressures" have their root in the psychology of the individual. In other words, many general attitudes are learned indirectly by children, for example, during their socialization. These attitudes are not arbitrary, however; they are profoundly related to the way in which man adapts to the world and to how he functions as a human being. For this reason, we will examine the experience of the individual as primary to the origins of attitudes and as a paradigm for the attitudes transmitted indirectly by him to society at large.[1]

We will begin, therefore, by discussing the meaning of an attitude viewed psychosocially. Milton Rokeach suggests the following definition: "An attitude is a relatively enduring organization of beliefs around an object or situation predisposing one to respond in some preferential manner." [2] Another definition, one which enumerates a range of potentialities, is that an attitude is "the sum total of a man's inclinations and feelings, prejudice or bias, preconceived notions, ideas, fears, threats, and convictions about any specific topic." [3] The important thing, as Rokeach points out, is the functional significance of an attitude, namely, that it is a predisposition to a preferential response, an "agenda for action," a way of reacting to some object and/or situation when it is encountered.[4] In addition to this general function, an attitude also serves several functions for the particular individual holding it. Daniel L. Katz's formulation includes four such functions of attitudes: "(1) instrumental, adjustive, or utilitarian; (2) ego-defensive; (3) value-expressive; and (4) provision of knowledge based upon the individual's need to give adequate structure to his universe." [5] It would seem that while all four of these functions are obviously interrelated, the value-expressive function is superordinate to the other three. "All of a person's beliefs and attitudes may be in the service of, or instrumental to, the satisfaction of one and another pre-existing, often conflicting, values: adjustive values, ego-defensive values, and knowledge and other self-realizing values." [6]

Clearly, an individual could not form or maintain a complete "inventory" of particular attitudes for each of the specific objects and situations that he is likely to encounter. The formation of attitudes, therefore, takes place in relation to categories of objects and situations; that is, the individual uses generalizations. In fact, using categories is crucial to the process of thinking and of forming judgments.

> We cannot possibly avoid the process. Orderly living depends on it. We may say that the process of categorization has five important characteristics. (1) It forms large classes and clusters for guiding our daily adjustments. . . . (2) Categorization assimilates as much as it can to the cluster. . . . (3) The category enables us quickly to identify a related object. . . . (4) The category saturates all that it contains with the same ideational and emotional flavor. . . . (5) Categories may be more or less rational.[7]

Categories applied to other people include, for example, the "generalized other" of George Herbert Mead.[8] Himes, in discussing Mead's concept, describes it as "the summary and universally applicable image of the persons, both known and unknown, with whom we come into contact." This category serves as a common base for other categories. "In the flow of social relations an individual tends to modify this generalized conception to conform to the recognized characteristics of the persons he confronts." [9] How these modifications are effected and more specific categories formed is described by Goffman.

> Society establishes the means of categorizing persons and the complement of attributes felt to be ordinary and natural for members of each of these categories. Social settings establish the categories of persons likely to be encountered there. The routines of social intercourse in established settings allow us to deal with anticipated others without special attention or thought. When a stranger comes into our presence, then, first appearances are likely to enable us to anticipate his category and attributes, his "social identity". . . .[10]

In addition, then, to the behavioral component of each belief within an attitude organization, there is also a cognitive component. That is, each belief ". . . represents a person's knowledge, held with varying degrees of certitude, about what is true or false, good or bad, desirable or undesirable." [11] Or, as it is expressed from the viewpoint of cognitive theory:

> In the general case the individual may be conceived as the site of a large and complexly organized set of perceptions, thoughts, and knowledge. This assemblage has been variously denoted the "image," the "mazeway," and so on; the term refers to the entire structure of the individual's cognition about himself and the surrounding world, including memories, abstract knowledge, and rules of thought. [12]

The point is that attitudes and beliefs become a part of an individual's "mazeway" as the result of information processing. Further, it can be seen, perception must play a primary role in the acquisition of information. For example, it has been proposed that there are six different ways of acquiring such information: ". . . blind trial-and-error, general perception, perception of others' responses, perception of the outcomes of others' explorations, verbal instructions relevant to behavior, and verbal instructions about objects' characteristics." [13]

As we know from several different theories of perception and concept formation, the way in which information is received and interpreted is a function of the overall psychological organization of the perceiver. More specifically, the performance of the perceptual tasks faced by the individual are affected by "the nature of the individual's relation to his environment (including other people), the way in which he manages his impulses and strivings, and the kind of conception he has of himself." And, therefore, "the pattern of adjustment worked out by a person helps determine the nature of his perception, in the sense of producing characteristic ways of perceiving. Perception thus contributes to adjustment and in turn reflects that adjustment." [14]

The way in which the perceptual object influences the

formation of impressions must, of course, also be considered. From gestalt theory we learn, as Asch points out, that the individual responds to "the interrelations among observed characteristics and the manner in which these characteristics modify each other." Applying this general assumption to the perception of persons, Asch also reports that "the following, more specific propositions emerge from investigation":

(a) The items of knowledge about a person do not remain isolated but interact and mutually alter each other.

(b) The interactions depend upon the properties of the items in their relation to one another.

(c) In the course of interaction the characteristics group themselves into a structure in which some become central and others dependent.

(d) The resulting interdependence creates a unitary impression which tends to be subjectively completed in the direction of becoming more consistent and coherent.

(e) It follows that a given item of information or a characteristic functions as a dependent part, not as an element.

(f) If so, the "same" trait in two persons is not necessarily the same.[15]

As Tagiuri, in his article "Person Perception," points out, the impressions that are formed about another person, whether directly perceived or inferred, include not only his appearance but also his intentions, attitudes, emotions, ideas, abilities, purposes, traits, thoughts, perceptions, memories, consciousness, and self-determination. In other words, "through [some combination of] inference and analogy, through sensory cues derived from empathic responses, and through the immediate response to external configurations and patterns that are expressions of qualities of a person 'out there,'" an individual perceiver will come to certain conclusions about the personality or inner state of another person.[16] In addition, it should be noted, the formation of these impressions is also influenced by the particular social situation in which the person is observed or encountered, the role of both the perceiver and the person perceived in that situation, and, finally, the attitude of the individual toward the situation.[17]

One of the primary uses to which the perceiver puts his impressions of others is to aid in placing the perceived person in categories. As we have seen, once an object of perception is categorized the perceiver then begins to relate to it as a member of that category and to the qualities that its members are thought to have. While this process of categorization is ultimately quite complex, it is usually accomplished very rapidly, especially when the other person possesses certain kinds of visible and conspicuous features.[18] Among those characteristics enumerated by Allport are skin color, cast of features, gestures, prevalent facial expression, speech or accent, dress, mannerisms, religious practices, food habits, names, place of residence, and insignia.[19] Applying the principle that what looks different is different to these traits[20] and using personal theories about what these traits suggest about another's personality,[21] the individual can easily satisfy himself that a person is a member of a certain larger group and that he will have certain other traits, react in certain ways, and so on.[22] This series of cognitive events, then, form the core around which an attitude is structured.

The third and final component of the beliefs within an attitude organization is the affective component. Rokeach writes that ". . . under suitable conditions the belief is capable of arousing affect of varying intensity centering (a) around the object of the belief, or (b) around other objects (individuals or groups) taking a positive or negative position with respect to the object of belief, or (c) around the belief itself, when its validity is seriously questioned, as in an argument." [23] Certain stimuli, therefore, will either activate the behavioral component and produce some action-response or set the cognitive components in motion in an effort to bolster the beliefs or to defend the attitude when contradictory evidence or beliefs are encountered.

Beliefs, however, are only the elements of attitudes. The organization of these beliefs within an attitude structure must, therefore, also be examined. Rokeach discusses a number of the characteristic dimensions of this organization. They can be briefly described as follows:

> *Differentiation*—degree of complexity; "an index of the total amount of correct and incorrect information or knowledge possessed about the focus of the attitude. . . ."
>
> *Integration*—degree of recognition and appreciation of similarities and differences; low integration would be compartmentalization, a failure to perceive contradictions in beliefs or attitudes.
>
> *Centrality*—degree of saliency, resistance to change, and effect on more peripheral beliefs or attitudes.
>
> *Time perspective*—orientation of beliefs or attitudes to the past, present, or future.
>
> *Specificity-generality*—". . . a function of the degree of differentiation, integration, and isolation of one belief from another and of one attitude from another."
>
> *Breadth*—the extent of "the total range, or spectrum, of relevant social reality that is actually represented within the whole." [24]

Based on this discussion, Rokeach observes that an attitude "is not a single predisposition but a set of interrelated predispositions focused on an attitude object or situation." [25] Throughout the balance of this chapter, we will explore the interrelations of the several predispositions that comprise attitudes toward blindness and blind people. We will begin this exploration by returning to an idea mentioned earlier, one which would seem to open the door to our subject very widely: expectation categories.

The idea of expectation categories is succinctly expressed by Allport. "Categories," he writes, "help us to identify a new object or person, and to expect from it (him) a certain kind of behavior to accord with our preconceptions." [26] What kind of expectations does the average individual have in a relatively normal situation? Simply put, he expects the other person to appear and behave in a "normal" way. That is, the other should conform to a large number of social "norms." These norms, that is, normative expectations, will vary, within certain rather narrow limits, in accordance with an equally limited number of "normal" situations. This normal characterization of the other, what Goffman terms the person's "virtual social identity," consists, in effect, of righteously presented demands.[27]

Since it is difficult to conceptualize the extent to which such normative expectations govern interpersonal relations, let us take an example of a common encounter between two people and just briefly note a few of the many norms that an individual will expect to be fulfilled. John Doe goes into his bank to make a deposit. When he reaches the teller's window, he will expect the teller's appearance to be within certain limits, not only his clothes, but the configuration of his face, hands, and body. Further, he will expect that the teller will be able to communicate with him (that he is not dumb and that he can speak the same language that John Doe does), that he will greet him in some way, ask how he may be of service, and, on the whole, conduct the exchange in the prescribed "bankerly" manner. In a somewhat different situation, but one that is nevertheless still relatively common (e.g., answering the doorbell, arriving at a cocktail party, queuing for a movie), most of the norms will be the same, some will shift, and a few will be applicable only to that particular situation.

Naturally, most normative expectations held by an individual are derived from various aspects of his cultural background or life conditions: his age, sex, race, occupation, social class, level of education, etc. There are, certainly, general human expectations (upright posture, distribution of hair, language, certain facial expressions, etc.), but, for the moment, these do not concern us. Social expectations and their attendant attitudes are, as Lukoff and Whiteman point out, determined largely by two factors, socialization variables and response tendencies. Of the first they write, "These are factors that influence an individual's attitudes by dint of his exposure to general social rules and the concrete behavior and expectations of the people around him." Of the second, "Any bit of behavior may reflect more generalized behavioral dispositions. Thus a specific aggressive act may reflect a general trait or motive for aggression, manifested by similar kinds of behavior exhibited in other situations, toward other people, and at other times." [28]

Turning now to the specific subject of blindness and blind people, we will begin by examining what happens when the other is perceived to be a person who is blind. What does the perceiver feel? What does he think? How does he react? Sommers describes a typical scene in a residential school for blind children:

> Frequently, when seeing persons visited one of these schools, a sense of tenseness and strangeness developed between visitor and student. The seeing visitor, who had never had any contact with blind people, became uneasy and self-conscious, fearful of saying or doing something tactless; the blind person, too, felt uneasy and self-conscious, his whole demeanor dominated by the fear of acting like a handicapped person. This was not the natural meeting of two individuals from similar planes of life; rather it was a meeting between representatives of two different worlds: that of the blind and that of the seeing.[29]

Ritter notes the tenseness and clumsiness that characterize such interactions and also points to the "simple, normal fear of doing or saying the wrong thing" as the stumbling block.[30] Siller and his associates report a number of reactions that they recorded in their interviews with sighted people: " 'I feel uneasy coming near a blind beggar'; 'It's difficult to remember that they're blind. . . . Makes you feel stupid when you make a gesture or point'; 'I feel uneasy watching them move about and am afraid they just might not make it'; 'If a person is completely sightless, you can't speak to him the way you would ordinarily to anyone else. . . .' " [31]

From these few examples, it is clear that much of the contact between sighted people and blind people involves interaction strain, a general disruption of the normal pattern of contact resulting from any of a number of expectation discrepancies. That is, the perceived image of the blind person in some way violates the normative expectations of the sighted person; the character of the interaction also does not fit into the expected pattern of interpersonal contact and exchange.[32] The particular discrepancies that may be experienced are several. First, and most obvious, there is the general expectation that the other person will have the full complement of five senses, that he will, in this case, be able to see. Then there is the appearance of the other person. Although the majority of blind people have no distinguishing physical traits, a few do have enlarged or protruding eyeballs, drooping or inflamed eyelids, watery eyes, or involuntary movement of their eyes.[33] Some blind people also have certain characteristic postures or ways of moving, often called "blindisms," that are distinctly atypical. It is important to remember, both with these differences and with those to be discussed shortly, that it is not simply their visibility that matters but the degree to which they obtrude themselves into the interaction, their ability to disrupt an otherwise normal situation.[34]

One theory of the origin of attitudes specifically related to physical deviance has been suggested by Winkler. His formulation states that unusual posture or movements are strange, disturbing emotional stimuli that block the establishment of an empathic relationship between the "normal" and the "deviant" person.[35] Although Winkler's experimental data are derived from studies involving crippled individuals, the basic stimuli do have certain parallels in the perceived characteristics of blind persons (as enumerated, for example, by Kooyman)[36] and, therefore, a breakdown in empathy should be considered as one source of attitudes toward blind people.

Within the interaction itself, there are two areas in which discrepancies may be encountered: (1) visual contact and (2) gestures, facial expressions, and other similar conversational cues.[37] In conversation, both parties are expected to look the other squarely in the eye. For many, such eye contact is very important and its lack may induce suspicion and mistrust.[38] The eyes also play a primary role in facial expressions and, to many, the emotional feedback derived from the silent expression of approval and disapproval is crucial to the smooth conduct of conversation. Cholden writes, ". . . in order for the individual to express feeling with any degree of comfort, he must be quite aware of the manner in which his communication is received. As the sighted person offers some indication of his emotions, he receives permission to proceed from the smiles, sympathetic faces, nods, etc. of his listener. . . ."[39] Now while there are a number of facial expressions that are by nature instinctual (those expressive of pleasure, pain, grief, etc.), the code of symbolic expressions (primarily facial, but also including the body as a whole and gestures) used in interpersonal relations are culturally determined and are learned largely by imitation.[40] This code, therefore, is not usually a part of the blind person's social behavior, much to the distress of the sighted speaker.[41] It is interesting to note that not only are the specific elements of the code of expressions culturally determined, but the importance of such a code also varies. In Japan, Imamura writes, ". . . it is the custom to avoid looking at people's eyes and not to display emotion through facial expressions. . . ."[42] Because of this cultural relativity of eye contact and expressive feedback, it might be argued that they are of minor importance. This, however, is not the case, for such cues are an expected, even demanded, part of behavior in Western culture and ". . . failure to sustain the many minor norms important in the etiquette of face-to-face communication can have a very pervasive effect upon the defaulter's acceptability in social situations." [43]

Another area of expectation within an encounter is the action or content of the exchange. Discrepancies can arise if the nature of the participants' behavior or their goals for the encounter are not consonant. This is what, in somatopsychological theory, is called the problem of the overlapping situation. Simply put, this problem involves the visibility-obtrusiveness question noted above. Most of the behavior of blind people is determined by the same factors that determine the behavior of sighted people. On the other hand, some of the behavior of blind people is determined by their blindness. Situations in which common determiners are involved create no problems (e.g., listening to the radio). The same is true of situations in which the seeing determiners and the blind determiners are not in conflict (e.g., dialing a telephone). Discrepancies can occur, however, when the two sets of determiners are contradictory and mutually exclusive (e.g., pouring a glass of water). More specifically, both sighted and blind people listen to the radio in the same way; their behavior is, in fact, identical. Sighted and blind people dial a telephone differently, but there is nothing in the way a blind person accomplishes the task that would particularly call attention to it or cause any kind of reaction. The behaviors in this case are consonant. To pour a glass of water properly (i.e., not half a glass and not to overflowing), a blind person will ordinarily hook his finger over the edge of the glass and pour the water until it reaches the tip of his finger. Putting one's finger inside the glass, however, conflicts with seeing determiners. In such a situation, the blind person's behavior, no matter which determiner he chooses to follow, will obtrude itself and, to one extent or another, violate the expectations of a sighted observer. While it is true that there are relatively few overlapping situations in which the potency of the seeing determiners is so great that the choices are completely antagonistic, there are nevertheless a great number of situations in which behaviors interfere with the natural and easy flow of social intercourse. Subjects about which the blind person can have little direct knowledge (e.g., an eclipse) may easily arise in conversation and cause an embarrassing moment of silence. A blind person may at some point not realize that certain non-verbal cues have been given that require action (e.g., rising when a woman enters the room or lighting someone's cigarette). In new or rapidly shifting situations the behavior of a blind person may lack the spontaneity that is normally expected.[44]

In a sense it is the new psychological situation which is central to the whole issue of social expectation, for it has certain characteristic properties that create difficulties for both blind and sighted people. First, the individual does not know in what direction the situation will move. Second, the alternatives he perceives for his own contribution are ambiguous; they may be positive or negative. Finally, his perception of the situation itself is also ambiguous and changeable.[45] For example, there can be a certain ambiguity in the perceptual figure of a blind person; as a person he may be whole-valued, yet physically he is incomplete, partial-valued.[46] A blind person in a new psychological situation does not know when or if his blindness will become obtrusive.[47] Because of this, many blind people take special care to prevent their blindness from looming too large in their relations with others or from being at all evident. They may re-learn motor propriety to make their movements less awkward. They may train themselves to look directly at someone who is speaking and to approximate those conversational feedback cues described above. Finally, they may so manage their encounters that things which would reveal their blindness or magnify their differentness are avoided.[48] Naturally, when covering and social management fail, the sudden revelation of blindness will often produce an even greater reaction, especially if it has succeeded for a while, than if the problems of interaction are dealt with straight-forwardly as they arise.

The ambiguities of a new situation involving a blind person can become quite serious when the sighted person approaches him with preconceptions about blindness and blind people.[49] Whether his notions are based on hearsay, previous experiences, or his own imagination, there is a good chance that the blind person will fail to fulfill such expectations completely. There are two factors involved in expectation discrepancies resulting from stereotypical ideas: the diversity of blind people and the often self-contradictory nature of most beliefs about blind people.

As with any group of people who are identifiable by a single characteristic, few actual blind individuals will possess any but a random number of the other characteristics imputed to blind people as a group. "The very act of classifying," writes Allport, "forces us to overlook all other features. . . ." [50] The more independent and well-adjusted a blind person is, the greater are the chances that his behavior will contradict the various cultural constructs concerning blind people.[51] Unfortunately, there is the matter of the role that expectations play in the socialization of blind people. Robert Scott, in his recent book *The Making of Blind Men,* demonstrates quite convincingly that blindness "is a social role that people who have serious difficulty seeing or who cannot see at all must learn how to play." [52] The individual's own attitudes toward blindness before his loss of sight and the attitudes of those around him, including workers in agencies for the blind, therefore, may result in the blind person's behavior conforming to some of the stereotyped behavior attributed to blind people.[53] Although this might in some cases lead to a sighted person's expectations being fulfilled, there remain nevertheless many blind people whose development is quite individual and not in line with the stereotypes.

One very potent source of discrepancy having to do with

stereotypes involves the participants' differing definitions of the encounter situation itself and of the roles of the participants in it.[54] The sighted person will most likely define himself and his role as "normal" and the situation as one in which he will be, for example, the initiator of actions and the aggressive one upon whom the blind person will depend. (As Imamura notes, "The expectation of dependency dominates the behavioral norms.")[55] The blind person, however, is also likely to think of himself as basically normal, that is, ". . . a human being like anyone else, a person, therefore who deserves a fair chance and a fair break." [56] These conflicting conceptions and expectations result, as Graham and Clark put it, in "a poor fit all around." [57] Gowman writes, "Once the stereotype falters, the sighted person is without any pattern of stable expectations, and his behavior may become bizarre or inappropriate. . . ." [58]

The second factor, the ambiguous and often self-contradictory nature of stereotypical attitudes about blindness and blind people, has been alluded to both in the introduction and in the first chapter. As we have seen in this chapter, it is necessary for man to create and use categories in order to function. Further, the categorization of people is to some degree reinforced by the natural separation of people into groups that share the same language, religion, foods, educational level, occupation, or other similar traits.[59] The tendency to regard blind people as a group is of long standing.[60] The implications, however, of categorizing blind people as a genuine group, that is, that they are different from sighted people and that they are similar to one another, cannot be supported objectively beyond the single fact of blindness.[61] There are several reasons why the similarities imputed to exist generally among blind people are not only false but also often contradictory. (It is well to remember at this point that the falsity or ambiguity of an individual's attitudes in no way compromises their reality for that individual.) First, blindness is sufficiently uncommon that most people have little direct experience with it.[62] Because of this, there is, secondly, a broad range of other data that will be used by an individual in filling out his categorization, among them, secondhand information, imagination, directly received past attitudes, superstitions, associations, and so on.[63] How much information is known is not really important, for ". . . most individuals feel able to make at least a guess about the characteristics of almost any defined social group on the basis of information that a social scientist would consider quite inadequate." [64] Further, whatever data are used will be influenced by the individual's age, level of education, and various psychological and environmental factors.[65] It is not surprising, therefore, that an individual's definition of "blind people" as a category will be ambiguous, that few individuals will agree completely on the "real" characteristics of blind people, and that clear-cut patterns of behavior in dealing with people will be lacking. Specifically, variations in attitudes toward blind people exist in the area of their personal attributes, the effect that blindness has on their lives in general, and the way in which blind people should be treated in personal interaction.[66] It is interesting to note, as Meyerson points out, that the conclusions of various researchers also reflect these ambiguities. Evidence has been found to both affirm and negate the following hypotheses: there is a special psychology of the blind; blind people have certain characteristic personality traits; blind people can, through adjustment, achieve normality; blind people have severe adjustment problems; and so on.[67]

Another factor contributing to the ambiguous nature of the category "blind people" has only recently begun to emerge, particularly during the last 25 years, namely, the increasingly successful rehabilitation of blind people and the decreasing acceptability of dependency and helplessness as social roles. Finer differentiations are being required of the public; the old categories are becoming even less appropriate now than they were in the past. This shift is also creating problems for many blind people; those who had formerly known their social role and could expect their actions to elicit certain responses are now being required to find new roles and to revise their own self-images. The present situation, therefore, is one of confusing transition.[68]

One final note on the so-called "halo" effect, the tendency of a category based on one characteristic to lead to assumptions about other characteristics. Physical attributes are particularly subject to such treatment. "Throughout recorded history, and probably before, man has been intrigued by the possibility that the outward characteristics of physique might in some way be a guide to the inner nature of man, to his temperament, his character, his personality." Palmistry and phrenology are the most noticeable forms of this kind of thinking. "Most of the inferences about personality based on physical signs have found no factual support in systematic investigation. Where relationships are revealed, the correlations are typically low." [69]

Throughout the foregoing discussion of expectation discrepancy, the affective aspects of the interaction have been noted, but not really examined. It will be recalled that sighted people reported having feelings of uneasiness, self-consciousness, tenseness, and self-doubt. The most immediate reaction to an expectation discrepancy, particularly when it is encountered suddenly and without warning, is surprise or perhaps even shock. The emotional element of a first encounter with a blind person is described by Townsend as follows:

> Unconsciously the fear of the unknown rushes to [the sighted person's] mind and a host of verbal traditions with which he is familiar. He feels something is expected of him but is at a loss to meet a circumstance for which he is so poorly prepared.[70]

Gowman writes, "Of the many disabilities, few are as capable of disturbing the studied rationality of man as is blindness." [71] In fact, the ubiquity of emotionality interferes with the rational assessment of blind people and with the efforts to assist blind people in their adjustment and rehabilitation. And not just the emotionality of the public, for it intrudes itself even among professional workers for the blind.[72] Some have even pointed to this problem as a paramount block to the full acceptance and integration of blind people into society.[73] Indeed, the necessary interdependence of intellect and emotion only highlights the degree to which there has been a general failure to come to terms with the affect produced by the idea of blindness.[74]

Although we will deal shortly with the specific emotions elicited by blindness and, in the next chapter, with the influence of blindness as an image or symbol, we can note at this point that "blind man" is what Allport calls a "label of primary potency," one of those linguistic symbols that "act like shrieking sirens, deafening us to all finer discriminations that we might otherwise perceive." [75] The many negative connotations of the word *blind* itself are a permanent part of the language and, necessarily therefore, are constantly being reinforced in the mind of the public.[76] The analogical situation thus created by the juxtaposition of "blind man" with "blind fury," "blind alley," "blind drunk," and so on is similar in effect to the negative connotations of *black* and its association with Negroes.

The primary potency of the word and image "blind man" also brings us back again to the visibility-obtrusiveness problem. Clearly, in some cases, the very existence of a blind person will be obtrusive, will disrupt the flow of social intercourse. Usually, however, obtrusiveness is a matter of degree. For example, it has been discovered by Lukoff and Whiteman that people in general respond to blindness in a somewhat different way than they respond to a blind person. "The image of blindness held by many people is more severe than the image they have of blind people, probably because blindness has more personalized connotations." [77] Elsewhere they suggest, "One possibility is that the reactions to people having a given attribute more effectively conjures up new and modifying characteristics which are not suggested by the attribute itself. . . ." [78] Jervis also found that ". . . the public does not respond to blindness per se but reacts to the way an individual blind person lives his life." [79] The degree of obtrusiveness seems to be related to how easily the individual's blindness can be disattended. If the only sign of a person's blindness is his dog guide or cane, it may be possible to note this and then ignore its implications. Lack of eye contact, on the other hand, may repeatedly interfere and keep the person's blindness in the forefront. [80] As long as the blindness of another is dominant in the mind of the perceiver its emotional ramifications, its valuation as a discrediting and nondesirable trait, will play a greater or lesser role in the interaction.

From our discussion so far, it can be seen that two different kinds of expectation discrepancy may occur in the interaction between a sighted and a blind person. The sighted person may expect that the other person will be sighted or, if he knows that the other person is blind, that he will behave in a certain way and have certain characteristics. As noted at the very outset of this chapter, it is in the primary reactions of sighted people to blind people that we are looking for the source of attitudes. Although we have noted that part of the strain of interacting with blind people is a result of perceived discrepancies in the category "blind person," our main emphasis in the following discussion of how people react to blind people will be on the sightedness-blindness discrepancy.

Because of the potency of blindness as a cue in an encounter, one of the immediate reactions of a sighted person to a blind person is a riveting of attention on that characteristic. As Gowman puts it, ". . . the sighted individual makes a drastic cognitive shift. He assumes that his usual reactions cannot be appropriately mobilized and searches for the special variety of interactive behavior which he feels is demanded." [81] Further, any strain in the interaction will likely be attributed to the deviation, even though other factors could be shown to be responsible.[82] As we have seen, however, the obtrusiveness of blindness may vary both in intensity and in duration. The potency of blindness in the interaction, and therefore the reason it obtrudes itself, results to a large extent from its strangeness, from the very fact that it is a discrepancy from the expected and usual. Heider's balance theory of sentiments is based on this idea.[83] Dr. Wright restates the theory briefly as positing "an interdependence between a person's liking for another (sentiment relation) and the connection of belongingness (unit relation) he perceives with that person. . . ." As she points out, however, ". . . the evidence that similarity and familiarity induce liking is much more consistent than that dissimilarity and unfamiliarity induce disliking. . . ." [84] We will return to this idea at a later point, though in a slightly different context.

One of the requirements of man's daily life is that it make some sense, that its many somewhat disparate parts sum to a comprehensible whole. When the out-of-the-ordinary, the unexpected, is encountered, it creates a disturbance and the average individual will make some effort to fit it into his world of experience and to reconcile it with his other beliefs. According to Wright, this is usually accomplished by revising one's expectations (that is, altering one's beliefs to accommodate the new evidence) or by altering the apparent reality (in effect, changing the evidence in some way so that it agrees with one's beliefs).[85] Throughout the rest of this chapter, we will examine the ways in which people confronted by an expectation discrepancy involving blindness attempt to reconcile it and the factors influencing that effort.

Broadly speaking, the difference between expectation revision and other means of resolving discrepancies is that while the former is a kind of learning, an expansion of one's knowledge, and a clarification of some aspect of reality, the latter efforts tend to distort reality and to narrow one's perception of it. Expectation revision, therefore, is the more desirable of the two reactions. Efforts to alter the apparent reality of a person or situation cannot, however, be unequivocally condemned, for, as we shall see, the forces and very human failings and inadequacies that motivate or even necessitate these alterations must be appreciated and accepted. Man's range of choice concerning the acceptability of certain aspects of reality is often severely limited.

Expectation revision is most likely to occur when an individual perceives the coping aspects of a person's adjustment to blindness.[86] In other words, when a person recognizes the problems and limitations caused by blindness, but can nevertheless acknowledge that "persons who are blind are more similar to, than different from, those who are sighted . . . ,"[87] he will be able to make adjustments in his expectations without compromising the blind person's humanity in any way. The result can, of course, be quite important to the individual blind person himself, for, as Lowry says,

> The blind person has a right to a strong and honest expectation from those in his relationship environment—honest, not only in terms of his handicap but also in terms of broader social standards or norms.[88]

Knowledge about blind people, but apparently only that derived from direct experience with blind people, is of primary importance in encouraging the revision of expectations.[89] The fact that blind people comprise such a small minority of the general population and that face-to-face encounters between blind and sighted people are, therefore, relatively uncommon surely accounts for the low incidence of expectation revision as compared with alteration of the apparent reality.[90]

If, as a result of an expectation discrepancy involving blindness or a blind person, an individual, for whatever reason, does not alter or revise his own expectations, he will in some way alter the apparent reality of the object. In other words, if he does not accept the discrepant phenomenon, he must to some degree reject it. "When evidence conflicts with categories," writes Allport, "it may be distorted . . . so as to seem to confirm the category." [91]

Why does this occur? Do some individuals have categories to which they find difficulty in admitting exceptions? The key to answering these questions would seem to lie in the individual's attitude toward such categories. It will be recalled from our earlier discussion of the nature of attitudes that the value-expressive function is superordinate to the other functions. With this in mind, then, it is clear that those categories directly related to an individual's personal set of values will be the ones toward which his attitudes will be the strongest. In other words, the organization of an individual's attitudes toward himself, along with the categories related to those attitudes, will be highly differentiated and central. Their degree of integration, specificity, and breadth, however, will depend on the person's level of maturity and degree of personality development.

> The most important categories a man has are his own personal set of values. He lives by and for his values. Seldom does he think about them or weigh them; rather he feels, affirms, and defends them. So important are the value categories that evidence and reason are ordinarily forced to conform to them.[92]

The tendency to alter the apparent reality of phenomena inconsistent with one's set of personal values can be viewed as an example of what Gerard terms the "action sequence."

> Any action engaged in by the person is designed to come to terms with his changing stimulus environment so that his outcomes (satisfactions) will be maximized. He will want to transact with objects having positive value for him and will avoid objects having negative value.[93]

At this point, the objection might be raised that both a person's set of values and his definition of a situation or object will

largely be culturally derived.[94] Tajfel, however, warns that
". . . it is easy to underestimate the extent of free play that a
cultural system of values and beliefs gives to individual varia-
bility." [95] This is not to say that cultural values do not play an
important role in such situations, but only that an individual
may very well go against those values when his more personal
values are at stake.

The point we are trying to make, put very simply, is that
a discrepancy in an expectation category that is perceived as
a threat to the personal values of an individual will be avoided
altogether if possible or, failing that, its apparent reality will
be altered in some way to lessen its threat. Siller and his associates cite two studies involving the relationship between a
"normal" individual's personal values and his attitudes toward
disabled persons. Steingisser found that well-adjusted individuals tend to have more positive attitudes toward blind people
than do those who are poorly adjusted.[96] Jabin found a high
correlation between rejection of the disabled and the degree to
which the disabled represent a threat to the self-concept and
security of the individual.[97] In their own studies, Siller and his
associates found that ". . . ego strength and the attainment
of stable object relationships are necessary for nondistorted
(accepting) feelings toward people with disabilities." [98] Still
other studies, concerned with the tendency of certain individuals to be prejudiced (that is, to hold negative attitudes based
on overgeneralizations) have discovered that personality structure plays a primary role.[99] Klineberg, in his review of the
literature, and others as well cite *The Authoritarian Personality* as the most important of these.[100] The exact relationship
between personality structure and attitudes toward disability
is, however, unknown, largely because of the limitations of
attitude and personality measuring instruments.[101] The influence of pathological conditions, traumatic experiences, and
even the pressure of social norms further complicate the problem.[102] For these reasons, we will confine ourselves in the fol-

lowing discussion to certain well-known and very general areas of personal values common to most people and eschew matters related to individual variations or idiosyncrasies.

"An attitude develops within a certain kind of individual, one who is exposed to certain social experiences and attributes certain meanings to these experiences." [103] Taking, first, the phrase concerning exposure to certain social experiences, we can begin this part of our investigation by asking the question: What will a perceptive and unbiased observer learn about a typical blind person in a face-to-face encounter? As was noted above in our discussion of expectation revision, a nondistorted view of an average blind person is that he is more similar to, than different from, those who are sighted. There are differences, but not really significant ones. Even if it is said, as Weelden does, that "the relations of the blind to objects, to their own selves, and to their fellow man are qualitatively different from those of the sighted," [104] the important point is that a blind person does have a relationship, is in touch with objects, himself, and other people. Further, somatopsychological studies have shown that these relationships are more similar to, than different from, those maintained by sighted people.[105] In other words, the unbiased observer will find that an average blind person is emotionally adjusted to his blindness;[106] his sensory and motor activities have reorganized themselves and are functioning efficiently;[107] his mental faculties have accommodated themselves to the loss of vision and are functioning quite as well as before the loss;[108] his self-concept is neither excessively positive nor negative;[109] in short, he will consider himself, except for his blindness per se, quite normal and complete.[110] When maladjustments are discovered, they will very rarely ever be directly a result of the loss of sight, but, rather, their causes will be the same as those that produce maladjustments in the sighted.[111] The only characteristic that all blind people share, therefore, is blindness. (Even blindness is not shared equally among all those who are called blind, for the term may refer to a range of severe visual impairments extending from total blindness—no visual perception at all—to functional blindness—no useful vision. Throughout this study, as we have noted before, we will take blindness to mean total blindness.) And if blindness, the absence of sight, is the only part of an individual's perception of a blind person's characteristics that differs from his own characteristics and would be unacceptable, then perhaps the next step in our study of attitudes toward blindness should be to examine attitudes toward sight.[112]

The sense of sight has often been called the "queen" of the senses,[113] but even without waxing poetic the importance of its role in the life of man cannot be denied. "It is, along with our other senses," Seeman writes, "a shield against danger and a fundamental weapon of survival. On a most primitive level, sight is a means of detecting food and, equally, of avoiding becoming food." [114] Gesell calls the eye "the crown jewel of organic evolution" [115] and, with his associates at Yale, has demonstrated the intimate relationship between vision and the development of man's entire action system.[116] Cutsforth says, "The most objective sort of human experience is visual experience. It gives detail which no other sense can provide; at the same time it brings objects into simultaneous relations of position, distance, size, and form." [117] These qualities of visual experience cited by Cutsforth have led, as Chevigny and Braverman note, to the linguistic equation of mental conception and sight, that is, to imagine something is to picture it. Likewise, comprehension is expressed as "seeing a point" or "viewing a situation." [118]

The relationship of sense perception, particularly sight, to knowledge has, in fact, been considered by philosophers. Molineux presented the following question to his friend, John Locke: Would a man who was born blind and who could distinguish between a cube and a sphere by touch be able to identify the two shapes correctly by sight alone if he were to have his blindness cured suddenly? In a sense, what Molineux was asking is does one see things and thus learn about them or must one learn to see in order to use sight for learning? Locke, in short, agreed with Molineux's suggested answer:

> Not. For though he has obtained the experience of how a globe, how a cube affects his touch, yet he has not yet obtained the experience, that what affects his touch so or so, must affect his sight so or so; or that a protuberant angle in the cube, that pressed his hand unequally, shall appear to his eye as it does in the cube.[119]

Bishop Berkeley also concurs, writing:

> . . . a man born blind, being made to see, would, at first, have no idea of distance by sight; the sun and stars, the remotest objects as well as the nearer, would all seem to be in his eye, or rather in his mind. The objects intromitted by sight, would seem to him (as in truth they are) no other than a new set of thoughts or sensations, each whereof is as near to him, as the perceptions of pain or pleasure, or the most inward passions of his soul. For our judging objects perceived by sight to be at any distance, or without the mind, is . . . entirely the effect of experience, which one in those circumstances could not yet have attained to.[120]

A modern psychologist, R. L. Gregory of Great Britain, reports that of the 60 or so recorded cases of congenitally blind persons recovering their sight (ranging from one in 1020 to one investigated by Gregory in the early 1960's), some reacted as Molineux had predicted. Others, however, could see quite well almost immediately. He concludes, "it is extremely difficult, if not entirely impossible, to use these cases to answer Molineux's question." On the other hand, based on his experiments with systematic distortions and displacements of retinal images (using prism-eyeglasses, mirrors, and other devices), Gregory did find that ". . . perception in man is susceptible to modification by learning . . . , but it is very difficult to establish just what is given and what is learned in infancy." [121]

In other words, therefore, the equation "seeing equals understanding" is not really valid. Nevertheless, the slightly more complex, but equally inaccurate, equation "understanding equals visualizing equals seeing" does seem to retain a hold on the imagination of many people.[122]

The net result of this kind of thinking and the other factors concerning the role of vision in man's life is that the importance of vision becomes greatly overestimated and it is deemed absolutely essential to life. In a certain sense, this is true, for the dependence of many people on sight is so complete that their other senses are relegated to an inferior role.[123] "The senses of smell, taste, and touch are primarily protective senses, biologically necessary for our existence. . . ." [124] Or, "The world of touch is the world of the lowest animals, the original primeval world of simple reflex actions and circumscribed life. . . . The world which opens to the seeing mind, on the other hand, is a unified, infinitely extended, beautifully colored, and variegated world." [125] Man is often said to be the most eye-minded of all living creatures.[126] Owing to the primary role of sight as a censor and tester of reality, the sighted person may assume that "without vision there can be no real grasp of reality." [127]

The overestimation of the importance of sight is, without denying its real value, quite unjustified. First, as Lowenfeld says, ". . . the non-visual senses are also actual as well as potential sources of experiences, and these experiences are not only as necessary but may also be as strong, vivid, and pleasurable as visual ones." [128] From the biological point of view, Whiteman writes,

> Where man excels is in the elaboration, interpretation, and ability to assign meanings to the sensory information fed into him by his sense organs. Once he gets that sensory information, in some form or other, the essentially human part of him begins to work it over, analyze, and conceptualize it. Indeed, evolutionary development is distinguished by the ability of the higher organisms, culminating

in man, to escape from the dominance of sensory control. . . . Rigid sensory control over behavior in the lower forms gives way to flexible, symbolic control in man.[129]

As noted above, Gesell and his associates have shown the fundamental interdependence of vision and the development of behavior in children. On the other hand, they also studied the effects of uncomplicated congenital anophthalmia on the patterning of a male infant, M. F.

> The developmental career of M. F. justifies the general conclusion that blindness in itself does not produce a serious degree of retardation. It profoundly alters the structure of mental life, but not the integrity of a total growth complex. . . . the basic patterns of body posture, manipulation, locomotion, exploitation, language, and adaptive and personal-social behavior have taken progressive form, thus establishing conclusively the fundamental role of maturation in the mental growth of the blind infant.[130]

What about the role of vision in personality development?

> . . . personality differences are not based on the way a person *senses*, but on the way a person *perceives*, or gives meaning to his sensations. Therefore blindness, insofar as it interferes only with visual *sensation*, need not cause personality alteration.[131]

It must be noted that Nagera and Colonna have studied the often "marked retardation and unevenness in the development of the total personality as shown in the Lines of Development" in some congenitally blind children.[132] (The Lines of Development is a concept, developed by Anna Freud, setting forth certain norms found in the psychological development of ego processes, drive development, object relationships, etc.)[133] Developmental retardation, they conclude, "is in part due to the lack of sight . . . and in part to environmental interferences such as pity and overprotection." [134] Nowhere do they suggest that lack of vision *prevents* psychological maturation.

Finally, whether the importance of sight is accurately appraised or not, most sighted individuals are firmly convinced that what they are able to accomplish is due largely to the fact that they can see and that their success would have been impossible without sight. (It is interesting to note at this point, as Whiteman observes, that no one counts as a visual handicap the inability of man to perceive ultraviolet or infrared light or other lengths of energy waves outside the narrow band of the visible spectrum. This, he goes on, ". . . attests to the force with which the culture selects particular psychological capacities for valuation and devaluation.")[135] This conviction is partly a result of the common experience of being clumsy and disoriented when one is in total darkness. "This kind of 'blindness,'" writes Father Carroll, "is within our experience, and so we generalize from it about the unknown experience of real blindness." [136]

We can see, therefore, that sight plays an important role in man's conception of his own ability to function and to survive. When a blind person is encountered, the sighted person may feel threatened in two ways that are closely related to this ability. First, the blind person reminds him of the vulnerability of his sight (related to the instinctive fear of being hurt or maimed in some way) and, by extension, his personal productivity and defense.[137] The practice of discarding the non-productive, especially in economically marginal societies or in societies under constant threat of attack, might be unconsciously feared even in the more benevolent and enlightened society of today.[138] Secondly, a perhaps more common reaction is the threat posed by someone who is blind and who is perceived as a functioning and productive person. In this instance, the highly valued sense of sight is shown in its true light, that is, as not absolutely essential. "These persons," writes Clunk, "are so proud of their daily achievements and responsibilities that they abhor the suggestion that a blind person can participate in the same activity and can contribute as much to a program of services as the Adonis-like competitor." [139]

Vision also is an important element in man's conception of "body-whole" and "body-beautiful." Despite the general emphasis in Judeo-Christian philosophy on the spiritual side of man, physical perfection and functional normality are highly valued traits in modern Western society and one of the requirements for full status as a human being.[140] There is even the well-known allegory of the body in the Bible in which it is said, "If one organ suffers, they all suffer together. If one flourishes, they all rejoice together" (1 Corinthians 12 : 14–26). The idea of a well-ordered body image is apparently universal throughout mankind,[141] although there is cultural variation in the exact characteristics considered to be indispensable.[142] Loss of vision, for reasons to be discussed shortly, is certainly a serious deviation from the norm.[143] When, therefore, a blind person is encountered, the sighted person's ". . . unconscious body image of himself may be threatened . . . inasmuch as he identifies to some extent with that person." [144] Further, when it is perceived that the blind person probably does not really feel incomplete, deviant, or marred, the viability of physique as a tool for determining social and personal distinctions is also threatened.[145]

The important role of vision in the body image of man is enhanced by the fact that the organs of sight are located in what many people consider the seat of personality, the region of the face and brain.[146] The close association of physique and identity[147] becomes, in this case, a threat to one's very individuality. The power of this belief is dramatically illustrated in the reactions of the sighted person who suddenly loses his sight. First, there is a period of shock: the person goes into a state of psychological immobility, of being unable to think or feel. "He reacts," Cholden writes, "to the feeling of imminent chaos and disintegration by an emergency constriction of his ego." [148] This is followed by a period of apathy and depression.

The patient is then reacting emotionally to his loss. He recognizes the loss of his vision and begins a period of mourning for his dead eyes. We all recognize the need for mourning the loss of a loved object. This is an apt comparison, for indeed the patient must die as a sighted person in order to be reborn as a blind man.[149]

It is perhaps understandable then that when contemplating another's blindness a sighted person may say to himself something like, " 'If blind, I would no longer be my recognizable self and therefore am horrified at the possibility of losing my ego. For all practical purposes I would then be dead because the self I know would not exist. . . .' " [150] Such a reaction in a person newly blinded and, therefore, presumably in the imagination of a sighted person, is especially pronounced in those individuals who are characterized as field-dependent.[151] In other words, blindness as "death" poses an extreme threat to those who "tend to be characterized by passivity in dealing with the environment; by unfamiliarity with and fear of their own impulses, together with poor control over them; by lack of self-esteem; and by the possession of a relatively primitive, undifferentiated body image." [152] When such a sighted person perceives that a blind person obviously does not feel "dead" (for it must be realized that the shock and depression induced by blindness are sooner or later transcended as the person adjusts to his blindness), it would seem that his own dependence, fears, low self-esteem, and poor body image are highlighted and brought forcefully into consciousness. Chevigny, writing about man's intense fear of blindness, says, "We stand in awe of the man who emerges from dangers we don't understand. . . ." [153] And, it will be recalled, *awe* is "an overwhelming feeling of reverence, admiration, fear, etc." or "the power to inspire fear or reverence." [154] In other words, the seemingly impossible adjustment of a person to blindness may threaten an individual by emphasizing his own weaknesses.

These, then, are some of the ways in which sighted people feel threatened when they encounter a blind person. We can now turn to some of the ways in which they react to these felt threats. It will be remembered that individuals often react to perceptions that they find threatening and, therefore, unaccept-able, by altering the apparent reality of the object of those perceptions. There are, as we will see shortly, a number of ways in which this may be done. Regardless of the way the apparent reality is altered, this kind of reaction, as Wright notes, "requires some fluidity in the perception of the reality, i.e., what is perceived cannot be bound too tightly to the ob-jective reality but must be responsive to the manipulations of the wishes and beliefs of the subject [the perceiver]." [155] As a result, the altered reality is often built around attributes that are nonessential or "noisy." [156]

It might seem that the alteration of the perceived reality of another person or group of persons would be recognizable as such to any other person. Apparently this is not the case. Many beliefs about blind people that have no basis in reality were seen, in the two preceding chapters, to enjoy wide accept-ance. Workers for the blind, who it would seem would have ample opportunity to test the reality of their beliefs about blind people, often are found to ascribe to mistaken notions. Meyer-son refers to these concepts as "vague feelings" and "strong beliefs." [157] Asenjo has strongly criticized agencies for the blind for "presenting to the public a portrait of the blind which bears little correspondence to the truth." [158] Sommers, in her investigation of the attitudes of parents of blind children, found that the adjustments made by these parents and their attitudes toward their child fall into five categories: accept-ance, denial, overprotectiveness, disguised rejection, and overt rejection.[159] In other words, even parents, whose perception of their own children might be thought to be favorably influenced by the natural ties of parent and child, can find the apparent reality of their perception unacceptable and react by denying its negative implications (denial reaction) or its positive as-pects (overprotection) or by rejecting the child himself.

To summarize, then, we see that when a sighted person objectively perceives a person who is blind he will learn that, except for his blindness per se, the person who is blind is more similar to, than different from, himself. This perception will, in turn, be considered threatening to a number of components of the sighted person's system of personal values. As we have seen, the threat to the individual's valuation of his sight is paramount. More specifically, the felt threat may involve the individual's beliefs concerning the importance of sight to his grasp of reality, to his ability to function and to survive, to his conception of wholeness as a physical and psychological entity, or to his identity as an individual. To reconcile this threatening discrepancy, the sighted person may completely alter the situation itself by placing the blind person outside the realm of normal expectations. He will, to use Wright's terminology, "anormalize" the blind person and attribute certain unusual characteristics, even supernatural ones, to him. This reaction is most likely to occur when, for whatever reason, the reality of the perception would be especially difficult to deny or to alter.[160] Here, then, is the mechanism through which the various compensatory powers are attributed to blind people. To say that a blind person, because of his blindness, is exceptionally religious in temperament, that he has a sixth sense, or that his remaining senses are unusually acute "means that he transcends the laws of ordinary mortals so that expectations relevant to normal persons do not apply." [161] Once this is done, the blind person's ability to function and his adjustment to his blindness are no longer seen as threatening. "After all," the sighted person may say, "he is not really like me at all."

The sighted person, as we have seen, places a high value on his vision. When he perceives that a blind person is not utterly miserable because he lacks vision, the sighted person's valuation is threatened. In this situation, the sighted person may simply demand that the blind person admit that he is miserable and that his apparent non-misery is a sham, a brave front, a mask. To rationalize this somewhat grotesque demand, the sighted person must, first of all, reverse the usual values connected with the perceived reactions to difficulties and misfortune. Normally, one who is seen to be coping with a problem is placed high on the scale of adjustment, while one who succumbs to difficulties is placed low on the scale. In this case, succumbing features are emphasized because they reinforce the values of the perceiver; at the same time, the coping aspects of the blind person are devalued or even blanked out and their existence denied.[162] The sighted person may invoke his own sympathetic response to the blind person. "Sympathy," Wispé writes, "is the capacity to apprehend the pain, suffering, or signs of negative emotions in man or animals and to respond to these with appropriate negative feelings." In other words, the sighted person will portray his sympathetic response as having greater veracity than even the statements or actions of the blind person. Sympathy, it should be noted, is not qualitatively the same as empathy. Wispé writes, "Empathy may be defined as the self-conscious effort to share and accurately comprehend the presumed consciousness of another person. . . . In empathy one attends to the feelings of another; in sympathy one attends to the suffering of another, but *the feelings are one's own*" [emphasis added].[163] This brings us to the idea of what Dembo calls "asset values." The invocation of asset values means that the sighted person's reaction to the blind person will be based on a demand for actions that are deemed appropriate to the situation.[164] In other words, the sighted person self-righteously demands that the blind person be miserable because that is the appropriate and, in this case, the only acceptable way for him to react to being blind. Another way of rationalizing the demand that the blind person admit his misery is to make misery a positive value. This can be done, for example, by repeating the popular belief that from suffering can come deep understanding and wisdom. While it might be argued that soul-*searching* experiences may be necessary to "enlightenment," there does not appear to be any reason to assume that soul-*torturing* experiences are necessary for such a result or for soul-searching experiences.[165] A reference to "enlightenment through suffering" is, in this instance, transparently self-seeking. It may be noted, finally, that this overwhelming need to pity a blind person may be attenuated when and if these rationalizations fail. Unfortunately, the sighted person may attribute this absence of misery to some extraordinary gift or power possessed by the individual; that is, the blind person is anormalized and his imagined suffering is, thus, magically assuaged.[166]

The fact that a blind person does not necessarily feel miserable also probably means that he is able to be objective about his blindness. For the sighted person who is consciously or unconsciously fearful of blindness, such a perceived attitude may be felt as threatening to any one of several of his values. For example, it may be important to the individual to believe that those who suffer misfortune have done something to deserve it, that fate does not strike indiscriminately.[167] Since the average blind person will neither agree that his blindness is a punishment nor exhibit any of the traits that might be thought deserving of such punishment, the sighted person may become highly suspicious of him, accuse him of hiding some deep, dark secret, and find evidence that betrays his immorality. Or, some may identify blindness itself with the horrible thing that they think is responsible for it. In this case, the blind person may be perceived as being repulsive. Finally, the individual may react negatively to his own judgment of a blind person as a sinner or monster. In this case, his own self-value is questioned and he asks, "Why is he blind and I am not?" He may then be led to consider his own sight an undeserved grace and the blind person an innocent victim. He reacts with shame and self-revulsion and pities the poor, miserable blind person.[168] In an extreme form, these guilty feelings may lead him to become a "typhlophile," one of "the overprotective, overkind friends of the blind [who] feed the 'positive' bias. . . ."[169] In other words, he perceives only pristine goodness and purity in the blind person and idealizes him to the point that, were it not for the sighted person's true feelings, we might be inclined to include this reaction with those classified above under anormalization.

Because the average individual places great value on his abilities and his accomplishments and because these values are a part of his overall self-esteem, he may feel threatened when he perceives that a blind person's abilities and accomplishments make it possible for him to be judged successful also and thus to acquire the status associated with success on a par with the sighted person. Here again the reaction may be denial: the sighted person may deny that the blind person is able to function and reject all evidence to the contrary. Apparently, however, the threat felt in this case is much more insistent or the reality much more resistant to alteration, for the sighted person may resort to a great variety of devices to reinforce his conviction that blind people are helpless, useless, and generally inferior to himself. First, he may try to rationalize his conviction by making certain assumptions about blindness and its effects. For example, he may say that blindness is, by its very nature, personally frustrating and that, therefore, the blind person is prevented from ever accomplishing anything.[170] While frustration may generally be considered a negative experience, ". . . a second look reveals that [it] is an inevitable part of life and a third look leads to the conclusion that it is capable of leading to highly desirable as well as to undesirable results." [171] Next, he may focus on some common human weakness or failing that the blind person also has and try to attribute it to some deficiency in the blind person, usually his blindness. This is what Heider calls the problem of attribution. Normally, if everyone has difficulty with a problem, the problem is considered difficult; if most people can cope with or solve the problem, the person who falls short is held at fault.[172] When an individual is rationalizing a belief, however, he will alter the reality of the situation by carefully overlooking the fact that a certain failing is rather common or, in this case, not at all peculiar to blind people. Along the same line, the individual may invoke comparative values. Wright, in discussing Dembo's theory of comparative values, says:

> . . . when we compare an object with a standard, we are interested in only certain characteristics of the object (e.g., physique). Because these characteristics are within our field of concern, they become potent and have the power to impose their properties upon our perception and evaluation of other characteristics not being compared at the moment and which, therefore, are vague and unstructured. If physical normalcy is taken as a standard and a disability is viewed as far below standard, other vague characteristics and the person himself are regarded as below standard.[173]

This is what is sometimes called the "halo" effect, meaning that the attributes of one characteristic "spread" to other characteristics. Lowry has noted that social caseworkers working with blind people may even sometimes be guilty of using inappropriate comparative values in assessing an individual client. He may be devalued, ". . . because he is functioning less adequately than some other blind persons do." [174] Finally, there is the common and very disarming mental device of admitting exceptions. "By excluding a few favored cases," writes Allport, "the negative rubric is kept intact for all other cases. In short, contrary evidence is not admitted and allowed to modify the generalization; rather it is perfunctorily acknowledged but excluded." [175]

In addition to these efforts to explain away the apparent reality, the individual may take various forms of action to bolster what to him is a more acceptable "reality." He may make disparaging allusions about blind people, or deprecate or ridicule them. He may carefully emphasize the word "blind" in saying "a blind man" to avoid any hint that he might merely be using the short-cut phrase "a blind man" for the psychologically sounder "a man who is blind." The latter phrase, or the short-cut version of it, "connotes that a person with a disability [in this case, blindness] is first a person with many unspecified characteristics in addition to a particular disability." [176] The short-cut phrase itself tends to reduce the life of the individual to only a single aspect—his blindness—but it especially does so when the word "blind" is emphasized. The sighted person may espouse segregated employment (and, perhaps, recreation and housing) for blind people because, it is reasoned, they need special protection and help. [177] In other words, they are to be excluded from normal society "for their own good." This kind of rejection, this deliberate blanking out of positive values and forcing the blind person to be dependent is often seen in the parents of blind children. [178] Their overprotectiveness will usually quite effectively prevent the child from becoming independent, just as a similar attitude in employers will effectively keep a blind worker from ever proving his ability. [179]

When the belief that blind people as a group are helpless and useless reaches the point at which it becomes rigid and exceptions are only grudgingly admitted, it would seem that we may correctly call the concept a stereotype. According to Allport, ". . . a stereotype is an exaggerated belief associated with a category. Its function is to justify (rationalize) our conduct in relation to that category." [180] Within the context of the present discussion, it may also be mentioned that a stereotype is usually simple rather than complex or differentiated, erroneous rather than accurate, and resistant to modification by new experience. [181] On the other hand, it would seem that a part of the power of the stereotype as a device for rejecting an individual (on the basis of his membership in a certain category) lies in the fact that the stereotype may have its origin in a kernel of truth. [182] That there are contradictory stereotypes of blind people, as has been noted several times, only emphasizes the point that true group traits are not involved (the kernel of truth notwithstanding). "The point at issue," writes Allport, "is rather that a dislike requires justification, and that any justification that fits the immediate . . . situation will do." [183]

Because stereotypes play such an important role in prejudice, the preceding discussion leads us to ask whether or not blind people are ever the victims of prejudice. Taking Allport's definition of prejudice—". . . an antipathy based upon a faulty and inflexible generalization [which is] . . . felt or expressed [and is] . . . directed toward a group as a whole, or toward an individual because he is a member of that group"— and his description of its net effect—placing "the object of prejudice at some disadvantage not merited by his own misconduct"—the answer must clearly be in the affirmative. [184] Social discrimination, one of the active components of prejudice in which individuals are systematically and unfairly excluded from certain activities, [185] may include denial of opportunity, segregation, and "barriers to the acquisition of full self-respect and intrapsychic harmony. . . ." [186] As we have seen, blind people are often discriminated against in these ways. "Critical to the whole idea of social discrimination," Yinger writes, ". . . is the fact that it is embedded in social structures and sustained by group practices. . . ." [187] Here again it can be seen that the unfair treatment of blind people is often built into situations. Environmental supports, the tendency to perceive only situations in which blind people will confirm the overgeneralization that forms the basis of a discriminatory practice, are widely employed in the service of prejudice against blind people. [188] In other words, discrimination is sustained and extended through self-fulfilling prophecies. [189]

The fact that blind people are often discriminated against raises the additional question of whether or not any of the results of the extensive research on ethnic prejudice are applicable to prejudice toward blind people. There are some similarities between the two objects of prejudice. For example, blind people are in a minority compared to the sighted population; they are usually easily identifiable; through overgeneralization they are assumed to have many traits in common.[190] Cowen, Underberg, and Verrillo report, "Significant correlations between negative attitudes to blindness and Anti-minority, Anti-Negro, and pro-authoritarian attitudes were found" in their study.[191] Lukoff and Whiteman write, "The conditions that foster *ethnic* tolerance and acceptance may also foster *blindness* tolerance and acceptance." [192] On the other hand, there are several important differences. For example, it has been noted that blind people do not really constitute a group in the same sense as individuals with the same ethnic background, religion, social class, etc., form a group. "Blind persons are derived from the dominant group, the sighted. In their primary social relations, therefore, they are intimately linked to the sighted world and share in the general cultural heritage. Other minority group members, connected to each other by descent and kinship, are more dissociated from the dominant social fabric." [193] Another difference is the lack of a widely accepted attitude structure. "This suggests that the extension of some of the experience from minority group research and theory may not be as useful as heretofore thought, unless considerably modified. Blind persons do not meet very consistent attitudes; nor are they organized by sighted persons in ways suggested by current theory in the field of minority research." [194] Because of these and other drawbacks to comparing blind people as a minority group with ethnic minorities, Jordan suggests defining them as and comparing them with a disadvantaged group. The members of a disadvantaged group, as defined by Jordan, have one trait in common that "influences [their] psychological and social orientation . . . and is the means by which they are identified." [195] While this construct does eliminate most of the objections to considering blind people in a class with ethnic minority groups, the paucity of research on the dynamics of attitudes toward the disadvantaged prevents our elaborating on the suggestion any further than this brief mention of it.

Returning to the subject of altering the apparent reality, it can be observed that there is a common feature throughout the alterations already discussed. In most instances, the sighted person has been seen to perceive something in the behavior of a blind person which threatens certain of his personal values and to which he reacts by denying the reality of that behavior. In each of these instances, however, the initial perception is that the other person is blind, that he is, in this respect, different from the observer, who is sighted. The whole difficulty in acknowledging that in all other respects the blind person is more similar to, than different from, the sighted observer can be considered, therefore, to originate in this unalterable reality, the person's blindness. So far we have only considered the sighted person's reaction to the behavior of a blind person, including not only the blind person's actions, but also his state of mind and its outward behavioral manifestations; we have not considered the hypothesis that apart from the blind person's behavior, the perception that a blind person is indeed a person may also be threatening. In other words, it is suggested, a sighted person may be unable to accept the fact that an individual who cannot see is nevertheless equal in his humanness to one who can see. The blind person's expressed or implied insistence on his right to "fellow humanity" may be felt to threaten the sighted person's criteria of those with whom he will admit basic equality. His reaction to this claim will be fearfulness and he will want to avoid contact with the blind person. In an effort to justify this avoidance he may resort to a great variety of mental devices and, because denying the humanness of another person is not at all easy and not usually socially acceptable, the devices may be quite extraordinary. Actually, as we shall see, fear may be masked and avoidance managed in such a way that the question of their acceptability is rarely ever raised.

In this case, the alteration of the apparent reality primarily involves the other person's blindness; the physiological inability to perceive light waves is transformed into a sign indicating that its possessor is inferior, not quite human, discredited. In short, the blind person is ". . . an individual who might have been received easily in ordinary social intercourse [but he] possesses a trait that can obtrude itself upon attention and turn those of us whom he meets away from him, breaking the claim that his other attributes have on us. He possesses a stigma, an undesired differentness from what we had anticipated." [196] In its original sense, as used by the Greeks, the word "stigma" referred to signs burnt or cut into the body to identify the bearer as a slave, criminal, traitor, or any other kind of person who was to be avoided. Today, it refers both to the sign and to the disgrace or other discrediting quality it signifies. Since the signs that may now be thought to be stigmas no longer carry with them a clear indication of their discrediting meaning, those who believe in them must ". . . construct a stigma-theory, an ideology to explain [the stigmatized person's] inferiority and account for the danger he represents, sometimes rationalizing an animosity based on other differences, such as those of social class." [197]

In considering the theories and ideologies used to support the stigmatization of blind people, it should first be noted that there may be varying degrees of discredit associated with the stigma. For example, based on the idea that because blind people are different, they should be treated differently,[198] they may be assigned to a marginal position in society, one that lies outside the normal social continuum, ". . . where they function as strangers in an uneasy social limbo." [199] At the other extreme, it might be suggested that because lower life forms defile their disabled (a conclusion involving the "principle of genetic reductionism"—in this case a false conclusion), more Draconian measures for blind people may be considered sanctionable.[200]

One common kind of rationalization used in discrediting blind people may involve what Franz Alexander has termed an "emotional syllogism." Simply put, an emotional syllogism is the elementary process in man by which certain cause and effect sequences and connections are immediately apprehended. Further, the resulting conclusions are felt to be self-evident and to require no further elaboration or argument.[201] For example, cause and effect qualitatively resemble each other; disability is negative, evil, undesirable; therefore, the cause of disability must be negative, evil, undesirable. If the cause of disability is negative, evil, undesirable, then disability itself may, in turn, produce additional negative, evil, undesirable consequences in the disabled person. In short, blindness is bad, therefore, the blind person is bad. Or, in terms that a primitive might use: blindness is evil; evil is caused by evil spirits; therefore, a blind person is "possessed" by an evil spirit (and further evil, it is understood, may be expected from the evil spirit–blind person).[202] Given its base in man's emotions and feelings, in his sense of what is appropriate and "right," the logic is unassailable. It can also be seen that this kind of thinking is similar to the process of anormalization discussed above; the difference being that here the result is more patently negative.[203] One explanation, suggested by Meng, for the fear and avoidance of the physically disabled places their origin in three deep, often unconscious, mechanisms, the first of which, to use the terminology from the preceding discussion, is an "emotional syllogism":

> (a) belief that physical distortion is a punishment for evil, and hence that a disabled person is evil and dangerous; (b) belief that a disabled person has been unjustly punished and therefore is under pressure to do an evil act in order to balance the injustice, and hence is dangerous; (c) projection of one's own unacceptable desires upon the disabled, and hence the belief that he is evil and dangerous.[204]

Here we find that an individual's sense of the relationship between evil and punishment and of the nature of justice and injustice may play an important role in how he perceives a person with a physical handicap. Further, the introduction of the idea of projection, which will be considered in more detail in the next chapter, reminds us of the many complex ways in which the psychological state of the perceiver may alter the apparent reality of much of what he encounters without his being aware of it.

If a sighted person believes that blindness is a stigmatizing condition, there is, in a sense, one sociologically sound reason for wanting to avoid contact, especially intimate contact, with blind people. That reason is that ". . . in certain circumstances the social identity of those an individual is with can be used as a source of information concerning his social identity, the assumption being that he is what the others are." [205] In other words, it is part of the nature of stigmas that their discrediting effect will spread to those who associate with stigma-bearers, but only in the eyes of those who also consider the same characteristic to be stigmatizing. This raises another very interesting point. If an individual himself does not consider blindness a stigma, he may nevertheless be aware that many other people do. Because of the spreading effect of stigma, therefore, he may be reluctant to associate with blind people. It has been found that readiness to interact with blind people decreases as the degree of social intimacy increases.[206] In other words, a sighted person will often want to avoid those situations in which he is more likely to be identified as being "with" a blind person than those in which their association is more distant or impersonal.

There is one way in which the complex behavior involving avoidance is sometimes bypassed: the stigmatized person is granted a "phantom" normalcy which, if he cooperates (and his reciprocation is essential), leads to a "phantom" acceptance. This arrangement is described in detail by Goffman, but we can briefly say that it involves the blind person (the stigma-bearer) limiting his actions and demands so that his blindness may be ignored. By conforming to these limits, he will in no way threaten the values of those involved with him and will, to some extent, confirm their expectations for him. In return, he is granted a limited degree of acceptance; he becomes an "honorary" normal. In assessing such phantom relationships, Goffman writes:

> The irony of these recommendations is not that the stigmatized individual is asked to be patiently for others what they decline to let him be for them, but that this expropriation of his response may well be the best return he can get on his money. If in fact he desires to live as much as possible "like any other person," and be accepted "for what he really is," then in many cases the shrewdest position for him to take is this one which has a false bottom; for in many cases the degree to which normals accept the stigmatized individual can be maximized by his acting with full spontaneity and naturalness as if the conditional acceptance of him, which he is careful not to overreach, is full acceptance. . . . Any mutual adjustment and mutual approval between two individuals can be fundamentally embarrassed if one of the partners accepts in full the offer that the other appears to make; every "positive" relationship is conducted under implied promises of consideration and aid such that the relationship would be injured were these credits actually drawn on.[207]

Here, once again, the blind person's individuality is denied. His blindness is like a mask, an impenetrable curtain, that always takes precedence over his identity as a person. For most blind people, as Weelden says, it may be only among their closest friends that they can fully attain fellow humanity. "Here at last, freed from social impediments, he can address the others and be addressed by them as a man." [208]

What is it about blindness that gives it this dominating influence, this great capacity for gripping men's minds? As we have seen in this chapter, sighted people feel threatened by the thought of blindness and by contact with blind people. And while we have investigated some of the reasons for this reaction, there still seem to be unanswered questions. Sighted people commonly overestimate the importance of sight and thus feel threatened by its loss. On the other hand, other overestimated aspects of people's lives do not elicit the affect-laden response that blindness does. Loss of sight threatens a person's idea of his wholeness, and yet other losses of senses or even limbs or areas of functioning are feared much less than blindness. We could recapitulate any number of similar factors about which the same parallels could be noted, but the point is that sight and blindness carry some affective "charge" that goes well beyond the explanatory capacity of our discussion so far. Sight and blindness obviously mean much more than the ability to see and the inability to see. It is to this deeper layer of meaning that we will now turn to discover, if possible, the fundamental values and significance of sight and its loss.

4 The Meaning of Blindness

IN THE TWO PRECEDING CHAP-
ters we have reviewed the
two ways in which attitudes are most commonly thought to
develop. As we have seen, the beliefs and misconceptions underlying a number of attitudes are passed on from generation
to generation with the individual learning them as part of
the ongoing process of socialization. Many attitudes are also
a product of actual encounters with blind people, with the
sighted person, either as an observer or as a participant, reacting to his perceptions both of the blind person and of the encounter. Although these explanations reveal many of the factors influencing the formation of attitudes, they nevertheless
leave many questions unanswered. For example, it has been
noted that the attention given to blind people (in folk tale and
legend in the past, in the large number of agencies and amount
of funds devoted to work for the blind in the present), is out of
all proportion to their actual numbers (see above, p. 2).
Why? What is it about blindness that creates this "interest"?
Despite more than 50 years of extensive public information
programs aimed at correcting misconceptions about blindness,
its causes, and its effects, a person's blindness is still perceived
to the exclusion of his other qualities and traits. Why? What
is it about blindness that even after false ideas are supposedly
cleared away, there remains a barrier to the acceptance of the
blind person as simply a person who cannot see? We have
learned that the overestimation of the importance of sight is
basic to many of the attitudes. We have not learned, however,

why this is true of sight in particular or why there is such an extreme reaction to the loss of sight. Finally, little light has been shed upon the feeling of many that blind people are mysterious, magical, and to be feared.

Admittedly these are difficult questions and ones that are not readily investigated through the tests, surveys, and questionnaires of social scientists and psychologists. It is understandable then why they are so seldom raised and almost never seriously pursued. The little notice that has been given to this dimension of attitudes toward blindness and blind people is, nevertheless, informative. Gerhard Schauer, in discussing the frictions and difficulties encountered in interactions between blind and sighted people, suggests that there may be an unconscious side to the problem in addition to the conscious one.[1] Father Carroll notes that attempts to examine attitudes rationally are greatly hampered by powerful and often conflicting emotions.[2] Chevigny and Braverman write that the practical basis through which each organ, limb, and sense of the body is given value is complicated by the fact that each of these also has irrational meanings.[3] (Two of these authors, Father Carroll and Sydell Braverman, have speculated on the deeper meaning of blindness: the former, in the context of the adjustment of the newly blinded individual, cites a blindness-death parallel; the latter, using the theories of Freud, relates the fear of blindness to castration anxiety. These two theories will be considered in more detail at a later point in this chapter.) Alan Gowman, who briefly notes several of the notions about this dimension of attitudes, makes a very interesting and suggestive comment, that many of the common reactions are "to the symbolic content of blindness."[4] What emerges from these few authors is an indication that underlying the attitudes toward blindness and blind people there are unconscious, highly emotional, and irrational factors related to the symbolic meaning of blindness.

Given this, how then shall we proceed to discover the nature and meaning of these factors and the role they play in the formation of attitudes? As we have said, these are areas with which most students of human behavior do not concern themselves. The unconscious, emotional, and non-rational world of symbolic content and meaning is, admittedly, not subject to the precise definition, complete objectivity, and syllogistic logic that are usually considered necessary to scientific consideration. Further, the average scientist has largely disavowed the heuristic value of superstition and myth and may see his role as one of freeing the world of their primitive, irrational influence. The observations recounted above, however, indicate the continued, very active influence of this "other" world of phenomena on modern man.[5] Fortunately, symbolism has, during the last 75 years, been subjected to scientific inquiry through the investigations of the depth psychologists. And it is to their findings that we will turn for aid in our investigation.

We will begin, then, as the psychologist does, with the basic phenomena of the individual's reaction to a blind person. This reaction is, as we have seen, highly emotional and irrational, and seemingly involves unconscious factors. Such a reaction usually signifies the existence of a disruptive complex of some sort. The complex is described as "an autonomous set of impulses grouped around certain kinds of energy-charged ideas and emotions; it is expressed in *identity, compulsiveness* and *primitivity, inflation,* and *projection.*" [6] By taking each part of this description of the complex in turn and applying it to the phenomena of attitudes toward blindness, we can determine the usefulness of the concept of the complex for our study. First, we have "an autonomous set of impulses." Certainly, the reactions of many sighted people are impulsive, that is, not under conscious control or regulation. They are also autonomous in the sense that the reaction apparently stems from a source beyond that of the personal psychology of the individual. Blindness is certainly an "energy-charged" idea. "Identity" is a state in which the individual does not distinguish between his own reactive capacity and his impulses and drives. In other words, he does not recognize the autonomous and impulsive nature of certain of his reactions. Those who fear and avoid blind people often exhibit this unconscious identity. In this state of identity, the impulses from the unconscious are "compulsive" and "primitive," that is, they possess the individual even though he feels that he is having them and, because there is little conscious intervention in the expression of these impulses, they are uncontrolled, destructive, inappropriate, undifferentiated—primitive. Compulsiveness and primitivity can be observed in the feeling of repugnance and in the out-and-out prejudice against blind people that is exhibited by some sighted people. "Inflation" results from the compulsive nature of the complex when the energy behind the compulsion is mistaken for personal power or a sense of total assurance in the rightness of one's actions and feelings. This phenomenon can be observed in the overestimation of the value and benefits of sight and in the belief that the loss of sight is utterly devastating and results in abject misery and despair. Finally, the complex will involve "projection," that is, it will be encountered as though it existed as a characteristic of another person (or object). Projected characteristics can be distinguished from the person's actual characteristics (although not usually by the individual experiencing it) by their strong emotional coloring and by a complete inability to react to the person in an acceptable, reasonable way.[7] As Whitmont writes:

> Where we do not project, we may see something which displeases us but we can decide for ourselves whether it is necessary or important or relevant that we go and do something about it. We may choose to do so for reasons of our own. However, when we see something which displeases us and are compulsively involved in how we feel about it and can neither take it or leave it, then we are projecting. Projection denies us freedom of choice. To the extent that projection recedes we can choose the appropriate time and place for action or nonaction, even for relationship or no relationship.[8]

It can be seen that projection is involved in such affect-laden beliefs about blindness and blind people as the "world of darkness" and sinfulness and immorality. Also it would seem that the overly insistent pitiers and helpers of blind people are reacting to projections, that is, to their own sense of inferiority or helplessness. The idea of the complex, therefore, appears to be useful in describing those reactions and attitudes toward blindness and blind people that we are investigating in this chapter. Our next step then is to try to discover how this complex of behavior can be analyzed and how the specific psychological meaning it expresses can be revealed.

The complex has usually very distinct parts: a "shell" and a core. Of the former, Whitmont writes that they "are largely shaped by childhood events, childhood traumas, difficulties and repressions and so can always be reductively traced to one's personal past and explained in terms of cause and effect . . . these associational patterns are the concrete manifestations of the complex in the here and now. They explain and express the complex as an autonomous pattern of behavior and emotion. . . ." [9] Our discussion in the two preceding chapters has, when viewed in this light, been an explication of this outer layer of the attitude-complex. We have, for example, noted the influence on attitudes of a sighted person's experience of the dark, of stories and tales he heard as a child, and of possibly embarrassing or awkward encounters with blind people. Since this discussion nevertheless leaves certain questions unanswered, the meaning of blindness must lie beyond this personalistic layer of the complex, that is, in the core of the complex.

As might be expected, the complex, as a basic structural element of the psyche, is grounded in the instincts. Defining the instincts as basic aptitudes or preformed tendencies toward typical reaction modes,[10] leads us to the idea that reactions to blind people are, in some sense, instinctual. This is not to say that there is an instinct specifically related to blind people.

That, needless to say, would be missing the point. We have already established that attitudes toward blindness and blind people are a result of a reaction not so much to the fact of blindness, of someone not being able to see, as to the meaning of blindness, its symbolic significance. Further, this significance, as Chevigny and Braverman point out, seems to have varied little throughout history or from culture to culture,[11] a positive indication of its close relationship with the instinctual side of man. Returning then to the formulations of analytical psychology, or, as it was once called, complex psychology, "The core of the complex . . . consists of the nucleus of a universal pattern which is called an *archetype* of the collective unconscious or of the objective psyche. . . . The archetypes are collective in the sense that they are no longer purely personal contents belonging to this or that person in terms of individual associations and histories, but belong rather to the trends toward certain types of symbolic representations inherent in all of us." [12] Or, as another author, Erich Neumann, expresses it, the archetypes "are the pictorial forms of the instincts, for the unconscious reveals itself to the conscious mind in images which, as in dreams and fantasies, initiate the process of conscious reaction and assimilation." [13] Undoubtedly, the concept of the archetype is one of the most significant discoveries made by C. G. Jung and one of the most controversial. There are a great many misconceptions about what an archetype is and what its ramifications as a concept are. This, however, is certainly not the place to review all of the evidence that led Jung to this hypothesis or to weigh all of the arguments and objections raised against it.[14] For the purposes of this discussion, it would seem that the archetype, like the complex, is a useful hypothesis, and one which will explain certain things and help us to understand some of the factors influencing attitudes toward blindness. As M.-L. von Franz writes:

> We are still far from understanding the unconscious or the archetypes—those dynamic *nuclei* of the psyche—in all their

implications. All we can see now is that the archetypes have an enormous impact on the individual, forming his emotions and his ethical and mental outlook, influencing his relationships with others, and thus affecting his whole destiny.[15]

The archetype, as the central element or core of the complex, is expressed in images. These images are most readily accessible to us through reference to myths, symbols, folk lore, and legends—the forms in which archetypal images are recorded. Although myths and symbols can, on an objective, rationalistic level, be thought of as fabrications and error-filled superstitions, they can also be viewed as a picture language in which the myth-motifs express metaphysical, psychological, and sociological truths.[16] As Heaton says, ". . . they point to the ground from which both the person and his world arise. They are the *gestalt* from which the self differentiates itself from its world, while at the same time being in the world." [17]

To discover the symbolic meaning of blindness, therefore, we will take the key ideas underlying attitudes toward blindness and investigate their mythological, or archetypal, significance. More specifically, we will explore the symbolism of light and darkness, the eye, and the loss of the eye or sight in order to determine the unconscious factors involved at the core of the attitude-toward-blindness complex. It must be noted, however, that because of the very nature of symbolism and of the unconscious (from where its meaning is derived), we cannot approach such matters directly. When dealing with things which to our logical and rational sensibilities are irrational (actually, non-rational would be more accurate), ever-changing, and, most important, charged with the emotion of living experience, it must be acknowledged that any effort at strict systematization of such material will lead us to either concretization (and betrayal of the dynamic quality of the material) or superficiality (a lack of awareness that much of the

meaning is ultimately unknowable). Von Franz explains the
situation as follows:

> Modern depth psychology has reached the same limits that con-
> front microphysics. That is, when we are dealing with statistical
> averages, a rational and systematic description of the facts is pos-
> sible. But when we are trying to describe a single psychic event,
> we can do no more than present an honest picture of it from as
> many angles as possible. In the same way, scientists have to admit
> that they do not know what light is.[18]

' The main source of all our knowledge about symbolism
is dreams, where symbols occur spontaneously.[19] Unfortunately, we have practically no data on dream imagery directly
involving blindness. The literature on the dreams of blind persons, potentially a rich source of symbols related to blindness,
is singularly deficient in reports of imagery and its interpretation.[20] In addition, there is little in the literature on dream
imagery in general that relates directly to the blind person as
a symbol. It is for these reasons that we have chosen the
images of light, the eye, and loss of the eye and that our main
sources of information about them will be myths, legends, and
folk tales.

Light and Darkness

One of the primary aspects of the world that has inelec-
tably influenced the evolution of life is the diurnal alternation
of light and dark. For man, this experiencing of the world soon
assumed dramatic proportions because:

> . . . at night the world sleeps, dangers lurk, and the mind plunges
> into a realm of dream experience, which differs in its logic from
> the world of light. . . . Dawn, and awakening from this world
> of dream, must always have been associated with the sun and sun-
> rise. The night fears and night charms are dispelled by light,
> which has always been experienced as coming from above and as
> furnishing guidance and orientation. Darkness, then, and . . . the

dark interior of the earth, of the jungle, or of the deep sea, as well as certain extremely poignant fears and delights, must for millenniums have constituted a firm syndrome of human experience, in contrast to the luminous flight of the world-awakening solar sphere into and through immeasurable heights. Hence a polarity of light and dark, above and below, guidance and loss of bearings, confidence and fears . . . must be reckoned as inevitable in the way of a structuring principle of human thought.[21]

It is not surprising, therefore, that the myths of Creation throughout the world are connected with this powerful, primary pair of opposites. Out of chaos, out of nothingness, out of a state of complete nondifferentiation, light and darkness, heaven and earth, are separated. Archetypally, the nondifferentiated state is symbolized by the uroboros (a serpent with its tail in its mouth), a closed, unitary system. Creation is symbolized by the separation of the World Parents, as in Egyptian mythology when Shu, the god of the air, parts Nut (the sky) and Geb (the earth) by stepping between them. Or similarly, the story at Genesis I : I–4. Within the context of the evolution of human consciousness, Creation symbolizes the emergence of the nascent ego from the nondifferentiated, preconscious period. Once this differentiating has begun, both for mankind in the prehistoric period and for the individual human being as a child, there is a steady increase in the number of pairs of opposites that grow out of the primary pair (light and darkness).

The inward as well as the outward development of culture begins with the coming of light and the separation of World Parents. Not only do day and night, back and front, upper and lower, inside and outside, I and You, male and female, grow out of this development of opposites and differentiate themselves from the original promiscuity, but opposites like "sacred" and "profane," "good" and "evil," are now assigned their place in the world.[22]

In many of these pairs, as indicated by the last two noted above, the idea that one side is to be sought and the other avoided arises. By virtue of the orderliness that the emergence of consciousness brings, the original unconscious state is felt to be negative and threatening. That is, although it is through consciousness that light and darkness are separated, once they are separated light and the separation of light are taken to symbolize consciousness and darkness the unconscious.[23] Further, because ego consciousness is at first very weak and because it must "wrest libido [psychic energy] from the unconscious for its own existence," the unconscious is experienced as a power threatening to overcome or "devour" consciousness.[24]

With their profound ties both with the perceptual development of life through the eons and with the psychic development of mankind and of every individual human being, light and darkness have become extraordinarily powerful symbols. As symbols, their realms of meaning and significance have expanded to include many related ideas. For example, *light* can mean "mental or spiritual illumination or enlightenment" and "information, ideas, or mental capacities possessed," while *to see* can mean to understand, to recognize, to learn, and to have insight.[25] In the entry for *light* in Cirlot's *Dictionary of Symbols,* we find that light can be equated with spirit, manifestations of morality, intellect, or virtue, and with spiritual strength.[26] Others have noted that light may symbolize life itself, or that which transcends life, the ecstatic, or even God.[27] The time of light—day—is often considered propitious or opportune.[28] White, associated with the sun, day, and light, is an auspicious sign, one signifying purity, innocence, and the absence of malice.[29] "The function of white is derived from that of the sun: from mystic illumination—symbolically of the East; when it is regarded as purified yellow . . . , it comes to signify intuition in general, and, in its affirmative and spiritual aspect, intuition of the Beyond." [30]

Dark, on the other hand, can mean "gloomy, cheerless, dismal," "sullen, frowning," "evil, iniquitous, wicked," "destitute of knowledge or culture," "hard to understand, obscure," "hidden, secret," or "silent, reticent." To be *in the dark* is to be "in ignorance, uninformed." [31] *Black* can have many of these same meanings plus it is often associated with inner or subterranean zones, with time, tragedy, and death.[32] The time of darkness—night—symbolizes "a state or time of obscurity, ignorance, misfortune, etc." [33] Darkness as the "shadow" represents man's negative side, his primitive and instinctive nature.[34] It is important to note, however, that darkness is not wholly negative, not the mere absence of light. In the occult sciences, black, night, and darkness can symbolize the initial, germinal stages of all processes, the maternal, fertile principle of potentiality, and the Hidden Source of wisdom.[35]

Such basic symbols as light and darkness are naturally present in the mythology of every culture past and present. To mention a few outstanding examples, we can note the Yin-Yang principle from the Orient upon which the 64 hexagrams of the classic *I Ching* are based. There is Lucifer, the Light Bearer, who became, after his fall out of heaven, the Angel of Darkness. Heaton notes, "In the *Tibetan Book of the Dead* the lama exhorts the newly dead person in these words: 'Reverend Sir, now that thou art experiencing the Fundamental Clear Light, try to abide in that state which now thou art experiencing.' " [36] In the Old Testament we read, "I set myself to look at wisdom and at madness and folly. Then I perceived that wisdom is more profitable than folly, as light is more profitable than darkness: the wise man has eyes in his head, but the fool walks in the dark." (Ecclesiastes 2 : 12–14) and "I, the Lord, have called you with righteous purpose and taken you by the hand; I have formed you, and appointed you to be a light to all peoples, a beacon for the nations, to open eyes that are blind, to bring captives out of prison, out of the dungeons where they lie in darkness" (Isaiah 42 : 6–7). In the New Testament, "A man may say, 'I am in the light'; but if he hates his brother, he is still in the dark" (1 John 2 : 9). In

Teutonic mythology the tension between light and darkness is portrayed in the story about the god Balder mentioned in chapter two, above. As will be recalled, the giant Loki plotted to destroy Balder. However, when Balder was born, his mother Frigg, had elicited solemn promises from all the materials in the world from which weapons are made that none would harm Balder. She neglected to get a promise from the lowly mistletoe and Loki learned of her oversight by tricking her. Because of his invulnerability, Balder amused his friends by inviting them to attack him, throw spears at him, and so on. Höd (or Hoder), Balder's blind brother and an archer before his loss of sight, did not participate. Loki, feigning concern for the fact that Höd was excluded from the sport, offered his assistance. Loki gave him a mistletoe arrow, guided his aim, and Höd shot and killed Balder.[37] Symbolically, therefore, Balder (who in his Eddic character is a summer sun-god and thus associated with light) is destroyed by Loki (the Scandinavian Mephistopheles, or Prince of Darkness) through the agency of the mistletoe (a plant associated with the dark Northern winter) and the blind Höd (as Munch notes, "Hod is originally an ancient term for war or battle . . .").[38] Höd is slain by Balder's followers for shooting the arrow, although it is clear that it is known that he was tricked by Loki. Further, it is not to be assumed that Höd was associated with either darkness or evil, but only, as noted, with war and strife. In fact, after the Twilight of the Gods, Balder and Höd are the only gods who are resurrected and together they occupy the hall of their father, Odin.[39]

The Eye

The structure of the eye physically has been determined by the nature and behavior of light. As the primary receptor of light in the body, the eye is symbolically associated with light and the act of seeing. And, by virtue of man's great depend-

ence on vision, the eye has come to symbolize the benefits of
vision, that is, discernment, intelligence, awareness, and so
on.[40] "Hence," writes Cirlot, "the 'divine eye' of the Egyptians
—a determinative sign in their hieroglyphics called *Wadza*
—denotes 'He who feeds the sacred fire of the intelligence of
Man'—Osiris, in fact." [41] Arnold Gesell observes, "Nothing
does [man] treasure more than the apple of his eye. Myth, language, folklore, proverbs, art, and poetry abound in allusions
to the magic, the mystery, the power, the evil, and the charm
of the eye." [42]

A prominent feature of neolithic religious art in the Near
East and Europe is the depiction of earth-mother goddesses
with wide-open, staring eyes. O. G. S. Crawford has traced the
migrations of early Mediterranean peoples through archaeolog-
ical evidence of these "eye" goddesses, dating from the seventh
millennium on, found in Syria, Anatolia, Cyprus, Crete,
Greece, the Balkans, Italy, Sicily, Malta, northern Africa, the
Canary Islands, the Iberian peninsula, England, Ireland, and
northern Europe.[43] Among the most important of these sites is
Tell Brak in the Khabur valley in eastern Syria. Here the so-
called Eye Temple, dating from about 3,000 B.C., was exaca-
vated in 1937–38 by Professor M. E. L. Mallowan.[44] Hundreds of figurines, all characterized by very prominent eyes,
were found; they are believed to have been used in the worship
of Ishtar, a Mesopotamian fertility goddess.[45]

This association of the eyes with the idea of fertility, creative energy, or magical power seems to be a nearly universal
one.[46] The circle, often used as a symbol of the sun and also,
therefore, its life-giving energy, has also been seen as the iris
with the pupil at its center. The eye as a whole is similar in
shape to a mouth with the iris and pupil within—called, for
example, by the Egyptians the "sun in the mouth" (that is, the
creative Word).[47] Finally, there is the ancient mystical idea
that light or energy of some sort is emitted by the eyes. As
Baynes explains it:

> . . . the world is illumined with meaning through the efficacy of the psyche, which creates the world of images inhabited by consciousness. According to the introverted philosophy, the whole world starts from within, from an energic focus of unextended intensity. . . . The eye, therefore, is conceived of as the hole or gateway through which this inner psychic intensity emits its rays upon an otherwise meaningless universe.[48]

This idea is expressed at Acts 3 : 4–5, where Peter and John transmit the spirit of Christ to a crippled beggar and cure his lameness by fixing their eyes upon him. In Revelation, we read, "His head and his hairs were white like wool, as white as snow, and his eyes were as a flame of fire" (1 : 14). In the *Upanishads* the eye is said to possess the fiery heat of Indha, kindler of fire, or the shining radiance of Viraj, wife of Indha, the shining one.[49] A Micronesian story tells of a miraculous birth from the eye and in a Chinese myth, day is created by the opening of the creator's eyes.[50]

Perhaps the most complex and highly developed mythology involving the eye was that found in ancient Egypt. In the Heliopolitan cosmogony, Atum, a primordial creator-god, was symbolized by light and known as the "completed one." He had one eye that was physically separable from him. When Shu (air) and Tefnut (world order) became lost in the dark wastes of the waters of Nun (chaos), Atum sent his eye to find and bring them back to him.[51] Ra, father of the gods and their king, is a later, more developed Atum-like creator-god, who also had a single and independently acting eye. Once when the Eye of Ra failed to return to him, he sent Shu and Tefnut to retrieve it. The Eye resisted them and, in the struggle, shed tears from which it was thought the first men grew.[52] (It may be noted here that the idea of an eye that can exist apart from the body is not peculiar to the Egyptians; it is a motif found in Greek mythology—the three Graeae shared one eye—and in the folk literature of the North American Indians, in Angola, Spain, and South Africa.)[53] Sekhmet, an Egyptian mother-goddess, who was the daughter of Ra and the consort of Ptah, was identified with the Eye of Ra, as was the predynastic Tauerot (or Thoeris or Apet), also a mother-goddess, who was portrayed as a hippopotamus deity.[54] The city of Thebes, created by Amon on the primeval mound, "was the Eye of Ra, and it oversaw all other cities (just as the Eye of Atum oversaw Shu and Tefnut in the waters of Nun)." [55]

The Eye of God, as a symbol of creative energy and of divine omniscience, is commonly associated with the sun. In India, it is Sûrya, the eye of Varuna, or *Siddhaśila,* the spiritual eye of the universe; in Persia, of Ahuramazda; in Greece, Helios, the eye of Zeus (or of Uranos); in Islam, of Allah; in Assyria and Babylonia, Ninigiku. Among primitive tribes the sun and moon are often thought of as the eyes of heaven.[56] Some individual gods are often portrayed as having only a single eye: Shiva, Horus, Zeus, Odin.[57] The significance of a non-divine being having only one eye is ambivalent; as Cirlot writes:

> . . . on the one hand it implies the subhuman because it is less than two (two eyes being equated with the norm); but on the other hand, given its location in the forehead, above the place designated for eyes by nature, it seems to allude to extra-human powers which are in fact—in mythology—incarnated in the Cyclops.[58]

A third eye, as the foregoing implies, is symbolic of the divine. It often stands for intuition, which, added to the symbolism associated with the right and the left eye (to be discussed below), is indicative of the more than human.[59] Having multiple eyes, signifying eternal watchfulness, is exemplified in Greek mythology by Argus Panoptes, a giant with 100 eyes. Similar examples exist in Hindu and Chinese mythology.[60] Perpetual attention is also symbolized by open, staring eyes, as the eyes of a fish, a symbol widely used by the alchemists. These shining, staring eyes were, for them, not only the eye or eyes of God, but heaven, the Holy Ghost, or sometimes the soul-sparks of divine illumination.[61] They themselves often referred to the vision recounted in Zechariah (3 : 10 and 4 : 4–5):

> Here is the stone that I set before Joshua, a stone in which are seven eyes. I will reveal its meaning to you, says the Lord of Hosts. . . . "These seven," he [the angel of the Lord] said, "are the eyes of the Lord ranging over the whole earth." [62]

For the alchemists, the presence of these eyes in the *lapis,* the Philosopher's Stone, is thought to have symbolized the idea that the *lapis* is in the process of evolution and that it is pervaded by the Creator's consciousness.[63] Multiple eyes displaced to sites other than the normal ones or disembodied altogether is also a common motif.[64] The alchemists spoke of eyes in the stars, in the clouds, in the water, and in the earth.[65] In the *Svetasvatara Upanishad* (III : 4), it is written, "The Supreme has a thousand heads, a thousand eyes, a thousand feet." [66] In the Bible, we find eyes on the rims of the wheels in Ezekiel's vision (Ezekiel 1 : 18, cf. 10 : 12), on one of the horns of the beast in Daniel's vision (Daniel 7 : 8, cf. 7 : 20), and, in Revelation, all over the beasts round the throne at the opening of the sealed book (4 : 6–8) and on the lamb marked for slaughter (5 : 6). Such phenomena in mythology and dreams are called the "multiple luminosities of the unconscious" by Jung. He writes:

> By this I mean the seeming possibility that complexes possess a kind of consciousness, a luminosity of their own, which, I conjecture, expresses itself in the symbol of the soul-spark, multiple eyes (*polyophthalmia*), and the starry heaven.[67]

Returning to the two ideas mentioned above, the significance of the shape of the eye and the number of eyes, it has been observed that the circle of the iris with pupil-center is prototypical of the mandala, "a concentrically arranged figure, usually round or square, with a center, which both in myths and dreams is widely used as a symbol of unity." [68] As we have seen, unity as symbolized by the uroboros serpent (also a circle) is a characteristic of the nondifferentiated state of the unconscious. Very often in mythology, the darker, negative aspects of this unconscious state are encountered as terrible, one-eyed giants threatening a heroic figure (who represents consciousness or the ego). In Greek mythology, Odysseus faces Polyphemus, a Cyclops (*cyclops* in Greek means "wheel-eye," indicating the idea of the mandala); other heroes who face such giants or monsters include Bissat (a Tartar hero), Lugh (Celtic), and Sinbad (Arabian). (There is even a folk tale from northern England in which one "Old Harry" tricks the Devil, as Odysseus did Polyphemus, and puts out his eyes.) [69] In one sense, therefore, "the single eye depicts a very archaic type of experience. . . ." [70] This is also the case with the third or "pineal" eye, thought by Descartes to be the seat of the soul or by Baynes to be an organ of psychic vision, a teleological eye corresponding to the wholeness of purpose characteristic of unconscious unity. [71] In another sense, the single "pineal" eye, which does not actually exist physically (although there are remnants of such an organ in certain lizards), [72] can be seen as symbolic of inner vision or, as the alchemists and other mystical philosophers would express it, the eyes of the spirit. [73] As Jung writes, the alchemists felt that to understand certain truths, "one must open wide the eyes of the soul and the spirit and observe and discern accurately by means of the inner light." [74] This, of course, is a common theme in both the Old and New Testament. There are at least three references in Isaiah alone to the idea that the people of Israel have eyes but cannot see (42 : 18–19; 43 : 8; 56 : 9–11). Jesus, in speaking of what modern depth psychology has identified as psychological projection, [75] uses the very effective metaphor of seeing the speck in the other's eye but not the plank in one's own eye that blocks true vision (Matthew

7 : 3–5 and Luke 6 : 41–42). The difference between outer
and inner vision is also mentioned at John 9 : 39–41 and at
Ephesians 1 : 18. Finally, there is also the familiar figure of
Fortuna (or Justice) who is blindfolded, yet can distinguish
the just from the unjust.[76]

The external, physical eyes, while differentiated from the
inner eyes, have traditionally been considered the "windows"
of the soul. In the preceding chapter, we made brief note of
the fact that eye-contact is an important part of the face-to-
face communication between people. Perhaps as a result of
this, "People are said to have dancing eyes; eyes are spoken
of as somber, dark, and impenetrable, as merry or sad. . . .
What we find there is a complete displacement of what is actually perceived elsewhere about the physiognomy and the rest
of the body." [77] Despite the fact that this last assertion has undoubtedly been proven in the laboratory, the symbolism associated with the eyes and their appearance is, nevertheless, still
quite potent. "Many people, though firmly believing themselves to be utterly without superstition or prejudice are convinced that they can judge a person by the appearance of his
eyes." [78] The eye was considered the seat of the soul by the
Egyptians.[79] Shakespeare and many other authors have used
vivid imagery to describe the eyes and what can be seen
there.[80] The "shifty-eyed" are thought to be untrustworthy; the
"squint-eyed," dishonest; blue eyes mean gentleness and yield-
ing; brown, strength and thought; ". . . a man with small
ears must have large, noble eyes or he is full of conceit"; "eyes
with long, sharp corners which do not turn downward are
sanguine and full of genius";[81] staring eyes are associated with
mystical experiences and visions (for example, at Numbers
24 : 4); "the man who narrows his eyes is disaffected at
heart . . ." (Proverbs 16 : 30); and "the Commandment of
the Lord shines clear and gives light to the eyes" (Psalm
19 : 8).

Just as light may symbolize consciousness, so too may

the eye itself: "Consciousness, like the sun, is an 'eye of the world.' " [82] In English, this symbolism is reinforced by the homophony of the word *eye* and the personal pronoun *I*.[83] In Genesis, the eyes play an important role in the emergence of consciousness in Eden: the forbidden fruit is "pleasing to the eye" and, after having eaten the fruit, "the eyes of both of them were opened" (Genesis 3 : 4–7). In the Sermon on the Mount, Jesus says, "The lamp of the body is the eye" (Matthew 6 : 22–23 and Luke 11 : 34–36). In the *Chandogya Upanishad,* it is written, "The person who is seen in the eye, he is the self" (IV : 15.1).[84] Not only does the eye stand for consciousness, but the two eyes, whose working together produces binocular vision, may each symbolize different aspects of the conscious personality. "Traditionally," writes Heaton, "the sun and the active part of the personality correspond to the right eye, and the moon and the passive part to the left. . . ." [85] These designations are found in the mythologies of Ancient Egypt and China, in the folklore of the Maori, on Samoa, and in the writings of the alchemists.[86]

In an interesting study done at the C. G. Jung Institute in Zurich, A. R. Pope explores the idea that the eyes symbolize the two kinds of consciousness; that is, the right eye, associated with the sun, represents *logos* consciousness, the left, associated with the moon, *eros* consciousness. The author, however, also insists that the eyes symbolize not only ego-consciousness, but the whole person—the conscious and the unconscious components.[87] It is to this that the idea, noted earlier, that the eyes are the "windows" of the soul owes its potency. The correspondence of the left eye to the eros side of man, to his passive feminine, unconscious aspects and of the right eye to the logos side, to his active, masculine, conscious aspects, is well illustrated by a Tibetan myth recounted by Pope. The blind king, Indrabodhi, receives a wish-granting gem. He asks that the vision in his left eye be restored and it is. At the same time, a self-born babe is found in a lotus blossom floating on the lake. The infant speaks of wisdom (his father), of voidness (his mother), and of perplexity (which sustains him). As a result, the vision in the king's right eye is restored.[88] What has happened, psychologically speaking, is that through the restoration of the sight in the king's left eye, he is made receptive to the dynamic contents of the archetypal world of the unconscious. Through this enlightenment, consciousness, the awareness of the perplexity of the world of opposites, can emerge— symbolized here by the restoration of the sight in the king's right eye.[89]

Allusion was made earlier in this section to the creative power of the eye and to the idea that the eye emits energy. We return now to this subject in order to explore it somewhat more fully. Symbolically, the eye has both an active, penetrating, and fertilizing or wounding function and a passive, receptive mode in which it can be fertilized or wounded.[90] Both the active and passive aspects are exemplified in the *communio,* the highly personal communication between the eyes of two individuals. In Ancient Egypt, extremely lifelike eyes were included in a funerary statue of the dead king, portrayed as Osiris. The statue was placed near the door of the tomb so that it was possible for the son to stare into these eyes through a special slit in the door. The *communio* was, therefore, between the spirit (of the father become Osiris) and the soul of the son, the eyes of man receiving magical power from the eyes of God. A similar eye communion (between an idol and the people) was also carried out periodically on a collective scale in the Old Kingdom of Egypt. Seeing likewise played a central role in the religion of Ancient Greece: *theoria* means going to the temple, looking at the statues, and looking through them to see the divinity itself. Through contemplation, the object becomes filled with meaning.[91] This brings us once again to the connection between the eyes and the inner world of the unconscious with the added idea here, however, of the eye as a point of access between the outer and inner worlds.[92] In superstition, for example, a throbbing of the right eye can be a favorable omen or simply an indication that the mother or sister is coming, while a throbbing of the left eye indicates that the husband or brother is coming.[93] The eye is here a site for the reception of magical knowledge that could be viewed as coming from the unconscious or from some outer spirit, god, or demon.

The *communio* of the eyes is most widely known in its negative aspect—the evil eye. Here we find the eye in both its active and passive roles and in a context that reveals its emotional component. The basis for the belief in the evil eye involves both the idea that the eye can project energy or some sort of influence and that it can receive such influences.[94] The Greek theory of vision as a projection from the eyes, noted above, has lent specious support to the evil eye.[95] On the other hand, the belief that individuals who are undergoing some change in life (for example marriage or pregnancy) or who are for some other reason in a state of weakened consciousness (such as childhood) are most susceptible to the evil eye indicates that the evil eye is part of a larger belief in malevolent powers or demonism, the very powers that rites of passage are meant to protect one from.[96]

The idea that the eye can be an organ of destruction is very ancient and linked to the symbolism of the single eye and of the third eye.[97] In Ancient Egypt, the *uraeus,* usually portrayed as a cobra and located on the forehead of the pharaoh or god, is actually the left eye of Ra. In a number of variant myths, this eye, representing the burning, scorching power of the sun, is prevented from destroying the earth and is transformed into the *uraeus.*[98] In Sumer and Babylonia, certain gods and demons could kill or injure with a glance.[99] In Ancient Greece, the Gorgon Medusa could turn to stone all who met her gaze.[100] In Jewish legend there is Keṭeb, a demon the sight of whom could kill.[101] Lania, a medieval witch, used the evil eye to entrap and destroy young men.[102] The glance of a menstruating woman was thought to be very powerful: the Bushmen of South Africa believe it will fix a man in whatever position he happens to be and St. Thomas Aquinas thought it would tarnish the brightness of a mirror.[103] Even the ancient belief that what a pregnant woman sees can affect her child, either by some mark on its body or some condition, is related to the belief in the power of the evil eye.[104]

While the idea of the evil eye is undoubtedly grounded in these myths and legends and in the belief that such gods and demons could possess an individual, its currency throughout both the primitive and more advanced parts of the world [105] indicates that some fundamental dynamism is involved. To be more accurate, we would have to say that both the evil eye and the related myths and legends noted above have arisen out of some aspect of the symbolism of the eye and vision. That is, there are certain qualities of the eye and of vision that arouse instinctive emotional responses. Heaton offers the following, very convincing explanation:

> . . . when we become aware of another person watching us, we cease to perceive his eyes; perceiving an eye and sensing that it is watching us are two mutually exclusive phenomena. This is because to perceive is to look at; there is a distance between us and what is perceived. Sensing that we are being watched, on the other hand, is to be aware of oneself as a vulnerable object occupying a limited space and time; we may even have this experience without seeing the other person's face or eyes, as when we become aware that we are being watched from behind. . . . "The look" may turn a person into an object; it may make him feel that he is merely a passive, mechanical, dissectable thing. . . .[106]

A look at the history and lore of the evil eye certainly lends a great deal of weight to this explanation. The "evil" eye is, in its original meaning, the envious eye. ". . . Good fortune, wealth, and personal attractiveness were believed to draw the attention of the evil eye and to increase vulnerability, and those with most reason for feeling envious were most likely to be suspected of possessing an evil eye." [107] In Latin, the word meaning "to look maliciously at" or "to cast an evil eye at" is *invidere,* from which the English words *envy* and *invidious* are derived.[108] The evil eye of envy is mentioned often in the Bible (for example, at Proverbs 23 : 6–8 and 28 : 22, Matthew 20 : 15, and Mark 7 : 20–23). According to Jewish legend, the first tablets given on Mount Sinai had to be broken, for the great ceremonies attending them "had the evil effect of directing an evil eye toward them. . . ." The second tablets were, therefore, received in quiet humility.[109] Thiselton–Dyer notes that the evil eye of envy is mentioned in an exchange between Aaron and Timora in Shakespeare's *Titus Andronicus.*[110]

In the course of time, the evil eye has been associated with abnormal or unusual conditions of the eye, such as squints, inflamed eyes, or a missing eye, with certain configurations of eyebrows, and even with missing eyeteeth or general physical malformations (hunchback, dwarfism, etc.).[111] In these instances, the person was usually said to have been afflicted with the so-called "natural" or involuntary evil eye. That is, the condition was considered congenital. Others, however, were thought to have a voluntary evil eye, one received in a pact with the Devil or resulting from possession by demons, witches, or evil spirits.[112] As a result there are two separate types of influence for which the evil eye can be blamed or at least suspected. First, the visitation of misfortune and illness on the prosperous and successful was associated with the natural evil eye; this influence was produced involuntarily or even unconsciously by the carrier. Voluntary fascination, involving the casting of evil spells, was malevolent and directed by conscious malice. Among the many conditions attributed to the influence of both kinds of evil eye (and almost any unusual or unexpected occurrence or one accompanied by mysterious circumstances could arouse suspicion) are eye diseases, cholera, syphilis, the Black Death, loss of function (especially the sexual function), abortions, congenital defects, smallpox, fevers, convulsions, yawning, hiccoughing, and headaches.[113] Animals, especially domestic animals, could be affected by the evil eye and wild animals, such as scorpions, snakes, spiders, grasshoppers, lions, tigers, wolves, hares, eagles, owls, ravens, magpies, cocks, and peacocks, were thought to possess the evil eye.[114] Among the great variety of amulets and talismans that have been devised to ward off the evil eye, there are the caduceus of Hermes, various representations of the eye (including the magic eye above a pyramid in the Great Seal of the United States), the phallus, bells, rings, precious stones, replicas of swords and animals, salt, and garlic.[115] The eyes of statues and paintings, when they are associated with some superstitious source (as the pyramids in Egypt or some ancient temple or religious site) are often obliterated for this same reason.[116] Elworthy recounts the story of a Slavic peasant who, believing that he was afflicted with the evil eye, blinded himself rather than endanger those around him.[117]

Loss of an Eye or of Both Eyes

In earlier chapters, it has been noted that blindness is often portrayed as a divine punishment for some sin of the individual. Significantly, one of the sins with which blinding was often associated as a punishment was having seen (and, therefore, gained knowledge of) that which is forbidden. Here the transgression involves a trespass against the natural order —one for which punishment is demanded by *moira*, the impersonal ruler of gods and men that symbolized the balance of nature for the Ancient Greeks.[118] There is, for example, Lot's wife who was turned into a pillar of salt for looking at the destruction of Sodom (Genesis 19 : 26). Oedipus' self-blinding is, in a sense, a punishment for the knowledge he so unwisely sought. A messenger reports that as Oedipus was putting out his eyes, he said, "Nor more shall ye [his eyes]

behold such horrors as I was suffering and working! Long
enough have ye looked on those whom ye ought never to have
seen, failed in knowledge of those whom I yearned to know—
henceforth ye shall be dark!" [119] The blind seer, Teiresias,
was, according to legend, punished for forbidden knowledge.
In one legend, he inadvertently beheld the naked Athena at
her bath. In another version, he saw two serpents copulating.
He killed the female and was himself transformed into a
woman. For seven years, he lived as a celebrated harlot and
then he once again saw the same sight. This time he killed the
male serpent and his manhood was returned. Later, in a dis-
pute between Zeus and Hera over whether man or woman
most enjoyed sex, Teiresias was asked to decide the issue from
his own experience. He sided with Zeus in saying that woman
derives the most pleasure. In retaliation, Hera blinded him;
Zeus then granted him compensation in the form of an extended life and foresight.[120] In a Jewish legend in which the
superiority of Moses over all others is demonstrated, it is told
that while Isaac had beheld the Face of the Shekinah (the
Glory of God), the sight of it had dimmed his eyes. Moses,
on the other hand, had talked with the Shekinah face to face
and his sight had remained unimpaired.[121] In Northern European folklore, there is the legend of the Wild Hunt in which
a ghostly hunter and his retinue ride in a midnight chase. The
sight of the Wild Hunt blinds the observer.[122]

The meaning of blinding as a punishment for seeing-
knowing, however, can more easily be understood in the context of those myths in which there is a necessary and usually
voluntary sacrifice of an eye or of sight. "In general," writes
Baynes, "the mythological sacrifice of an eye has the character
of a payment from one god to another, whereby a new order
of nature is established or the original balance restored." [123]
That is, change or transformation carries a price. Symbolically,
this idea is portrayed by the "death" of the invincible sun each
evening, a death that is not a true death but a descent into the

dark waters from which the new sun is resurrected each day. The moon, on the other hand, must suffer fragmentation (as it wanes) and death before it is reborn.[124] In mythology, the Egyptian god Horus (symbolizing light) battles with Set (darkness). Horus castrates Set, but Set, in the form of a black pig, tears out the weak eye of Horus (the moon). Although the eye is restored to Horus, Set is thought to renew his attack continually and, therefore, to be responsible for the waning of the moon and eclipses.[125] In another Egyptian myth, Set tears out both of Horus' eyes and buries them. Through the aid of Hathor, a goddess (and later protectress of the eyes of mortals), Horus regains his vision. He then kept only one of his eyes for himself and gave the other to Osiris as a token of life.[126] In Teutonic mythology, Odin is usually portrayed as one-eyed. He had sacrificed his other eye as payment for a drink from Mimir's spring, whose waters, flowing from beneath Yggdrasil (the World-Tree), give inspiration and knowledge of things to come.[127] Mimir, by the way, means "he who thinks." [128] In the Apocrypha, Tobit's failing eyesight personifies the general loss of faith of the Jewish people of that time. Tobit is forced to turn inward and to invoke heavenly powers in order to heal this dissociation and to be spiritually enlightened.[129] This brings to mind a line from Plato's *Symposium*, "Remember, the intellectual sight begins to keen when the visual is entering on its wane." [130] Another example of enlightenment being accompanied by blinding, in this case temporary, is the story of Saul's conversion on the road to Damascus (Acts 9 : 3–9). Saul's three days of blindness could be viewed as a direct result of the vision itself (his sight being overcome by the brilliance of the light, as Acts 22 : 11 would suggest) or as an integral part of his conversion (reinforcing the importance of the vision and allowing him time to assimilate its message fully). In folklore (European and North American Indian) and in hagiography, the loss of the eyes is often a sacrifice for virginity, as for example in the cases of St. Lucy of Syracuse and of the Scottish virgins, St. Triduana and St. Medana.[131] Here, self-blinding is a reaffirmation of the spiritual vow of chastity. In *King Lear,* Kirsch contends, "The frequent use of the imagery of vision is clear evidence that the gaining of consciousness is the main dramatic intention of Shakespeare. . . ."[132] The blinding of Gloucester (Act III, Scene 7), therefore, can be seen as retribution for his unconscious, pleasure-loving attitude. On the other hand, it is also the means through which Gloucester achieves greater consciousness. In this way, Shakespeare personifies Lear's unconsciousness and elucidates the role that hardship, disaster, and sacrifice play in the achievement of consciousness.

The observations of many modern workers for the blind tend to confirm the fundamental truth contained in the preceding material. Dr. Louis Cholden, a psychiatrist noted for his work with blind people, has written that the inner person is altered by having experienced blindness. He also writes that the newly blinded person becomes a child again, that he is reborn,[133] much as it was thought in Egyptian mythology. ("The little image reflected in the pupil of the eye is a child again; the great god Osiris becomes a child in the eye of his son Horus.")[134] Gowman says, "While the education is harsh, blindness lends perspective to one's life and permits a consciousness which may be both sensitive and intense."[135] By far the most thorough treatment of the symbolic significance of the loss of sight is that of Father Carroll in his book *Blindness: What It Is, What It Does, and How to Live With It.* He writes:

> The "death" of blindness destroys a whole complex pattern of existence. We must be prepared to offer something whole in its place. For there *is* a new life ahead. But this is the paradox: the sighted person is "dead"; the blind person who is born can once more become the same person, but only if he is willing to go through the pain of death to sight.[136]

He goes on to point out that life for all men and women is filled
with these symbolic "deaths," the old ways being given up
to be replaced by the new. And it is because of this that the
"death" and "rebirth" of the sighted-become-blind person does
not give him any unusual or supernaturally granted powers of
reflection or contemplation.[137] He does, however, note the
possibility of spiritual growth resulting from blindness. Writing
of course within a Roman Catholic context, Father Carroll
concludes:

> What can be said, if we believe that growth in sanctity is measured
> by the degree to which we are able to conform our wills to the
> will of God, is that perhaps blind persons as a group have a
> greater *opportunity* for a higher degree of sanctity. We can say
> this (keeping in mind many other factors) on the basis that the will
> of God had demanded more of them—for them, complete sub-
> mission to the will of God includes submission to His permissive
> will with regard to a terrible and multiple handicap from which
> the rest of us are free.[138]

Although we can see, therefore, that blindness can symbolically represent a necessary sacrifice for the attainment of
greater knowledge, insight, sanctity, or consciousness (an idea
specifically encountered in certain attitudes toward blindness
and blind people), the emphasis on the symbolic losses represented by blindness is clearly dominant in both mythology
and in the attitudes of the public at large. For this reason, we
will now examine those symbolic losses in detail to determine
the specific role they play in the processes out of which attitudes toward blindness and blind people evolve.

Because sight plays a symbolically significant part in
man's ability to exercise power, its loss is seen as depriving him
of his "magic," of his ability to fascinate, to "devour," to destroy.[139] The stigma of blindness, therefore, undoubtedly arises
from this degrading of the individual, from his being deprived
of his effectiveness as a person.[140] This degradation is power-
fully reinforced by another aspect of the symbolism of vision,

and of light and the eye as well, namely, the creative principle. The active, aggressive quality of sight, which is particularly evident in the belief in the evil eye, is closely linked with the aggressive, phallic aspect of sexuality.[141] The loss of sight, therefore, is thought to arouse man's anxiety concerning castration. Grounded in the psychoanalytic theories of Freud, castration anxiety as the motive force behind attitudes toward blindness is the most widely cited and accepted theory in the literature on attitudes. It was apparently first suggested by Sydell Braverman in her 1951 article "The Psychological Roots of Attitudes Toward the Blind." [142]

In the first part of this theory, the eyes are seen to be symbolically equated with the sexual organs. As just noted, the piercing quality of vision is phallic in nature. The eye and its lids can be seen to resemble the female genitals, a symbolic similarity that is expressed, for example, by the Latin *pupillae,* the Greek *kophn,* and the Spanish *niña,* which in each instance means both "the pupil of the eye" and "maiden." [143] Because of these links between sight and the sexual function, blindness is thought to be a symbolic castration in itself.[144] And there are indeed striking similarities between feelings about one who is castrated and one who is blind that are explained by this theory. The sequence of emotions beginning with revulsion and leading to guilt, anxiety, and finally pity is present in both situations.[145] Gloom and melancholy are often associated with impotence as they are with blindness.[146] The castrated man is thought to be sinister and to have thoughts and impulses that the potent man would never entertain. He is not only sly and conniving, but also thought to be mentally subnormal.[147]

The second part of the castration anxiety theory involves the role that sight plays in the ego and sex instincts. Freud writes:

> At least a certain amount of touching is indispensable for a person in order to attain the normal sexual aim. . . . The same holds true in the end with looking, which is analogous to touching.

The manner in which the libidinous excitement is frequently awakened is by optical impressions, and selection takes account of this circumstance—if this teleological mode of thinking be permitted—by making the sexual object a thing of beauty.[148]

Accordingly, looking can be termed a partial instinct and the eye an erogenous zone.[149] Loss of sight, therefore, implies a consequent diminution in the individual's capacity to respond to stimulation.

More importantly, however, the act of looking can also be a means of gratification in and of itself. This function is, in fact, a normal part of human sexual development and occurs, according to Freud, in the early years of childhood.

We must admit . . . that the infantile sexual life, though mainly under the control of the erogenous zones, also shows components which from the very beginning point to other persons as sexual objects. Among these, we may mention the impulses for looking, showing off, and for cruelty, which manifest themselves somewhat independently of the erogenous zones and only later enter into intimate relationship with the sexual life; but along with the erogenous sexual activity they are noticeable even in the infantile years, as separate and independent strivings.[150]

Freud goes on to explain that through the development of shame these impulses to look are gradually controlled and suppressed.

Of particular importance for our purposes is the unresolved conflict that arises in nearly everyone between looking and not looking.[151] Apparently, as long as the impulse to look, a normal part of the sexual impulse, is balanced by the ego-instincts, everything is fine. Looking can, on the other hand, become a perversion—scoptophilia, or scopophilia. As Freud explains it:

If the sexual component-instinct which makes use of sight—the sexual "lust of the eye"—has drawn down upon itself, through its exorbitant demands, some retaliatory measure from the side of the ego-instincts, so that the ideas which represent the content of its strivings are subjected to repression and withheld from consciousness, the general relation of the eye and the faculty of vision to the ego and to consciousness is radically disturbed. The ego has lost control of the organ, which now becomes solely the instrument of the repressed sexual impulse. It would appear as though repression on the part of the ego had gone too far and poured away the baby with the bath-water, for the ego now flatly refuses to see anything at all, since the sexual interests in looking have so deeply involved the faculty of vision.[152]

In other words, looking may become compulsive, out of control, and, in the context from which the preceding quotation is taken, this compulsion may even result in a psychogenic disturbance of vision.

Applied to the larger context with which we are dealing, the act of looking is undoubtedly associated in the minds of many individuals with the "sin" of looking and with the potential loss of conscious control over an area of one's functioning. Freud goes on to point out that, in keeping with the talion laws ("an eye for an eye . . .") found in saga, myth, and legend, he who has "looked" (as the "peeping Tom" in the story of Lady Godiva) is blinded.[153] In turn, he who is blind must, in the minds of many, have been guilty of "looking." Also, one who is aware of his own "looking sins" may, since he is not blind, feel guilty when he encounters someone who is.[154] Finally, returning to our starting point in this part of the discussion, because this "looking" is, in a sense, a sexual act, the punishment is also of a sexual nature. Loss of sight is, thus, associated symbolically with castration or a loss of sexual potency.

The Meaning of Blindness

We have now reached a level of understanding at which we can see that blindness symbolizes a loss of power, of individual creativity, of control. It also symbolizes the terrible sacrifice that is often necessary for certain gains in knowledge, insight, revelation, or growth. To the sighted person, an encounter with blindness, whether it is a personal experience with his own vision, a face-to-face meeting with one who is blind, or a somewhat abstract consideration in his thoughts or in conversation, touches him personally or profoundly. He is touched because the threat to him that is symbolized by blindness is the loss of his own identity, of his sense of who and what he is; in short, the death of his consciousness.[155] Blindness is, therefore, a thing in itself, not an absence of sight, but the grip of darkness, the maw of the chasm, the obliteration of consciousness by the overpowering seduction of the unconscious.

After the long, harrowing, painful, but heroic struggle of the ego to establish its independence from the unconscious (the maternal uroboros), the threat of a collapse of that consciousness is indeed a dreadful one.[156] The fear of castration is but one part of the situation. The loss of the genitals or of the sexual function represents a loss of a part of the individual that he most closely identifies with his sense of self and a loss of one of the fundamental ways in which he expresses his own individuality, both in his relationships with the opposite sex and in "reproducing" himself in his children. In a wider sense, any general loss of power or control is feared. Consciousness, after all, is the "organ" in man through which he organizes his perceptions of the inner and outer worlds and his responses to those perceptions.[157] Such a loss of a sense of control may occur when the individual is in a state of depression and, therefore, lacks the psychic energy required for the efficient functioning of consciousness, or when he is in a position in which the power of that which threatens him seems to dwarf his own power to respond. Similarly, mental illness is feared because it means a loss of control; for example, in a mild form, being unusually subject to fits of rage is to be temporarily taken over—possessed—by an intense emotion, and, in an extreme form, being completely insane is to be permanently under the control of some part of the psyche other than consciousness.[158] Also, distortions of reality, whether produced by a disease, by drugs, or by some physical or mechanical means (for example, weightlessness or optical illusions that include the entire environment) are very unnerving for some people, because they threaten their sense of being in conscious control of the situation.

On the other side of the coin, we find that, although the loss of consciousness and of the power and control that is exercised through it is feared and avoided, it is not of necessity completely negative. For while it is in the nature of things that consciousness is the "good" toward which men strive, it is also "true" that many of the steps exact a price, a sacrifice. For example, the initial emergence of consciousness is symbolized in the Old Testament by the eating of the fruit of the Tree of Knowledge. The price, of course, is the loss of Paradise, of the blissful, nondifferentiated, closed system of the uroboros. By the same token, it is often only through sacrifice or even destruction that the next step is possible and that something new can emerge.[159] In mythology, there is the phoenix which, as death approaches, must be consumed in fire in order to be reborn out of its own ashes.[160] In the *Divine Comedy,* Dante acknowledges this principle quite graphically when he shows that to get to Paradise one must pass *through* the Inferno and Purgatory. In legend, Christ is said to have descended into Hell in order, on the third day, to be resurrected.[161] The first stage of the alchemical Opus involves the utter destruction of the materials (through calcination, solution, separation, conjunction, and putrefaction) which results in the *Nigredo,* the *prima materia.* Only with the achievement of this stage is it possible for the work on the Philosopher's Stone to continue.[162] That such sacrifices are necessary does not alter the fact that they are extremely painful, often dangerous, and avoided completely by all save those of whom they are required. Even the individual for whom this process is not necessary is, nevertheless, aware that there are many potent forces that continually threaten whatever consciousness he has developed. To cite but one example: the seductive attractions of what seems to be a paradisaical situation can easily draw the individual into its embrace and, as happened to Odysseus and his crew in the Land of the Lotus-Eaters, dissolve the individual's consciousness. Blindness, therefore, can be seen as a symbol of all these threats to consciousness. [Attitudes toward blindness, in turn, will reflect much about an individual's insight into himself and the ways in which he has learned to cope with or to come to terms with those things which threaten his sense of self. Needless to say, so fundamental and powerful a threat as that which blindness symbolizes is bound to produce some anxiety in even the most well-adjusted and secure individual.

The symbolic meaning of blindness, however, takes on an entirely new dimension when the blindness is encountered as an attribute of another person, when it is, so to speak, embodied in a human being. Roughly speaking, the situation appears to be one in which all of the unknown and terrifying aspects of the threats to consciousness that blindness symbolizes are constellated in the blind person. In other words, through his blindness he represents the potentialities, both positive and negative, of the loss of the eyes. When a sighted person encounters a blind person, therefore, he responds less to the individual person before him than to the archetypal patterns that are aroused within him.[163]

In many instances, the sighted person's reaction to the blind person involves emotionally toned valuations that are clearly not related to actual traits and qualities found in the blind person. If the configuration of valuations are such that they reflect the negative or undesirable traits (either personally or culturally determined) of the perceiver, then he has encountered his own unconscious projection of his other self, of all that he cannot admit as a part of himself. Because of its negative quality, Jung named the dark counterpart of every individual's conscious personality the Shadow. The archetype of the Shadow is encountered whenever an individual over-emphasizes the positive aspects of his own life and personality, for in doing this he will completely deny his own weaknesses and negative qualities and repress them. Such repression, of course, does not eliminate the negative side, but serves only to remove it from consciousness. The unconscious, which serves in a compensatory fashion to consciousness, "reminds" the conscious mind of that which it has denied by "projecting" these qualities onto another person. The conscious mind, therefore, encounters this projection and because its specific negativity is precisely that which the individual is least able to accept in himself, he reacts as though the finger of accusation were pointing directly at him (which in fact it is). If the individual can recognize his perception in its true light (often a most disagreeable business), it is then possible for him to re-integrate that part of himself which he has denied and re-establish a portion of his own wholeness.[164] The specific nature of the projection that a sighted person may encounter in a blind person would, of course, depend on his own psychological makeup. On the other hand, the fundamental (that is, archetypal) symbolism of blindness and its role as the "hook" upon which the projection is "hung" would seem to indicate that the compensatory function of the projection would often be to remind the individual that his consciousness is not impregnable but quite susceptible to "blinding." In other words, blindness in this context symbolizes the very real dangers that confront every individual and that every individual should strive to admit and come to terms with in his own life, however much he would rather not think about them. These are, specifically, that we all have our "blind spot," are "in the dark" about many things, and are, therefore, exposed to dangers from unknown directions; that we are often not in complete control of either ourselves (when, for example, we are in a fit of "blind rage") or the situation (which may be subject to "blind chance"); that we have eyes, but cannot see; that we have all committed the "sin" of looking at what is forbidden and are subject to the talion (the punishment—in this case blinding—that is reciprocal to the offense—looking); that we are attracted by the submergence of our consciousness—by "blinding"—in sensual pleasure, in irresponsibility, and in compulsiveness.

A somewhat more uncommon archetypal pattern that can be encountered as a projection carried by a blind person is that of the Stranger. Stated simply, the Stranger "stands for the possibility of unseen change, for the future made present, or for mutation in general." [165] The ordinary individual reacts to this configuration with a certain amount of wariness and suspicion. The Stranger, by simply appearing, raises questions about the status quo and may require changes of one sort or another. In and of itself, the blind person as the Stranger is not likely to elicit an overly emotional response. If, however, the Stranger is, in actuality, the extremely powerful archetype of the Wise Old Man, the situation is on a completely different footing. The Wise Old Man, the archetype of spirit, usually appears at a time of spiritual crisis and compensates for a stalemated condition of consciousness by providing some sort of guidance.[166] He is both a positive and a negative figure— personified by the alchemists as the *Mercurius duplex,* the two-faced, dual "spirit Mercurius." [167] In his positive aspect, the Wise Old Man is one who is invested with wisdom, authority, knowledge, insight, or intuition, as, for example, a scholar, professor, teacher, sage, philosopher, doctor, magician, grandfather, even a tramp or beggar.[168] In his negative aspect, he can be a gnome engaged in mischief or a black magician who has evil intentions.[169] Naturally, the blind person is not the Wise Old Man, nor does he necessarily actually have any of the characteristics of this archetypal figure. As in the case of the Shadow, the fact that blindness is again the "hook" upon which the projection is "hung" is most significant. The guidance given by the Wise Old Man is in response to a critical stasis of some sort in the consciousness of the individual and it often invokes severe demands on the individual, including the requirement of painful sacrifices, dangerous hardships, and tasks that are unpleasant in the extreme. In other words, the Wise Old Man is associated with many of the situations which, on the archetypal level, are also associated with blindness: specifically, placing consciousness (sight, the eyes) in great jeopardy or even requiring its apparent sacrifice in order that a higher consciousness (enlightenment, a "vision") may be achieved.[170] Speaking in more concrete terms, he who encounters a blind "Wise Old Man" is confronted by the wisdom, authority, knowledge, insight, or intuition that he requires for progress or that he desires personified in such a way that he is forced to admit the possibility that such an advancement might entail a loss of consciousness (blindness). That the loss is temporary or even illusory or that the result more than compensates for the terrors of the attempt is not in the reckoning, for the sacrifice does not insure the result (indeed, it may be fatal) and the prospect of voluntarily relinquishing consciousness (of blinding oneself) is in no way depotentiated by the possibility of gain. The gain is, after all, only potential, an abstraction, while the loss is horrifyingly real. If an individual is, in fact, personally confronted by the Wise Old Man (an admittedly somewhat rare occurrence and one not likely to occur as a projection anyway), he must respond to this "divine" guidance through profound reflection and a deep insight into the mysteries of his own psyche. Even for the individual who is not so confronted, the numinosity, the awe-inspiring transpersonal power, of the Wise Old Man is, nevertheless, of such a proportion that he is made uncomfortably aware of the dark possibilities that blindness symbolically represents.

Conclusions

Taking all of the discussion in the preceding three chapters into account, not only the symbolic meaning of blindness, but also the historical and psychosocial factors, we can see that the origins of the attitudes discussed in the first chapter lie in the very fabric of man's existence. As enduring symbols of perhaps the most vital aspect of human evolution and the human condition—consciousness—sight and blindness are infused into our literature and art. They influence the conduct of our daily lives, as they have apparently done throughout man's past. They are an important part of the way we perceive ourselves and others. Insofar as our attitudes are negative, our reactions to sight and to its loss reflect our own uncertainties and anxieties. By turns, our beliefs about them can be colored by our emotionality, our fears and terrors, our inflated sense of our own worth, and our sense of inferiority. Most importantly, however, we often fail to distinguish between the symbolic and the actual, between the meaning of sight and blindness and the physical sense of sight and the actual loss of that sense, between the Shadow or the Stranger and the unique, individual human being who happens to be blind.

The question that naturally arises from these conclusions is: How might an understanding of the meaning of blindness be applied to the problem of changing and improving attitudes toward blindness and blind people? Although a full consideration of this question lies beyond the scope of this study, the following brief discussion may suggest some possibilities.

5 Attitude Change

THE GOAL OF EFFORTS TO change attitudes toward blindness is to improve the way in which blind people are viewed and treated. The emphasis, which varies somewhat according to the particular attitude being dealt with, is largely upon establishing the fact that blind people are more similar to, than different from, sighted people. Recognizing the fact that, to one degree or another, most negative attitudes involve misinformation, false beliefs, or unfounded fears, agents of change seek to disseminate accurate information about the true nature of visual loss and the effects of that loss upon the individual. The assumption is that once the public is accurately informed and has had its fears dissipated, it will find its negative attitudes untenable and will perforce begin thinking of blind people as equals and treating them fairly.[1]

Such an information program typically includes a presentation of the medical aspects of blindness, some statistics on prevalence and rate, and a description of the training and rehabilitation services that are available. Specific beliefs or stereotypes may be repudiated. In the better programs, the real problems and limitations of blindness are discussed and assessed. Practical guidelines for what to do and what not to do in interactions involving blind people may be offered. Individual blind people may be shown going about their normal routines at home, in school, or on the job. Some effort may also be made to "police" the media by preventing, or at least protesting, the portrayal of blind people in distortedly negative, stereotypical, or unrealistic ways. By all these means, the ability of blind people to be happy, productive, and responsible individuals is emphasized. Although the chief advantage of this approach is the relative ease with which it can be implemented, there still remain those who make no effort in this direction or even exploit the stereotypes and fears of the public.

In theory, a large proportion of negative attitudes should be amenable to the effects of accurate information. Insofar as attitudes are a function of learning, of information processing, and of the social adjustment of the individual,[2] it is reasonable to assume that new attitudes can be learned and that the individual will correct or modify his opinions and beliefs as his awareness is increased.[3] This has undoubtedly been the case during the last century or so. Overt attitudes toward blind people have in many ways improved and there has been some reduction in the social barriers that blind people face. In fact, as Imamura has observed, the advancement of blind people into new lines of employment has created certain problems involving status dilemmas, that is, clashes between new roles and old stereotypes.[4]

On the other hand, purely informational campaigns have one important, built-in limitation. Insofar as overt attitudes represent a "symbolic substitute for covert attitudes taken in the inner struggle," [5] providing information will do little to alter them, "since the target audience will select, accept, ignore, or even distort the meaning of the available content in order to keep it consonant with preconceptions." [6] Or, as Allport so succinctly puts it, "Defeated intellectually, prejudice lingers emotionally." [7] While it is admitted that not all attitudes are externalizations and of functional significance for the individual, those that are will be quite resistant to change. Through some form of rationalization (as demonstrated in the third chapter), the new data are easily accommodated without there being any significant alteration in the attitudes or beliefs.[8] It is not surprising, therefore, to find that covert attitudes toward and emotional responses to blind people by sighted people have been changed very little by the extensive public education programs of the past and present.[9]

Because they do reflect such fundamental psychological orientations, negative attitudes toward blindness are, as many have observed, inevitable and nearly universal.[10] This is not to say that there is no way to alter these attitudes, but only that the usual approach of information and education programs is largely ineffective. To be more specific, it is the thinking in such programs that any attitude based in the emotions can be depotentiated, deprived of its "charge," by rationally analyzing it, reducing it to its basic components, and demonstrating this "true" nature of the attitude to the individual holding it. For example, we know that many people feel that a blind person lives in a depressing "world of darkness." The response to this attitude will usually include the following: (1) a statement to the effect that the experiential state of being blind is not one of being in darkness, but in grayness; (2) a demonstration of the fact that this belief is grounded in a mistaken analogy: the sighted person without light perceives darkness; since sight is the ability to distinguish between light and dark, one without sight can perceive neither light nor dark; and (3) an explanation that because of the significance of light as a symbol of life, consciousness, etc., being without light is viewed with fear and dread and felt to be depressing. Once realizing all of this, it is thought, the sighted person will no longer entertain the mistaken notion that blind people live in a depressing "world of darkness."[11] And, intellectually, he may accept the evidence and cease to hold such a belief. Emotionally, however, the specific idea of a "world of darkness" will still fill him with dread and he will still react as if the blind person were one who inhabits that depressing realm. Given man's manner of being in the world, from which such ideas stem, no other result is possible. No matter how strenuously it is argued, blindness is still darkness and both blindness and darkness are still depressing. A blind person is demonstrably more similar to, than different from, those who have sight. Nevertheless, he is perceived to be quite different, all denials to the contrary notwithstanding.[12]

What, then, is to be done? Are we to accept the fact that public education programs can only have limited success in improving attitudes toward blindness and blind people? Toward blindness, probably. Toward blind people, not necessarily. That is, it seems unlikely that any way can be found to alter the belief that both physical and symbolic blindness are extremely serious matters, ones to be feared and avoided, for indeed that is their nature. It does seem, however, that certain changes in the approach of programs aimed at improving attitudes might be able to affect the way blind people are viewed and treated.

The *sine qua non* of this new approach is a recognition of the fact that some attitudes toward blindness and blind people involve the influence of a disruptive complex. As will be recalled from our discussion in the first part of the fourth chapter, an important characteristic of the complex is identity, the inability of the individual to differentiate between his perceptions and reactions to outer reality on the one hand, and, on the other, those of his perceptions and reactions that are highly colored or distorted by the compulsive and primitive impulses that are expressive of the complex. In other words, in meeting a blind person, the sighted person will react as much to the symbolic meaning of blindness as to blindness as a physical impairment. Furthermore, because of the phenomenon of projection, the complex and all the psychic conflicts that it entails will be encountered as if they were characteristics of the blind person. Being a carrier of these projections, the blind person and his true characteristics cannot be clearly perceived by the sighted person; he becomes a mere character in the internal drama of the perceiver.[13] "Projections of all kinds," writes von Franz, "obscure our view of our fellow men, spoiling its objectivity, and thus spoiling all possibility of genuine human relationships." [14] (It is interesting to note that an analogous situation occurs as a normal part of an individual's adjustment to blindness. That is, he is overwhelmed by the symbolic meaning of blindness and is, at first, incapable of recognizing or dealing with the practical, personal ramifications of his visual loss.) [15] The problem in improving such negative attitudes toward blindness, therefore, is one of dissolving this state of identity and of separating the sighted person's projection from the blind person.

What is required of the individual in solving the problem of identity with unconscious impulses and their projection onto others is first a recognition and acceptance of the fact that this is what is occurring. Projection, as an outward manifestation of identity, can be recognized with relative ease by a truly objective third party, but the task of recognizing one's own projections and of achieving a non-distorted view of the actual person who has been obscured by them is not at all easy. To achieve such a separation the individual must recognize not only the real characteristics of the other person, but also, and more importantly, the fact that the content of the projection itself is real. This, then, is precisely where the difficulty lies, for what is encountered in the projection is that which the individual is unable or unwilling to identify as his own; it is, in short, from his unconscious. [16]

What role can an outsider have in promoting the dissolution of a projection? First, he can point out and emphasize the true characteristics of the person carrying the projection. Second, he can demonstrate that there is a disparity between the true characteristics and those that the individual believes are present. Finally, the outsider can raise certain questions about the projected characteristics and their meaning for the individual. The essential point, it must be emphasized, is that the reality of the contents of the projection is never denied. While such a denial might seem the rational thing to do, it is self-defeating. For example, if a sighted person believes that blind people are evil and immoral, we gain nothing by saying that such a belief is nonsensical. It is nonsensical, but only insofar as it refers to actual blind people; symbolically, it is quite accurate. Because of this, the sighted person will, through a powerful, inner necessity, dismiss the third-person evidence and reaffirm his belief.

Accepting the reality of the projection does not necessarily mean that it can be differentiated from its carrier, but it is a step in the right direction. By doing so, there is then a chance that the sighted person will begin to reflect on the implications of his belief. As we have said, even admitting that there is a possibility of a projection is extremely difficult; it requires quite a degree of self-awareness and a great degree of moral courage. Recognition of the projection, however, does not solve the problem, for a further effort must then be made to make its contents conscious, a process that is often disagreeable or even painful.

In dealing with projection and identity, it should be remembered that the complex underlying them has both a shell and a core. The significance of the projection of the impulses involved in the state of identity are related to both these parts. Through his personal associations with the various specific qualities involved in the complex, the individual can make great headway in becoming conscious of those parts of himself that had formerly been completely unconscious. Eventually, however, the archetypal core of the complex will need to be confronted if there is to be a genuine growth in consciousness and a consequent dissolution of the state of identity. This is accomplished by determining the meaning of the complex within the context of the individual's own life and development. As Whitmont explains it:

> Only when the personal (the ontogenetic) is fully explored can the archetypal core of the complex effectively be reached, because the personal shell of the complex is the form in which the eternal

mythological motif incarnates itself and makes itself felt in our personal life and our personal nature. Unless we can deal with the mythological core in personal terms we have nothing *real* to deal with. Unless, however, we deal with the personal history in mythological terms we do not touch its driving power and *meaning,* nor do we reach that which is to be transformed.[17]

To be more specific, the sighted person must come to terms with the personal significance of blindness for him and also with the archetypal meaning of blindness (discussed in the fourth chapter, above). His ability to transform the complex will largely be determined by the circumstances of his life and his qualities as an individual.[18] Whatever the degree of his success, however, the recognition of the situation and any effort to deal with it will have a beneficial effect on the individual [19] and an ameliorative effect on his negative attitudes toward blind people.

This is not to say that negative attitudes can only be improved through the intervention of a psychotherapist. Only when attitudes are of such an intensity and rigidity that they are symptomatic of mental illness is therapy the only approach. The goal of therapy, it must be remembered, is a growth in consciousness, in self-awareness, but this is also the goal of public education programs. Both seek to induce changes in the individual by "laying all the cards on the table," by making known that which was unknown and revealing that which was hidden. Nevertheless, it is reasonable to ask how much effect a public education program would have if it attempted to deal directly with the archetypal core of the blindness complex from whence these attitudes come. First, it should be recalled that the archetypes correspond to basic aptitudes or preformed tendencies toward typical reaction modes and that they are collective, not purely personal, in content.[20] Given this, it is clear that a public education program could not literally "deal directly with the archetypal core," but it most decidedly could acknowledge, elucidate, and comment upon these universal reaction modes and preformed tendencies. In fact, in a somewhat parallel situation, the provision of adjustment services to the newly blinded individual (parallel because all of the individual's former attitudes toward blindness play a significant role in his reaction to blindness), it is emphasized that the individual is not expected to minimize his handicap or to exaggerate it, but "Rather he is to see it as it is, *in its full meaning.*" [21] By the same token, the difficult task of helping the sighted person to overcome his negative attitudes requires that he be encouraged to reflect upon the meaning of blindness. Father Carroll expresses this idea as follows:

> There is no easy way to find how to give true sympathy, help, love. But the approach that tries to see the meaning of blindness and the meaning of some of our feelings about it is a beginning. If it does not necessarily and of itself lead to love, it can at least remove some of the difficulties that stand in the way of loving.[22]

The implication of this for public education programs is simply that full information about the meaning of blindness has got to be presented, both the outer meaning and the symbolic, inner, psychologically "true" meaning. To ignore or deny or repress this side, as has been done in the past, only means that the influence of consciousness is relinquished and that this side is allowed to continue reinforcing the negative attitudes and stereotypes. Since the inner meaning of blindness is related to one of the universal fears of mankind, its influence when left unconscious is inexorable. Only by addressing ourselves to it, by keeping it in the open where it can be dealt with, is there a possibility that it can gradually be made conscious by the individual. Josef Goldbrunner has written:

> To live a spiritually healthy life . . . one must consciously come to terms with the irrational forces within oneself, incorporating them into the total life of the soul, but never allowing them a perfectly free rein. . . . If the striving for perfection is to keep man's soul in wholeness and health, he will have to be led along the path of self-unfolding.[23]

The short-term, practical goal of an educational effort is to provide the orientation, the background, and the basic insights through which the sighted individual can be made aware of the origins of his negative attitudes. By adding such a component to an already sound program (as described at the outset of this chapter), it is relatively easy to promote the differentiation between the symbolic and the actual meaning of blindness and between the blind person himself and the projections that he carries.

Materials that are particularly important and highly effective for this purpose are myths, legends, and folktales. Here the archetypes are found in their most vivid and instructive form. Joseph Campbell has said that there are four functions of mythology: (1) "to reconcile waking consciousness to the *mysterium tremendum et fascinans* of this universe *as it is*"; (2) "to render an interpretive total image of the same, as known to contemporary consciousness"; (3) to enforce a moral order ("the shaping of an individual to the requirements of his geographically and historically conditioned social group"); and, most vitally and critically, (4) "to foster the centering and unfolding of the individual in integrity, in accord with (d) himself, (c) his culture (the mesocosm), (b) the universe (the macrocosm), and (a) that awesome ultimate mystery which is beyond and within himself and all things. . . ." [24]

In addition to this two-pronged attack on negative attitudes, a very useful way of further promoting differentiation between the symbolic and the actual is to increase as much as possible the face-to-face contacts between blind and sighted people. If both parties are fully aware of the role that the symbolic will play in their meeting, it is possible that they will both be able to recognize the basic humanity and individuality of the other.[25] There is, of course, the problem of there being so relatively few blind people. Indeed, as has been noted before, the small number of blind people and the consequent infrequency of personal contacts are primary factors in the maintenance of negative attitudes and stereotypes.

To summarize, the ideal approach to improving attitudes toward blindness and blind people is one which fully recognizes the multi-faceted nature of those attitudes and the many layers of significance that they have. It should, in the light of this recognition, seek to correct misconceptions and to put fears and anxieties in their proper perspective. Finally, it should be acknowledged that attitudes are, in large measure, an internal orientation of the individual and that, therefore, it is easier and more effective to aim toward helping the individual to change his own attitudes than to try to change his attitudes for him. Of course, it should also be realized that one who would thus help others must already have undergone these internal changes himself.

Bibliography

Abraham, Karl. "Restrictions and Transformations of Scoptophilia in Psychoneurotics: With Remarks and Analogous Phenomena in Folk Psychology." In *Selected Papers of Karl Abraham*. New York: Basic Books, 1953.

Adorno, T. W.; Frenkel–Brunswick, E.; Levinson, D. J.; and Sanford, R. N. *The Authoritarian Personality*. New York: Harper, 1950.

Alexander, Franz. "Remarks About the Relation of Inferiority Feelings to Guilt Feelings." *International Journal of Psychoanalysis* 19 (1938):41–49.

Allport, Gordon W. *The Nature of Prejudice*. Cambridge, Mass.: Addison-Wesley Publishing Co., 1954.

Anderson, Dorothy K. "The Social Caseworker's Relation to Concepts of Blindness." *Social Casework* 31(1950):416–20.

Asch, Solomon E. "Forming Impressions of Personality." *Journal of Abnormal Social Psychology* 41(1946):258–90.

———. "Gestalt Theory." In *International Encyclopedia of the Social Sciences,* vol.6, edited by David L. Sills, pp.158–74. [New York]: Macmillan and the Free Press, 1968.

Asenjo, J. Albert. "Philosophy of Adjustment." In *Proceedings of the 28th Convention of the American Association of Workers for the Blind, 1954,* pp.13–17.

Axline, Virginia M. "Understanding and Accepting the Child Who Is Blind." *Childhood Education* 30(1954):427–30.

Barker, Roger G. "The Social Psychology of Physical Disability." *Journal of Social Issues* 4(1948):28–38.

Barker, Roger G.; Wright, Beatrice; Meyerson, Lee; and Gonick, Mollie R. *Adjustment to Physical Handicap and Illness: A Survey of the Social Psychology of Physique and Disability*. Bulletin no.55. Revised edition. New York: Social Science Research Council, 1953.

Barnett, M. Robert. "Attitudes Toward the Blind." *Outlook for the Blind* 45(1951):165–69.

——. "20 Centuries B.C. vs. 20 Centuries A.D.—So What Else Is New?" Remarks delivered to the National Federation of the Blind in Annual Convention, Minneapolis, Minnesota, July 5, 1970. Mimeographed.

Barron, Louis. Introduction to *The Evil Eye: The Origins and Practices of Superstition,* by Frederick Thomas Elworthy, pp.ix–xv. 1958. Reprint. New York: Collier–Macmillan, Collier Books, 1970.

Barshay, Helen. *Empathy: Touchstone of Self-Fulfillment: A Creative Approach to Self-Understanding.* New York: Exposition Press, 1964.

Bateman, Barbara. "Sighted Children's Perceptions of Blind Children's Abilities." *Exceptional Children* 29(1962):42–46.

Bauman, Mary K. *Characteristics of Blind and Visually Handicapped People in Professional, Sales, and Managerial Work.* Harrisburg, Pa.: Office for the Blind, 1963.

——. "The Initial Psychological Reaction to Blindness." *New Outlook for the Blind* 53(1959):165–69.

Bayley, Harold. *The Lost Language of Symbolism: An Inquiry Into the Origin of Certain Letters, Words, Names, Fairy-Tales, Folklore, and Mythologies.* 2 vols. 1912. Reprint. London: Williams and Norgate, 1952.

Baynes, H. G. *Mythology of the Soul: A Research Into the Unconscious From Schizophrenic Dreams and Drawings.* 1940. London: Methuen & Co., 1949.

Bellamy, Edward. "The Blindman's World." In *The Blindman's World and Other Stories.* Boston: Houghton, Mifflin, 1898.

Berkeley, George. "A New Theory of Vision." In *A New Theory of Vision and Other Select Philosophical Writings.* London: J. M. Dent & Sons, 1910.

Bertin, Morton A. "A Comparison of Attitudes Toward Blindness." *International Journal for the Education of the Blind* 9(1959):1–4.

Best, Harry. *Blindness and the Blind in the United States.* New York: The Macmillan Company, 1934.

Blank, H. Robert. "Countertransference Problems in the Professional Worker." *New Outlook for the Blind* 48(1954):185–88.

——. "Dreams of the Blind." *Psychoanalytic Quarterly* 27(1958):158–74.

——. "Psychoanalysis and Blindness." *Psychoanalytic Quarterly* 26(1957):1–24.

——, and Rothman, Ruth. "The Congenitally Blind Child: Psychiatric and Case Work Considerations." From the *Proceedings of the Insti-*

tute of the Social Service Department, New York Guild for the Jewish Blind, February 29, 1952, pp.1–13. [New York: New York Guild for the Jewish Blind, 1952.]

"Blind From Birth." *Good Housekeeping,* February 1966, p.12.

Borchert, Charles R. "Blind Trainees Succeed in Industry." *Rehabilitation Record,* September–October 1966, pp.32–33.

Boswell, James. *Life of Samuel Johnson LL.D.* In *Great Books of the Western World,* vol.44. Chicago: Encyclopaedia Britannica, 1952.

Braverman, Sydell. "The Psychological Roots of Attitudes Toward Blindness." In *Attitudes Toward Blindness,* pp.22–32. New York: American Foundation for the Blind, 1951. (Originally published in *New Outlook for the Blind* 45(1951):151–57.

Briggs, K. M. *The Anatomy of Puck: An Examination of Fairy Beliefs Among Shakespeare's Contemporaries and Successors.* London: Routledge and Kegan Paul, 1959.

Brontë, Charlotte. *Jane Eyre.* 1847. London: J. M. Dent & Sons, 1908.

Burland, C. A. *The Arts of the Alchemists.* New York: Macmillan, 1968.

Burlingham, Dorothy. "Psychic Problems of the Blind." *The American Imago* 2(1941):43–85.

Campbell, Donald T. "Social Attitudes and Other Acquired Behavior Dispositions." In *Investigations of Man as Socius: Their Place in Psychology and the Social Sciences,* pp.94–172. *Psychology: A Study of a Science,* edited by Sigmund Koch, vol.6. New York: McGraw-Hill, 1963.

Campbell, Joseph. *The Flight of the Wild Gander: Explorations in the Mythological Dimension.* New York: Viking Press, 1969.

——. *The Masks of God: Creative Mythology.* New York: Viking Press, 1968.

——. *The Masks of God: Primitive Mythology.* New York: Viking Press, 1959.

Carroll, Thomas J. *Blindness: What It Is, What It Does, and How to Live With It.* Boston: Little, Brown and Company, 1961.

——. "Developing Public Understanding About the Blind." In *Proceedings of the 28th Convention of the American Association of Workers for the Blind, 1954,* pp.53–59.

Cason, Hulsey. "The Nightmare Dream." *Psychological Monographs* 46(1935):1–51.

Caulfield, Genevieve. "Friends Around the World." *Catholic World* 181(1955):339–44.

Chevigny, Hector. Foreword to *The Blind in School and Society: A*

Psychological Study, by Thomas D. Cutsforth. New edition. New York: American Foundation for the Blind, 1951.

———. *My Eyes Have a Cold Nose*. New Haven, Conn.: Yale University Press, 1946.

———, and Braverman, Sydell. *The Adjustment of the Blind*. New Haven, Conn.: Yale University Press, 1950.

Cholden, Louis. *A Psychiatrist Works With Blindness*. New York: American Foundation for the Blind, 1958.

Cirlot, J. E. *A Dictionary of Symbols*. Translated by Jack Sage. New York: Philosophical Library, 1962.

Clunk, Joseph F. "Employer Attitudes and the Adjustment of the Blind." In *Psychological Diagnosis and Counseling of the Adult Blind: Selected Papers From the Proceedings of the University of Michigan Conference for the Blind, 1947*, edited by Wilma Donahue and Donald Dabelstein, pp.53–64. New York: American Foundation for the Blind, 1950.

Connor, Gordon B. "An Educator Looks at Attitudes." *New Outlook for the Blind* 57(1963):153–56.

Coon, Nelson. "The Blind in Art." *Eye to Eye: Bulletin of the Graphic History Society of America*, no.6, September 1954, pp.1–7.

Cowen, Emory L.; Underberg, Rita P.; and Verrillo, Ronald T. "The Development and Testing of an Attitude to Blindness Scale." *The Journal of Social Psychology* 48(1958):297–304.

Cowen, Emory L.; Underberg, Rita P.; Verrillo, Ronald T.; and Benham, Frank G. *Adjustment to Visual Disability in Adolescence*. New York: American Foundation for the Blind, 1961.

Crawford, Fred L., and Lirtzman, Sidney. *Counseling and Placement of Blind Persons in Professional Occupations: Practice and Research*. New York: American Foundation for the Blind, 1966.

Crawford, O. G. S. *The Eye Goddess*. New York: The Macmillan Company, n.d. [1956].

Cruden, Alexander. *Cruden's Complete Concordance to the Old and New Testaments*. Edited by A. D. Adams, C. H. Irwin, and S. A. Waters. Grand Rapids, Mich.: Zondervan Publishing House, 1967.

Cutsforth, Thomas D. "Are We Truly Part of the Community?" *New Outlook for the Blind* 55(1961):121–25.

———. *The Blind in School and Society: A Psychological Study*. New edition. New York: American Foundation for the Blind, 1951.

Davidson, H. R. Ellis. *Scandanavian Mythology*. London: Paul Hamlyn, 1969.

Davis, F. "Deviance Disavowal: The Management of Strained Interaction by the Visibly Handicapped." *Social Problems* 9(1961):120–32.

Dearborn, George Van N. Editorial Introduction to *The Sense of Sight,* by Frank Nicholas Spindler. New York: Moffat, Yard & Company, 1917.

Dembo, T. "Devaluation of the Physically Handicapped Person." Paper presented at the American Psychological Association, Cleveland, 1953.

Dembo, T.; Leviton, G. L.; and Wright, B. A. "Adjustment to Misfortune—A Problem of Social Psychological Rehabilitation." *Artificial Limbs* 3(1956):4–62.

Dent, Oran B. "An Investigation of Attitudes Toward Work Adjustment of the Blind." *New Outlook for the Blind* 56(1962):357–62.

Deutsch, Elinor. "The Dream Imagery of the Blind." *Psychoanalytic Review* 15(1928):288–93.

Devereaux, Jane. "Attitudes Toward the Blind: How Can Social Casework Be Effective in Their Development?" *Outlook for the Blind* 45(1951):158–65.

Dickens, Charles. *American Notes and Pictures From Italy.* New York: E. P. Dutton, 1908.

Dickinson, Raymond M. "The Humanitarian Spirit in Work for the Blind." *New Outlook for the Blind* 47(1953):264–70.

Diderot, [Denis]. *An Essay on Blindness in a Letter to a Person of Distinction.* 1773. Reprint. London: Sampson Low, Marston, and Company, 1895.

Dishart, Martin. "Family Adjustment in the Rehabilitation Plan." *New Outlook for the Blind* 58(1964):292–94.

Dunton, William Rush, Jr. "Mental State of the Blind." *American Journal of Insanity* 65(1908):103–12.

Ecclesine, Margy Wyvill. "Father Carroll's Fight for the Blind." *Catholic Digest,* July 1962, pp.120–27.

Edinger, Edward F. "Christ as Paradigm of the Individuating Ego." *Spring* (1966):5–23.

Elworthy, Frederick Thomas. *The Evil Eye: The Origins and Practices of Superstition.* 1895. Reprint. New York: Collier–Macmillan, Collier Books, 1970.

Eriksen, Charles W. "Perception: Unconscious Perception." In *International Encyclopedia of the Social Sciences,* vol.11, edited by David L. Sills, pp.575–81. [New York]: Macmillan and the Free Press, 1968.

Farrell, Gabriel. "Community and Family Problems Related to Adjustment of the Blind." In *Psychological Diagnosis and Counseling of the Adult Blind: Selected Papers from the Proceedings of the University of Michigan Conference for the Blind, 1947,* edited by Wilma Donahue and Donald Dabelstein, pp.45–52. New York: American Foundation for the Blind, 1950.

Fenichel, Otto. "The Scoptophilic Instinct and Identification." In *Collected Papers of Otto Fenichel, First Series.* New York: W. W. Norton, 1953.

Fenton, Calvin W. "A Study of Social Workers' Attitudes Toward Blindness." Master's thesis. Adelphi College, 1962.

Fink, Edna. "Parental Attitudes Toward Blind Children." *Outlook for the Blind* 45(1951):24–25.

Fitting, Edward A. *Evaluation of Adjustment to Blindness.* New York: American Foundation for the Blind, 1954.

Foley, Kate M. *Five Lectures on Blindness.* Sacramento: California State Library, 1919.

Freeman, John. Introduction to *Man and His Symbols,* edited by C. G. Jung, pp.9–15. New York: Doubleday, 1964.

French, Richard Slayton. *From Homer to Helen Keller: A Social and Educational Study of the Blind.* New York: American Foundation for the Blind, 1932.

Freud, Anna. "The Concept of Developmental Lines." *The Psychoanalytic Study of the Child* 18(1963): 245–65.

Freud, Sigmund. "Psychogenic Visual Disturbance According to Psychoanalytical Conceptions." 1910. In *Collected Papers,* vol.2, pp.105–12. London: Hogarth Press and the Institute of Psychoanalysis, 1924.

———. "Three Contributions to the Theory of Sex." 1905. In *The Basic Writings of Sigmund Freud,* translated and edited by A. A. Brill. New York: Random House, Modern Library, 1938.

Fries, Emil. "The Social Psychology of Blindness." *Journal of Abnormal and Social Psychology* 25(1930): 14–25.

Gerard, Harold B. "Social Psychology." In *International Encyclopedia of the Social Sciences,* vol.14, edited by David L. Sills, pp.459–73. [New York]: Macmillan and the Free Press, 1968.

Gesell, Arnold; Ilg, Frances L.; Bullis, Glenna E. *Vision: Its Development in Infant and Child.* New York: Paul B. Hoeber, 1949.

Gibson, Eleanor J. "Perception: Perceptual Development." In *International Encyclopedia of the Social Sciences,* vol.11, edited by David L. Sills, pp.535–40. [New York]: Macmillan and the Free Press, 1968.

Gibson, J. J. *The Perception of the Visual World*. Boston: Houghton Mifflin, 1950.

Gifford, Edward S., Jr. "The Evil Eye in Medical History." *American Journal of Ophthalmology* 44(1957):237–43.

——. *The Evil Eye: Studies in the Folklore of Vision*. New York: Macmillan, 1958.

——. "Patron Gods of Vision." *American Journal of Opthalmology* 42 (1956):903–6.

Ginzberg, Louis. *The Legends of the Jews*. 7 vols. 1909. Translated by Henrietta Szold. Philadelphia: Jewish Publication Society of America, 1967–1968.

Goffman, Erving. *Stigma: Notes on the Management of Spoiled Identity*. Englewood Cliffs, N. J.: Prentice–Hall, Spectrum Books, 1963.

Goldbrunner, Josef. *Holiness Is Wholeness*. Translated by Stanley Goodman. New York: Pantheon Books, 1955.

Gowman, Alan G. "Blindness and the Role of Companion." *Social Problems* 4(1956):68–75.

——. *The War Blind in American Social Structure*. New York: American Foundation for the Blind, 1957.

Graham, Milton D. *Social Research on Blindness: Present Status and Future Potentials*. New York: American Foundation for the Blind, 1960.

——, and Clark, Leslie L. "The Social Management of Blindness." An unpublished manuscript (dated July 25, 1968) of a chapter prepared for a forthcoming book being edited by Eric Josephson.

Gregory, R. L. *Eye and Brain: The Psychology of Seeing*. New York: McGraw-Hill, 1966.

Grierson, E. "Children's Tales From Scottish Ballads: The Lochmaben Harper." *Caledonian* 12(1913):517–19.

Guillié, [Sebastian]. *An Essay on the Instruction and Amusement of the Blind*. 1819. Reprint. London: Sampson Low, Marston, and Company, 1894.

Haggard, H. Rider. *The Wanderer's Necklace*. 1914. Reprint. New York: Longmans, Green, 1922.

Haj, Fareed. *Disability in Antiquity*. New York: Philosophical Library, 1970.

Handel, Alexander F. "Community Attitudes Influencing Psycho-Social Adjustment To Blindness." *Journal of Rehabilitation* 26(1960): 23–25.

Harding, John. "Stereotypes." In *International Encyclopedia of the*

Social Sciences, vol.15, edited by David L. Sills, pp.259–62. [New York]: Macmillan and the Free Press, 1968.

Hart, Henry Harper. "The Eye in Symbol and Symptom." *The Yearbook of Psychoanalysis* 6(1950):256.

Haüy, [Valentin]. *An Essay on the Education of the Blind.* 1786. Reprint. London: Sampson Low, Marston, and Company, 1894.

Hawkes, Clarence. "Some Common Fallacies About Blindness." *The Outlook* 3(1915):573–74.

Hayes, Samuel Perkins. *Contributions to a Psychology of Blindness.* New York: American Foundation for the Blind, 1941.

Heaton, J. M. *The Eye: Phenomenology and Psychology of Function and Disorder.* Studies in Existentialism and Phenomenology Series, edited by R. D. Laing. London: Tavistock Publications, 1968.

Heider, F. *The Psychology of Interpersonal Relations.* New York: Wiley, 1958.

Henderson, Joseph L. "Ancient Myths and Modern Man." In *Man and His Symbols,* edited by C. G. Jung, pp.104–57. New York: Doubleday, 1964.

Herodotus. *The History.* Translated by George Rawlinson. In *Great Books of the Western World,* vol.6. Chicago: Encyclopaedia Britannica, 1952.

Himes, Joseph S. "Changing Attitudes Toward Blind People—From the Viewpoint of a Sociologist." In *Proceedings of the 32d Convention of the American Association of Workers for the Blind, Inc., 1958,* pp.158–63.

———. "The Measurement of Social Distance in Social Relations With the Blind." *New Outlook for the Blind* 54(1960):54–58.

———. "Some Concepts of Blindness in American Culture." In *Attitudes Toward Blindness,* pp.10–22. New York: American Foundation for the Blind, 1951. (Originally published in *Social Casework* 31[1950]: 410–16.)

Hochberg, Julian E. "Perception: Introduction." In *International Encyclopedia of the Social Sciences,* vol.11, edited by David L. Sills, pp.527–35. [New York]: Macmillan and the Free Press, 1968.

Holt, Alfred H. *Phrase and Word Origins: A Study of Familiar Expressions.* Revised edition. New York: Dover, 1961.

Homer. *The Odyssey.* Translated by Samuel Butler. In *Great Books of the Western World,* vol.4. Chicago: Encyclopaedia Britannica, 1952.

"The Homeric Hymns." In *Hesiod, the Homeric Hymns, and Homerica.* Translated by Hugh G. Evelyn–White. Loeb Classical Library, no.57. Cambridge, Mass.: Harvard University Press, 1964.

Hugo, Victor. *The Man Who Laughs.* 2 vols. New York: J. H. Sears, n.d.

Hutchinson, Elizabeth. "The Visually Handicapped Person in His Community." In *Proceedings of the 35th Convention of American Association of Workers for the Blind, 1961,* pp.38–42.

Ichheiser, G. "Misunderstandings in Human Relations." *American Journal of Sociology* 55(1949):(supplement to No.2) 1–70.

Imamura, Sadako. "A Critical Survey of the Literature on the Social Role of the Blind in the United States." Doctoral paper. Harvard University, 1955.

Ions, Veronica. *Egyptian Mythology.* London: Paul Hamlyn, 1968.

Jabin, Norma. "Attitudes Toward the Physically Disabled As Related to Selected Personality Variables." Doctoral dissertation. New York University, 1965.

Jablonski, Edward. "Man's Conquest of Blindness." *Blind Digest,* February 1966, pp. 2–6, 8.

Jacobi, Jolande. *Complex/Archetype/Symbol in the Psychology of C. G. Jung.* Bollingen Series, no.57. Princeton, N. J.: Princeton University Press, 1959.

——. "Symbols in an Individual Analysis." In *Man and His Symbols,* edited by C. G. Jung, pp.272–310. New York: Doubleday, 1964.

Jaffé, Aniela. "Symbolism in the Visual Arts." In *Man and His Symbols,* edited by C. G. Jung, pp.230–71. New York: Doubleday, 1964.

Jastrow, Joseph. "The Dreams of the Blind." *New Princeton Review* 5(1888):18–34.

Jervis, Frederick M. "A Comparison of Self-Concepts of Blind and Sighted Children." In *Guidance Programs for Blind Children: A Report of a Conference, April 1959,* edited by Carl J. Davis, pp.19–25. Watertown, Mass.: Perkins School for the Blind, [1959].

Johns, B. G. "How the Blind Dream." *National Review* 5(1885):309–19.

Jonas, Hans. "The Nobility of Sight: A Study in the Phenomenology of the Senses." In *The Phenomenon of Life: Toward a Philosophical Biology,* by Hans Jonas, pp.135–56. Reprint. New York: Dell, Delta Books, 1968.

Jordan, Sidney. "The Disadvantaged Group: A Concept Applicable to the Handicapped." *The Journal of Psychology* 55(1963):312–22.

Jung, C. G. *Aion: Researches Into the Phenomenology of the Self.* Translated by R. F. C. Hull. In *The Collected Works of C. G. Jung,* vol.9, pt.2. 2d edition. Bollingen Series, no.20. Princeton, N. J.: Princeton University Press, 1968.

——. "Approaching the Unconscious." In *Man and His Symbols,* edited by C. G. Jung, pp.18–103. New York: Doubleday, 1964.

——. *The Archetypes and the Collective Unconscious.* Translated by R. F. C. Hull. In *The Collected Works of C. G. Jung,* vol.9, pt.1. 2d edition. Bollingen Series, no.20. Princeton, N. J.: Priniceton University Press, 1968.

——. *Mysterium Coniunctionis: An Inquiry Into the Separation and Synthesis of Psychic Opposites in Alchemy.* Translated by R. F. C. Hull. In *The Collected Works of C. G. Jung,* vol.14. Bollingen Series, no.20. New York: Pantheon Books, 1963.

——. *Psychology and Alchemy.* 2d revised edition. Translated by R. F. C. Hull. In *The Collected Works of C. G. Jung,* vol.12. Bollingen Series, no.20. Princeton, N. J.: Princeton University Press, 1968.

——. *The Structure and Dynamics of the Psyche.* Translated by R. F. C. Hull. In *The Collected Works of C. G. Jung,* vol.8. Bollingen Series, no.20. New York: Pantheon Books, 1960.

——. *Symbols of Transformation: An Analysis of the Prelude to a Case of Schizophrenia.* Translated by R. F. C. Hull. In *The Collected Works of C. G. Jung,* vol.5. Bollingen Series, no.20. New York: Pantheon Books, 1956.

——, and Kerényi, C. *Essays on a Science of Mythology: The Myth of the Divine Child and the Mysteries of Eleusis.* Translated by R. F. C. Hull. Bollingen Series, no.22. Princeton, N. J.: Princeton University Press, 1969.

Katz, Daniel L. "The Functional Approach to the Study of Attitudes." *Public Opinion Quarterly* 24(1960):163–204.

——, and Stotland, Ezra. "A Preliminary Statement to a Theory of Attitude Structure and Change." In *Psychology: A Study of a Science,* vol.3, edited by Sigmund Koch, pp.423–75. New York: McGraw–Hill, 1959.

Keller, Helen. *The World I Live In.* New York: Century, 1908.

Kendler, Howard H., and Kendler, Tracy S. "Concept Formation." In *International Encyclopedia of the Social Sciences,* vol.3, edited by David L. Sills, pp.206–11. [New York]: Macmillan and the Free Press, 1968.

Kimmins, C. W. *Children's Dreams.* London: Longmans, Green, 1920.

Kipling, Rudyard. *The Light That Failed.* New York: Doubleday & McClure, 1899.

Kirsch, James. *Shakespeare's Royal Self.* New York: G. P. Putnam's Sons, 1966.

Kleck, R. "Emotional Arousal in Interactions with Stigmatized Persons." *Psychological Reports* 19(1966):1226.

——. "Physical Stigma and Nonverbal Cues Emitted in Face-to-Face Interaction." *Human Relations* 21(1968):19–28.

Kleck, R.; Ono, H.; and Hastorf, A. H. "The Effects of Physical Deviance Upon Face to Face Interaction." *Human Relations* 19 (1966):425–36.

Kleck, R.; Buck, P.; Goller, W. L.; London, R. S.; Pfeiffer, J. R.; and Vukcevic, D. P. "Effects of Stigmatizing Conditions on the Use of Personal Space." *Psychological Reports* 23(1968) : 111–18.

Klein, Milton H. "Observations on the Attitudes of the Blind Toward the Sighted." In *Proceedings of the 23d Convention of the American Association of Workers for the Blind, 1949*, pp.60–62.

Klineberg, Otto. "Prejudice: The Concept." In *International Encyclopedia of the Social Sciences*, vol.12, edited by David L. Sills, pp.439–48. [New York]: Macmillan and the Free Press, 1968.

Kooyman, W. J. J. "Het Houdings- en Bewegingsbeeld van de Blinde Mens" (Carriage and Mobility of the Blind Man). *De Lichamelijke Opvoeding*, March 7, 1959, pp.38 ff.

Kress, Ruth Irene. "Reactions of Employers in the St. Louis Shoe Industry to the Employment of the Blind." Master's dissertation. George Warren Brown School of Social Work, Washington University, 1948. Mimeographed.

Ladieu, Gloria; Adler, D.; and Dembo, Tamara. "Studies in Adjustment to Visible Injuries: Social Acceptance of the Injured." *Journal of Social Issues* 4(1948):55–61.

Langworthy, Jessica L. "Blindness in Fiction: A Study of the Attitude of Authors Towards Their Blind Characters." *Journal of Applied Psychology* 14(1930):269–86.

Larkin, H. "Attitudes of Blind Adolescents to Their Blindness." *The Teacher of the Blind* 1(1962):161–66.

Lee, Mrs. H. L. "The Social Impact of Blindness Upon the Individual." *Proceedings of the World Assembly of the World Council for the Welfare of the Blind, 1964*, pp.108–13. [London]: World Council for the Welfare of the Blind, [1965].

Lehman, Ann. "Employer Attitudes on Blind Workers." In *Proceedings of the 23d Convention of the American Association of Workers for the Blind, 1949*, pp.49–50.

Lende, Helga. *Books About the Blind: A Bibliographical Guide to Literature Relating to the Blind*. Revised edition. New York: American Foundation for the Blind, 1953.

Levy, W. Hanks. *Blindness and the Blind: or, A Treatise on the Science of Typhlology*. London: Chapman & Hall, 1872.

Liddle, Don. "Psychological Problems of Blindness." *The Utah Eagle*, March 1965, pp.1,15–16.

Lippmann, Walter. *Public Opinion*. 1922. Reprint. New York: Macmillan, 1944.

Locke, John. "An Essay Concerning Human Understanding." In *The Philosophical Works of John Locke*, edited by J. A. St. John, vol.1. London: George Bell and Sons, 1901.

London, Jack. *The Sea-Wolf*. New York: Grosset & Dunlap, 1904.

Lowenfeld, Berthold. "Mental Hygiene of Blindness." In *Psychological Diagnosis and Counseling of the Adult Blind: Selected Papers From the Proceedings of the University of Michigan Conference for the Blind, 1947*, edited by Wilma Donahue and Donald Dabelstein, pp. 35–44. New York: American Foundation for the Blind, 1950.

——. "A Psychological Approach to Blindness." *Journal of Exceptional Children* 16(1949):1–6,19.

——. "The Role and Status of the Blind Person." *New Outlook for the Blind* 58(1964):36–40.

——. "The Social Impact of Blindness Upon the Individual." *New Outlook for the Blind* 58(1964):273–77.

Lowry, Fern. "Basic Assumptions Underlying Casework With Blind Persons." In *Social Casework and Blindness*, edited by Samuel Finestone, pp.13–17. New York: American Foundation for the Blind, 1960.

——. "The Implications of Blindness for the Social Caseworker in Practice—Implications for the Study Process." In *Social Casework and Blindness*, edited by Samuel Finestone, pp.64–86. New York: American Foundation for the Blind, 1960.

Lukoff, Irving Faber. "A Sociological Appraisal of Blindness." In *Social Casework and Blindness*, edited by Samuel Finestone, pp.19–44. New York: American Foundation for the Blind, 1960.

——, and Whiteman, Martin. "Attitudes and Blindness: Components, Correlates, and Effects." Vocational Rehabilitation Administration, U. S. Department of Health, Education, and Welfare, Grant No. 835s, and The Seeing Eye, Inc. Mimeographed. 1963.

——. "Attitudes Toward Blindness—Some Preliminary Findings." *New Outlook for the Blind* 55(1961):39–44.

——. *The Social Sources of Adjustment to Blindness*. Research Series, no.21. New York: American Foundation for the Blind, [1970].

Maas, Melvin J. "Changing Attitudes Toward the Employment of the Blind." *New Outlook for the Blind* 52(1958):86–88.

McCartney, Fred Morton. "A Comparative Study of Dreams of the Blind and of the Sighted, with Special Reference to Freud's Theory." Master's thesis, Indiana Uniiversity, 1913.

McCollam, H. Kenneth. "Attitude of the Blind Toward Sighted." In *Proceedings of the 23d Convention of the American Association of Workers for the Blind, 1949*, pp.62–65.

MacFarland, D. C. "The Public Image of Blindness." *New Outlook for the Blind* 58(1964):150–52.

Mackenzie, Donald A. *Teutonic Myth and Legend*. London: Gresham Publishing Co., n.d.

MacLeod, Robert B. "Phenomenology." In *International Encyclopedia of the Social Sciences*, vol.12, edited by David L. Sills, pp.68–72. [New York]: Macmillan and the Free Press, 1968.

Mallowan, M. E. L. "Excavations at Brak and Chagar Bazar." *Iraq* 9(1947):206.

Mead, George Herbert. *Mind, Self, and Society*. Chicago: University of Chicago Press, 1934.

Meng, H. "Zur Sozialpsychologie der Körperbeschädigten: Ein Beitrag zum Problem der praktischen Psychohygiene." *Schweizer Archiv für Neurologie und Psychiatrie* 40(1938):328–44.

Meyerson, Lee. "Somatopsychological Aspects of Blindness." In *Psychological Diagnosis and Counseling of the Adult Blind: Selected Papers From the Proceedings of the University of Michigan Conference for the Blind, 1947*, edited by Wilma Donahue and Donald Dabelstein, pp.12–34. New York: American Foundation for the Blind, 1950.

Milton, John. "Paradise Lost" (1667). In *Great Books of the Western World*, vol.32, pp.93–333. Chicago: Encyclopaedia Britannica, 1952.

——. "Samson Agonistes" (1671). In *Great Books of the Western World*, vol.32, pp.339–78. Chicago: Encyclopaedia Britannica, 1952.

——. "Sonnet XVI." In *An Anthology of Famous English and American Poetry*, edited by William Rose Benét and Conrad Aiken, p.101. New York: Random House, Modern Library, 1945.

Milton, W. E. "A Forward Movement in Worker-Community Relations." In *Proceedings of the 29th Convention of the American Association of Workers for the Blind, 1955*, pp.92–94.

Munch, Peter Andreas. *Norse Mythology: Legends of Gods and Heroes*. Translated by Sigurd Bernhard Hustvedt. Scandanavian Classics, vol. 27. New York: American-Scandanavian Foundation, 1927.

Murphy, Albert T. "Attitudes of Educators Toward the Visually Handicapped." *International Journal for the Education of the Blind* 10 (1961):103–7.

Murray, Virginia. "Parental Attitudes Affect Growth and Development of the Young Blind Child." *New Outlook for the Blind* 52(1958): 8–10.

Nagera, Humberto, and Colonna, Alice B. "Aspects of the Contribution of Sight to Ego and Drive Development." *The Psychoanalytic Study of the Child* 20(1965):267–87.

Neumann, Erich. *The Origins and History of Consciousness.* Translated by R. F. C. Hull. Bollingen Series, no.42. New York: Pantheon, 1954.

The New English Bible With the Apocrypha. New York: Oxford University Press and Cambridge University Press, 1970.

New Larousse Encyclopedia of Mythology. Translated by Richard Aldington and Delano Ames. New edition. Buffalo, N. Y.: Prometheus Press, 1968.

Nikoloff, Oliver M. "Attitudes of Public School Principals Toward the Employment of Teachers With Certain Physical Disabilities." *Rehabilitation Literature* 23(1962):344–45.

O'Connor, Marguerite; O'Connor, John; and McNamara, Helen A. *A Pilot Study for the Blind Students in Education, Who Plan to Teach Sighted Children.* [DeKalb, Ill.: Northern Illinois University, 1961.]

Pascal, Joseph I. "The Changing Attitude Towards the Blind and the Partially Sighted." *American Journal of Optometry* 31(1954):319–24.

Paterson, Janet G. "The Blind in Fiction." *Outlook for the Blind* 6(1912):68–76.

Pierce, Robinson. *It Was Not My Own Idea.* New York: American Foundation for the Blind, 1944.

Plutarch. *The Lives of the Noble Grecians and Romans.* The Dryden Translation. In *Great Books of the Western World,* vol.14. Chicago: Encyclopaedia Britannica, 1952.

Pope, A. R. "The Eros Aspect of the Eye: The Left Eye." Thesis. C. G. Jung Institute, Zurich, Switzerland, 1960.

Potter, C. S. "Living in a Sighted World." *Minnesota Welfare,* August 1949, pp.14–17.

Potter, E. G., and Field, F. E. "Physical Disability and Interpersonal Perception." *Perceptual and Motor Skills* 8(1958):241–42.

Putnam, Peter. "If You Had a Choice." *Saturday Review,* October 26, 1963, pp.29,53.

The Random House Dictionary of the English Language, edited by Jess Stein. New York: Random House, 1966.

Raskin, N. J. "The Attitudes of Sighted People Towards Blindness." Paper presented to National Psychological Research Council on Blindness, March 17, 1956.

Rawls, Rachel F. "Parental Reactions and Attitudes Toward the Blind Child." *New Outlook for the Blind* 51(1957):92–97.

Read, Margaret. "Attitude Towards Health and Disease Among Preliterate Peoples." *Health Education Journal* 6(1948):166–72.

Richardson, S. A.; Goodman, N.; Hastorf, A. H.; and Dornbusch, S. M. "Cultural Uniformity in Reaction to Physical Disabilities." *American Sociological Review* 26(1961):241–47.

Ritter, Charles G. "Changing Attitudes Towards Blindness—From the Point of View of 20/20." In *Proceedings of the 32d Convention of the American Association of Workers for the Blind, Inc., 1958,* pp.163–65.

Robertson, Margaret. "The Gloucester Treatment: Punitive and Political Blinding in the British Isles." *New Beacon* 51(1967):64–67.

Rokeach, Milton. "Attitudes: The Nature of Attitudes." In *International Encyclopedia of the Social Sciences,* vol.1, edited by David L. Sills, pp.449–58. [New York]: Macmillan and the Free Press, 1968.

Rusalem, Herbert. "Attitudes Toward Blind Counselors in State Rehabilitation Agencies." *Personnel and Guidance Journal* 39(1961): 367–72.

———. "The Environmental Supports of Public Attitudes Toward Blindness." *Outlook for the Blind* 44(1950):277–88.

Satrustegui, Ignacio de. "The Social Impact of Blindness on the Individual." In *Proceedings of the World Assembly of the World Council for the Welfare of the Blind, 1964,* pp.104–8. [London]: World Council for the Welfare of the Blind, [1965].

Schauer, Gerhard. "Motivation of Attitudes Toward Blindness." In *Attitudes Toward Blindness,* pp.5–10. New York: American Foundation for the Blind, 1951. (Originally published in *Outlook for the Blind* 45[1951]:39–42.)

Schilder, P. *The Image and Appearance of the Human Body.* London: Kegan Paul, Trench, Trubner, 1935.

Scott, Robert A. *Adjustment to Blindness and Severe Visual Impairment: A Selected Bibliography.* New York: American Foundation for the Blind, 1967.

———. *The Making of Blind Men: A Study of Adult Socialization.* New York: Russell Sage Foundation, 1969.

Seeman, Bernard. *Your Sight: Folklore, Fact, and Common Sense.* Boston: Little, Brown and Company, 1968.

Shakespeare, William. *King Lear.* In *Great Books of the Western World,* vol.27. Chicago: Encyclopaedia Britannica, 1952.

Siller, Jerome; Chipman, Abram; Ferguson, Linda; and Vann, Donald H. *Attitudes of the Nondisabled Toward the Physically Disabled.* Studies in Reactions to Disability, no.11. New York: New York University, School of Education, 1967.

Siller, Jerome; Ferguson, Linda; Vann, Donald H.; and Holland, Bert. *Structure of Attitudes Toward the Physically Disabled: Disability Factor Scales—Amputation, Blindness, Cosmetic Conditions.* Studies in Reactions to Disability, no.12. New York: New York University, School of Education, 1967.

Simmons, Harry E. "The Attitudes of the Sighted Toward the Blind." In *Proceedings of the 23d Convention of the American Association of Workers for the Blind, 1949,* pp.54–57.

Singer, Jerome, and Streiner, B. F. "Imaginative Content in the Dreams and Fantasy Play of Blind and Sighted Children." *Perceptual and Motor Skills* 22(1966):475–82.

Smith, M. Brewster. "Attitude Change." In *International Encyclopedia of the Social Sciences,* vol.1, edited by David L. Sills, pp.458–67. [New York]: Macmillan and the Free Press, 1968.

Smith, M. Brewster; Bruner, Jerome S.; and White, R. W. *Opinions and Personality.* New York: Wiley, 1956.

Sommers, Vita Stein. *The Influence of Parental Attitudes and Social Environment on the Personality Development of the Adolescent Blind.* New York: American Foundation for the Blind, 1944.

Sophocles. *Oedipus at Colonus.* Translated by Sir Richard C. Jebb. In *Great Books of the Western World,* vol.5. Chicago: Encyclopaedia Britannica, 1952.

———. *Oedipus the King.* Translated by Sir Richard C. Jebb. In *Great Books of the Western World,* vol.5. Chicago: Encyclopaedia Britannica, 1952.

Sorter, Judi. "Blindness Seen Through Reactions." *The Blind Digest,* May 1968, pp.1,3,5–6.

Spindler, Frank Nicholas. *The Sense of Sight.* New York: Moffat, Yard & Company, 1917.

Standfast, Richard. *A Little Handful of Cordial Comforts and a Caveat Against Seducers, Whereunto Are Annexed "The Blind Man's Meditations" and "A Dialogue Between a Blind Man and Death."* London: 1684.

Steingisser, Edith. "The Influence of Set Upon Attitudes Toward the Blind As Related to Self-Concept." Master's thesis. University of New Hampshire, 1954.

Stevenson, Robert Louis. *Kidnapped*. New York: Charles Scribner's Sons, n.d.

——. *Treasure Island*. New York: Charles Scribner's Sons, 1911.

Sumner, William Graham. *Folkways: A Study of the Sociological Importance of Usages, Manners, Customs, Mores, and Morals*. 1906. Reprint. New York: New American Library, Mentor Books, 1960.

Super, Charles William. "Sight and Seeing in Ancient Times." *Popular Science Monthly*, May 1907, pp.413–28.

Tagiuri, Renato. "Perception: Person Perception." In *International Encyclopedia of the Social Sciences*, vol.11, edited by David L. Sills, pp.560–67. [New York]: Macmillan and the Free Press, 1968.

Tajfel, Henri. "Perception: Social Perception." In *International Encyclopedia of the Social Sciences*, vol.11, edited by David L. Sills, pp. 567–75. [New York]: Macmillan and the Free Press, 1968.

Tanaka, Mitsuo. "Historic Japanese Attitudes Toward Blindness." *New Outlook for the Blind* 52(1958):191–92.

Tenny, J. W. "The Minority Status of the Handicapped." *Exceptional Children* 19(1953):260–64.

Thiselton-Dyer, T. F. *Folklore of Women*. 1906. Reprint. Detroit: Singing Tree Press, 1968.

Thompson, Stith, ed. *Motif-Index of Folk-Literature*. 6 vols. Revised edition. Bloomington, Ind.: Indiana University Press, 1932–1936.

Thume, Lyle. "Symbols of Blindness." *New Outlook for the Blind* 51 (1957):245–47.

Thurstone, Louis J., and Chave, Ernest J. *Measurement of Attitudes: A Psychological Method and Some Experiments With a Scale for Measuring Attitudes Toward the Church*. Chicago: University of Chicago Press, 1922.

Townsend, M. Roberta. "Attitude of the Sighted Toward the Blind." In *Proceedings of the 23d Convention of the American Association of Workers for the Blind, 1949*, pp.57–60.

Traubitz, Gretchen. "A Word to the Normal." *Today's Health*, May 1956, pp.36–37,52.

Twersky, Jacob. *Blindness in Literature: Examples of Depictions and Attitudes*. New York: American Foundation for the Blind, 1955.

Urena, Manuel. "The Return of the Exile." *Braille Monitor*, July 1970, pp.22–32.

VanBuren, Mrs. A. E. Douglas. "Amulets, Symbols, or Idols?" *Iraq* 12(1950):139–46.

———. "New Evidence Concerning an Eye Divinity." *Iraq* 17(1955): 164–75.

Villey, Pierre. *The World of the Blind: A Psychological Study.* Translated by Alys Hallard. New York: Macmillan, 1930.

von Franz, M.–L. "The Process of Individuation." In *Man and His Symbols,* edited by C. G. Jung, pp.158–229. New York: Doubleday, 1964.

———. "Science and the Unconscious." In *Man and His Symbols,* edited by C. G. Jung, pp.375–87. New York: Dell, Laurel Editions, 1968.

Voorhees, Arthur L. "Attitudes of the Blind Toward Blindness." In *Proceedings of the 23d Convention of the American Association of Workers for the Blind, 1949,* pp.65–67.

Wagg, Henry J., and Thomas, Mary G. *A Chronological Survey of Work for the Blind.* London: Sir Isaac Pitman & Sons, for the National Institute for the Blind, 1932.

Wall, W. D. "Adjusting to a Handicap: Some General Considerations." *Teacher of the Blind* 35(1947):5–10.

Wallace, Anthony F. C. "Cognitive Theory." In *International Encyclopedia of the Social Sciences,* vol.2, edited by David L. Sills, pp.536–40. [New York]: Macmillan and the Free Press, 1968.

Weelden, Jacob van. *On Being Blind: An Ontological Approach to the Problem of Blindness.* Translated by Harm Jan Westerling and Jacob van Weelden. Amsterdam: Netherlands Society for the Blind, 1967.

Weiss, Carl. "Reality Aspects of Blindness as They Affect Case Work." *The Family* 26(1946):363–68.

Wells, H. G. "The Country of the Blind." In *The Country of the Blind and Other Stories.* London: Thomas Nelson and Sons, n.d.

Wheeler, Raymond H. "Visual Phenomena in the Dreams of a Blind Subject." *Psychological Review* 27(1920):315–22.

Whiteman, Martin. "A Psychological Appraisal of Blindness." In *Social Casework and Blindness,* edited by Samuel Finestone, pp.45–63. New York: American Foundation for the Blind, 1960.

———, and Lukoff, Irving Faber. "Public Attitudes Toward Blindness." *New Outlook for the Blind* 56(1962):153–58.

Whiting, J. W. M., and Child, I. L. *Child Training and Personality.* New Haven, Conn.: Yale University Press, 1953.

Whitmont, Edward C. *The Symbolic Quest: Basic Concepts of Analytical Psychology.* New York: G. P. Putnam's Sons, 1969.

Wilman, C. W. *Seeing and Perceiving.* Oxford: Pergamon Press, 1966.

Wilson, Eunice W. "Parental Attitudes." In *The Blind Pre-school Child: A Collection of Papers Presented at the National Conference on the Blind, March 13–15, 1947*, edited by Berthold Lowenfeld, pp.5–13. New York: American Foundation for the Blind, 1947.

Wilson, George S. "The Blind in Literature." In *Proceedings of the 18th and 19th Regular Meetings of the American Association of Instructors of the Blind, 1906 and 1908*, pp. 7–17.

Winkler, H. *Psychische Entwicklung und Krüppeltum*. Leipzig: Leopold Voss, 1931.

Wispé, Lauren G. "Sympathy and Empathy." In *International Encyclopedia of the Social Sciences*, vol.15, edited by David L. Sills, pp. 441–47. [New York]: Macmillan and the Free Press, 1968.

Witkin, H. A.; Lewis, H. B.; Hertzman, M.; Machover, K.; Meissner, P. Bretnall; and Wapner, S. *Personality Through Perception: An Experimental and Clinical Study*. New York: Harper & Brothers, 1954.

Wolman, Marianne J. "Interpreting the Needs of the 'Special Child' to the Parents and Children of the 'Normal' Group." *New Outlook for the Blind* 48(1954):267–69.

Wood, Maxine. *Blindness—Ability, Not Disability*. Public Affairs Pamphlet, no.295. New York: Public Affairs Committee, Inc., 1960.

Wright, Beatrice A. *Physical Disability: A Psychological Approach*. New York: Harper & Brothers, 1960.

Yinger, J. Milton. "Prejudice: Social Discrimination." In *International Encyclopedia of the Social Sciences*, vol.12, edited by David L. Sills, pp.448–51. [New York]: Macmillan and the Free Press, 1968.

Yuker, Harold E.; Block, J. R.; and Young, Janet H. *The Measurement of Attitudes Toward Disabled Persons*. Human Resources Study, no.7. Albertson, N. Y.: Human Resources Center, 1966.

Zarlock, Stanley P. "Magical Thinking and Associated Psychological Reactions to Blindness." *Journal of Consulting Psychology* 25(1961): 155–59.

Zubek, J. P. "Perception: Perceptual Deprivation." In *International Encyclopedia of the Social Sciences*, vol.11, edited by David L. Sills, pp.551–56. [New York]: Macmillan and the Free Press, 1968.

Notes

Introduction

1. I am not a worker for the blind in the usual sense of the word, but an editor who has worked in several positions that are ancillary to the field, including the editorship of two magazines for blind people (*Talking Book Topics* and *Braille Book Review*) and, most recently, associate editorship of the *New Outlook for the Blind*, the field's professional journal.

2. Gordon B. Connor, "An Educator Looks at Attitudes," p.156. (Full bibliographic citations for note references will be found in the bibliography.)

3. Richard Slayton French, *From Homer to Helen Keller: A Social and Educational Study of the Blind*, p.1; Hector Chevigny, *My Eyes Have a Cold Nose*, p.81.

4. Jerome Siller et al., *Attitudes of the Nondisabled Toward the Physically Disabled*, pp.50, 77; cf., p.54.

5. Thomas J. Carroll, *Blindness: What It Is, What It Does, and How to Live With It*, p.5.

6. Martin Whiteman and Irving Faber Lukoff, "Public Attitudes Toward Blindness," p.154.

7. *Random House Dictionary of the English Language*, attitude, def.1.

8. Siller et al., pp.61–62.

9. Irving Faber Lukoff and Martin Whiteman, *Attitudes and Blindness: Components, Correlates, and Effects*, p.141.

10. Ibid., p.152.

1 Attitudes Toward Blindness and Blind People

1. Harry Best, *Blindness and the Blind in the United States*, p.278; Mrs. H. L. Lee, "The Social Impact of Blindness on the Individual," p.108; Irving Faber Lukoff and Martin Whiteman, *The Social Sources*

of Adjustment to Blindness, p.239 (hereafter cited as *Social Sources*); Sadako Imamura, *A Critical Survey of the Literature on the Social Role of the Blind in the United States,* p.15.

2. Berthold Lowenfeld, "Mental Hygiene of Blindness," p.39; Jerome Siller et al., *Attitudes of the Nondisabled Toward the Physically Disabled,* p.52 (hereafter cited as *Attitudes of the Nondisabled*); Hector Chevigny and Sydell Braverman, *The Adjustment of the Blind,* p.166.

3. Irving Faber Lukoff and Martin Whiteman, "Attitudes Toward Blindness—Some Preliminary Findings," p.43 (hereafter cited as "Attitudes Toward Blindness").

4. Sydell Braverman, "The Psychological Roots of Attitudes Toward the Blind," p.23; Helen Barshay, *Empathy: Touchstone of Self-Fulfillment: A Creative Approach to Self-Understanding,* p.31; Siller et al., *Attitudes of the Nondisabled,* p.49; Charles G. Ritter, "Changing Attitudes Toward Blindness—From the Point of View of 20/20," p.163; Imamura, p.13.

5. Siller et al., *Attitudes of the Nondisabled,* p.49; Vita Stein Sommers, *The Influence of Parental Attitudes and Social Environment on the Personality Development of the Adolescent Blind,* p.48; Lowenfeld, "Mental Hygiene of Blindness," p.42; Fern Lowry, "Basic Assumptions Underlying Casework With Blind Persons," p.14; Bernard Seeman, *Your Sight: Folklore, Fact, and Common Sense,* p.175.

6. Arthur L. Voorhees, "Attitudes of the Blind Toward Blindness," p.65; Morton A. Bertin, "A Comparison of Attitudes Toward Blindness," p.3.

7. Harry E. Simmons, "The Attitudes of the Sighted Toward the Blind," p.56.

8. Manuel Urena, "The Return of the Exile," pp.26–27; Voorhees, p.66.

9. Joseph F. Clunk, "Employer Attitudes and the Adjustment of the Blind," p. 59.

10. Albert T. Murphy, "Attitudes of Educators Toward the Visually Handicapped," p.106. The categories of exceptionality in this study were visually handicapped, mentally retarded or slow, emotionally disturbed, physically handicapped (crippled), hearing handicapped, gifted and talented, speech disorders, and delinquents (overt-aggressive types).

11. Oliver M. Nikoloff, "Attitues of Public School Principals Toward the Employment of Teachers with Certain Physical Disabilities," pp. 344–45. The five categories were blind, deaf, crutch, stutter, and artificial limb.

12. Barshay, p.31; Braverman, p.26; Simmons, p.56; Hector Che-

vigny, *My Eyes Have a Cold Nose,* p.131; Thomas D. Cutsforth, *The Blind in School and Society: A Psychological Study,* p.125.

13. Alan G. Gowman, *The War Blind in American Social Structure,* p.104.

14. Cutsforth, p.126.

15. Chevigny and Braverman, p.47.

16. Louis Cholden, *A Psychiatrist Works with Blindness,* p.18; Ritter, p.163; Sommers, p.48.

17. Cutsforth, p.129.

18. Richard Slayton French, *From Homer to Helen Keller: A Social and Educational Study of the Blind,* p.16.

19. Seeman, p.4.

20. Thomas J. Carroll, *Blindness: What It Is, What It Does, and How to Live With It,* p.28 (hereafter cited as *Blindness*); J. Albert Asenjo, "Philosophy of Adjustment," p.14.

21. Cutsforth, pp.129–30; Carroll, *Blindness,* pp.30–31.

22. Don Liddle, "Psychological Problems of Blindness," p.1; Robinson Pierce, *It Was Not My Own Idea,* pp.14–15.

23. Pierce, p.15.

24. Liddle, p.1.

25. Barshay, p.31; Braverman, p.25; Chevigny, pp.130–31; Gowman, p.104; Berthold Lowenfeld, "A Psychological Approach to Blindness," p.5; Rachel F. Rawls, "Parental Reactions and Attitudes Toward the Blind Child," p.94; Judi Sorter, "Blindness Seen Through Reactions," p.1; Urena, pp.26, 27–28.

26. Clunk, p.60.

27. M. Robert Barnett, "20 Centuries B.C. vs. 20 Centuries A.D.—So What Else Is New?" p.5; Fred L. Crawford and Sidney Lirtzman, *Counseling and Placement of Blind Persons in Professional Occupations: Practice and Research,* pp.25,85; Ann Lehman, "Employer Attitudes on Blind Workers," pp.49–50; Siller et al., *Attitudes of the Nondisabled,* p.52; Jerome Siller et al., *Structure of Attitudes Toward the Physically Disabled: Disability Factor Scales—Amputation, Blindness, Cosmetic Conditions,* p.23 (hereafter cited as *Structure of Attitudes*); Simmons, pp.56–57; Martin Whiteman, "A Psychological Appraisal of Blindness," pp.56–57.

28. Lukoff and Whiteman, "Attitudes Toward Blindness," p.43; idem., *Attitudes and Blindness: Components, Correlates, and Effects,* p.139 (hereafter cited as *Attitudes and Blindness*).

29. Alexander F. Handel, "Community Attitudes Influencing Psycho-Social Adjustment to Blindness," p.24; Simmons, p.56.

30. M. Roberta Townsend, "Attitudes of the Sighted Toward the Blind," p.59.

31. Gowman, p.103; cf. Imamura, p.15.

32. Lukoff and Whiteman, *Social Sources*, p.239.

33. Chevigny, p.77.

34. Ibid., p.88.

35. Voorhees, p.66.

36. Urena, pp.28, 29-30.

37. Townsend, p.58; cf. Urena, p.29.

38. Cholden, p.20; Rawls, p.95; Simmons, p.56; Urena, p.26.

39. Chevigny, p.168.

40. Edna Fink, "Parental Attitudes Toward Blind Children," p.24; Sommers, p.45; Lowenfeld, "Mental Hygiene of Blindness," p.40.

41. Thomas J. Carroll, "Developing Public Understanding About the Blind," p.58.

42. Fink, p.24; Sommers, pp.46-48; Voorhees, p.66.

43. Lowenfeld, "Mental Hygiene of Blindness," pp.46-48.

44. Carroll, *Blindness*, p.14; H. Kenneth McCollam, "Attitude of the Blind Toward the Sighted," p.64; Robert A. Scott, *The Making of Blind Men: A Study of Adult Socialization*, p.21.

45. Scott, p.24.

46. Siller et al., *Attitudes of the Nondisabled*, pp.52-53; W. D. Wall, "Adjusting to a Handicap: Some General Considerations," p.6.

47. Urena, p.27.

48. Gowman, p.104; Townsend, p.58; Jacob Twersky, *Blindness in Literature: Examples of Depictions and Attitudes*, p.9.

49. Clunk, p.63.

50. Voorhees, p.27.

51. Lukoff and Whiteman, "Attitudes Toward Blindness," p.42; McCollam, p.65.

52. Urena, p.27.

53. Siller et al., *Structure of Attitudes*, pp.21-23.

54. For example, Frank Nicholas Spindler, *The Sense of Sight*, p.4.

55. Sorter, pp.3-5.

56. Siller et al., *Attitudes of the Nondisabled*, p.49.

57. Best, p.279; Irving Faber Lukoff, "A Sociological Appraisal of Blindness," p.25; Urena, p.30.

58. McCollam, p.64; Siller et al., *Structure of Attitudes*, p.23.

59. Urena, p.25.

60. Lowry, p.16.

61. McCollam, p.63.

62. Voorhees, p.66.

63. French, p.19.

64. McCollam, p.64, quoting Allen. No original source is cited. French (pp.26–27) states similar beliefs.

65. French, pp.16,17.

66. Best, p.279.

67. Dorothy Burlingham, "Psychic Problems of the Blind," pp.43–44; Chevigny and Braverman, p.viii; Simmons, p.56.

68. Clarence Hawkes, "Some Common Fallacies About Blindness," p.573; Lukoff and Whiteman, *Attitudes and Blindness*, p.138; Maxine Wood, *Blindness—Ability, Not Disability*, p.4.

69. Kate M. Foley, *Five Lectures on Blindness*, p.6; also, Samuel Perkins Hayes, *Contributions to a Psychology of Blindness*, p.45.

70. Foley, pp.32–33; Best, p.279; Carroll, *Blindness*, p.365; Urena, p.25; Voorhees, p.67; Lukoff and Whiteman, *Attitudes and Blindness*, p.138.

71. Siller et al., *Structure of Attitudes*, p.22; Voorhees, p.65.

72. Best, p.279; Burlingham, p.43; Lehman, p.50.

73. Lukoff and Whiteman, *Attitudes and Blindness*, p.137; cf. Voorhees, p.65.

74. Sorter, p.3.

75. H. Robert Blank, "Psychoanalysis and Blindness," p.1; also, Braverman, pp.26–27.

76. Voorhees, p.67.

77. Chevigny and Braverman, pp.viii–ix.

78. Carroll, *Blindness*, pp.15,20.

79. French, p.37; Joseph S. Himes, "Some Concepts of Blindness in American Culture," pp.14–17; Joseph I. Pascal, "The Changing Attitude Towards the Blind and Partially Sighted," p.319.

80. Gerhard Schauer, "Motivation of Attitudes Toward Blindness," p.9.

2 Attitudes Toward Blindness and Blind People in the Past

1. Milton Rokeach, "Attitudes: The Nature of Attitudes," p.450; Beatrice A. Wright, *Physical Disability: A Psychological Approach*, p.265.

2. Irving Faber Lukoff and Martin Whiteman, *Attitudes and Blindness: Components, Correlates, and Effects*, p.17c.

3. M. Robert Barnett, "20 Centuries B.C. vs. 20 Centuries A.D.—So What Else Is New?" p.2.

4. Berthold Lowenfeld, "The Social Impact of Blindness Upon the Individual," p.275; Sadako Imamura, *A Critical Survey of the Literature on the Social Role of the Blind in the United States,* p.12; Jacob Twersky, *Blindness in Literature: Examples of Depictions and Attitudes,* p.9.

5. Nelson Coon, "The Blind in Art," p.3.

6. Fareed Haj, *Disability in Antiquity,* p.40.

7. Herodotus, *The History* (Book 2, paragraph 84), p. 65.

8. Haj, pp.40–41.

9. Lowenfeld, p.273. Also, Hector Chevigny and Sydell Braverman, *Adjustment of the Blind,* pp.vi–vii, and Alan G. Gowman, *The War Blind in American Social Structure,* pp.213–14.

10. Jessica L. Langworthy, "Blindness in Fiction: A Study of the Attitude of Authors Toward Their Blind Characters," pp.271 and 283; Lukoff and Whiteman, p.17c; idem., *The Social Sources of Adjustment to Blindness,* p.1; Jacob Twersky, pp.26,36, and 45.

11. Richard Slayton French, *From Homer to Helen Keller: A Social and Educational Study of the Blind,* pp. 32–33; Milton D. Graham and Leslie L. Clark, "The Social Management of Blindness," paragraphs 3 and 7 (because the pagination of the manuscript of this article will probably not agree with that of the printed version, citations are therefore to paragraphs); the authors have gathered their anthropological data from the resources of the Human Relations Area Files, New Haven, Connecticut; Lowenfeld, p.273; Bernard Seeman, *Your Sight: Folklore, Fact, and Common Sense,* p.176.

12. Gowman, p.211.

13. Graham and Clark, paragraphs 8–10.

14. Janet G. Paterson, "The Blind in Fiction," p.75.

15. Twersky, p.10.

16. Biblical quotations used throughout this chapter are from the *New English Bible With the Apocrypha.*

17. Harry Best, *Blindness and the Blind in the United States,* p.299.

18. Gowman, p.212.

19. Haj, p.46, citing *Koran,* XLVIII, 17 and XXIV, 61.

20. Seeman, pp. 176–77; Lowenfeld, p. 273.

21. Gowman, p.212; Henry J. Wagg and Mary G. Thomas, *A Chronological Survey of Work for the Blind,* pp.1–2.

22. Wagg and Thomas, pp.3–4.

23. James Boswell, *Life of Samuel Johnson, LL.D.,* p.63.

24. Denis Diderot, *An Essay on Blindness in a Letter to a Prominent Person,* p.11.

25. Twersky, p.18.

26. Ibid.

27. Stith Thompson, ed., *Motif-Index of Folk-Literature*, motif X123.

28. Twersky, p.50.

29. Thompson, motifs X121, X121.1, X122.

30. French, p.38.

31. Sophocles, *Oedipus the King*, line 1360.

32. French, p.36.

33. Twersky, p.17.

34. Sophocles, lines 408–10.

35. Homer, *The Odyssey*, Book IX, lines 371–542; Twersky, p.17.

36. Diderot, p.16.

37. Quoted in Charles William Super, "Sight and Seeing in Ancient Times," p.423; cf. Twersky, p.27.

38. Charlotte Brontë, *Jane Eyre*, p.443.

39. Ibid., p.432.

40. Thompson, motif M225.

41. Victor Hugo, *The Man Who Laughs* (vol.1, pt.2, bk.2, ch.2), pp.209–10.

42. W. Hanks Levy, *Blindness and the Blind: or, A Treatise on the Science of Typhlology*, pp.1 and 373.

43. Robert Louis Stevenson, *Treasure Island* (ch.5), p.40.

44. Rudyard Kipling, *The Light That Failed*, pp.227 and 339.

45. Twersky, pp.40 and 47–48.

46. George S. Wilson, "The Blind in Literature," p.14.

47. Sophocles, line 1313.

48. John Milton, "Samson Agonistes," lines 80–82, 98–99, and 151–54.

49. Quoted by Levy, p.212.

50. Sebastian Guillié, *An Essay on the Instruction and Amusement of the Blind*, p.40.

51. Charles Dickens, *American Notes and Pictures From Italy*, p.32.

52. Hugo (vol.1, pt.2, bk.2, ch.2), pp.208 and 209.

53. Frank Nicholas Spindler, *The Sense of Sight*, p.4.

54. Sophocles, lines 346–50.

55. Ibid., lines 379–80 and 1316.

56. Thompson, motif J2133.9.

57. Guillié, p.1.

58. Brontë, pp.435, 439, 438–39, 449–50, and 455–56.

59. Hugo (vol.1, pt.2, bk.2, ch.3), p.211.

60. Levy, p.54.

61. Kipling, pp.222, 233, 271, and 228.

62. Paterson, p.75; Twersky, p.39.

63. Thompson, motif N338.

64. Louis Ginzberg, *The Legends of the Jews,* vol.1, p.116.

65. *New Larousse Encyclopedia of Mythology,* p.268.

66. Ginzberg, vol.1, p.330.

67. Kipling, p.224.

68. Ginzberg, vol.1, p.329.

69. Ibid., vol.2, p.282.

70. Ibid., vol.6, p.183 (note 17).

71. Haj, p.45.

72. Twersky, pp.20-21.

73. Alfred H. Holt, *Phrase and Word Origins: A Study of Familiar Expressions,* p.131.

74. William Shakespeare, *King Lear,* Act IV, Scene VI, lines 1-80.

75. Milton, "Samson Agonistes," lines 75-78 and 941-44.

76. Valentin Haüy, *An Essay on the Education of the Blind,* p.30.

77. Twersky, p.30.

78. Kipling, p.227.

79. Thompson, motifs K333.1, K1081.1, K1081.2, K1081.3, K333, R121.2, K2382.2, and J1169.1.

80. Twersky, p.16.

81. French, p.39.

82. Haj, p.109.

83. Milton, "Samson Agonistes," lines 563-67.

84. Ibid., lines 579-80.

85. Haüy, pp.5-6.

86. Twersky, p.33.

87. Paterson, p.68.

88. Levy, p.467.

89. Best, p.299.

90. Gowman, pp.211-12.

91. Sophocles, lines 453-54.

92. Best, p.299.

93. Gowman, p.106; Lowenfeld, p.273.

94. Gowman, pp.212-13 and 213.

95. Chevigny and Braverman, p.86.

96. Elizabeth Hutchinson, "The Visually Handicapped Person in His Community," p.38.

97. Best, pp.262-63.

98. Twersky, p.21.

99. Paterson, p.68.

100. Herodotus (Book 2, paragraphs 137 and 140), p.78.

101. Homer, Book IX, lines 475–93 and 500–42.

102. Gowman, pp.211–12; Edward Jablonski, "Man's Conquest of Blindness," p.3.

103. Twersky, p.15.

104. Plutarch, *The Lives of the Noble Grecians and Romans,* pp. 212–13.

105. Wagg and Thomas, p.3.

106. Twersky, pp.22–23.

107. Gowman, pp.211–12; Mitsuo Tanaka, "Historic Japanese Attitudes Toward Blindness," p.191.

108. Tanaka, p.191.

109. French, p.35.

110. Tanaka, p.191.

111. Boswell, p.171 and note.

112. Haüy, p.5; Wagg and Thomas, p.8; Guillié, p.3.

113. Guillié, pp.12–13.

114. Gowman, p.213.

115. Best, pp.313–14.

116. Levy, pp.382–495.

117. Graham and Clark, paragraph 72.

118. Twersky, pp.27–38.

119. Hugo (vol.1, pt.2, bk.2, ch.8), p.225.

120. Twersky, p.33.

121. Jack London, *The Sea Wolf,* p.275.

122. Wilson, p.13.

123. H. Rider Haggard, *The Wanderer's Necklace,* p.227.

124. Thompson, motif N886.

125. French, p.38; Pierre Villey, *The World of the Blind: A Psychological Study,* p.75; Twersky, p.15.

126. "The Homeric Hymns," III, lines 166–78; Homer, *The Odyssey,* Book VIII, lines 62–70, 484–90, and 470–81.

127. French, p.38.

128. Levy, p.69; Twersky, pp.16–17.

129. Villey, p.75.

130. Best, p.302.

131. Guillié, pp.2, 20, 28, 34, and 35; cf. p.40.

132. Levy, pp.62–63 and 65.

133. London, p.275.

134. Twersky, pp.46–47.

135. Langworthy, pp.272–73.

136. Roger C. Barker et al., *Adjustment to Physical Handicap and Illness: A Survey of the Social Psychology of Physique and Disability,* p.275.

137. Thompson, motifs D1313.4, U171.

138. Hector Chevigny, *My Eyes Have a Cold Nose,* pp.171–72.

139. Chevigny and Braverman, p.65.

140. Twersky, pp.15 and 16.

141. Sophocles, lines 1318–20.

142. Twersky, p.16.

143. Plutarch, p.212.

144. Ginzberg, vol.6, p.126 (note 730); vol.3, p.347; vol.4, p.48.

145. Twersky, p.24.

146. Milton, "Samson Agonistes," lines 202–5, 233–36, and 373–76.

147. Twersky, p.24.

148. Ibid., pp.29 and 31.

149. Hugo (vol.1, pt.2, bk.2, ch.2), p.210.

150. Gowman, p.17.

151. Chevigny and Braverman, pp.64–65.

152. Thompson, motifs C943, M13, Q451.7, Q559.2, S165.

153. Margaret Robertson, "The Gloucester Treatment: Punitive and Political Blinding in the British Isles," pp.64–67.

154. Graham and Clark, paragraph 2.

155. Thompson, motif J2074.

156. Graham and Clark, paragraph 2; Chevigny and Braverman, p.vii.

157. Emory L. Cowen et al., *Adjustment to Visual Disability in Adolescence,* p.5; Seeman, p.176.

158. Chevigny and Braverman, pp.v–vi.

159. Ginzberg, vol.3, p.78.

160. French, p.36.

161. Graham and Clark, paragraph 14; Chevigny and Braverman, p.vi.

162. Graham and Clark, paragraph 37.

163. Dickens, p.31.

164. Guillié, p.60.

165. Levy, pp.319 and 375.

166. Quoted in Twersky, pp.49–50.

167. Graham and Clark, paragraphs 12 and 3.

168. Thompson, motif K1984.5.

169. Diderot, pp.18–19.

170. Guillié, pp.2, 33–34, 36–38.

171. Kipling, pp.270–71 and 224.

172. Wilson, pp.13–14.

173. Ginzberg, vol.5, p.121 (note 116).

174. Twersky, p.19.

175. Ibid., p.27.

176. Ibid., pp.29–30.

177. Stevenson (chap.3), pp.24 and 24–25.

178. Robert Louis Stevenson, *Kidnapped,* pp.150 and 152–54.

179. Twersky, p.37.

180. London, p.287.

181. Twersky, p.50.

182. Ibid., p.37.

183. Stevenson, *Treasure Island* (chap.3), p.26, and (chap.5), pp. 40–41.

184. Stevenson, *Kidnapped,* pp.151, 153–54.

185. London, p.278.

186. E. Grierson, "Children's Tales From Scottish Ballads: The Lochmaben Harper," pp.517–19.

187. Thompson, motifs K436 ad., K1456.

188. Paterson, p.73.

189. K. M. Briggs, *The Anatomy of Puck: An Examination of Fairy Beliefs Among Shakespeare's Contemporaries and Successors,* p.185.

190. Twersky, pp.30–31.

191. Paterson, p.72; Twersky, p.31.

192. Hugo (vol.1, pt.2, bk.2, ch.2), p.208.

193. Twersky, p.35.

194. Langworthy, pp.278–79.

195. Ibid., p.276.

196. Wilson, pp.15–16.

197. Gowman, p.212.

198. Sophocles, *Oedipus the King,* lines 300–2.

199. Sophocles, *Oedipus at Colonus,* lines 1546–55.

200. Ginzberg, vol.1, pp.262 and 328.

201. Expressed in a letter written by Milton in 1652, quoted in Levy, pp.211–13.

202. Quoted by Ignacio de Satrustegui, "The Social Impact of Blindness on the Individual," p.108; also by Levy, p.214.

203. John Milton, "Paradise Lost," lines 51–55.

204. Both pieces are quoted by Levy, pp.217–18.

205. In Richard Standfast, *A Little Handful of Cordial Comforts and a Caveat Against Seducers* . . . , pp.110–17.

206. Brontë, pp.450–51.

207. Hugo (vol.1, pt.2, bk.4, ch.2), p.231, and (vol.2, pt.2, bk.4, ch.2), p.296.

208. Twersky, pp.32, 39, and 42, respectively.

209. Wilson, p.14.

210. Graham and Clark, paragraph 4.

211. Thompson, motif J33.

212. Graham and Clark, paragraph 4.

213. Thompson, motifs D1331–1331.3.2, D1821.4, F362.1, and A2332.6.1.–2332.6.6, and D1505–1505.8.1, F952–952.2.

214. Graham and Clark, paragraph 5.

215. W. E. Milton, "A Forward Movement in Worker-Community Relations," p.93.

216. Stanley P. Zarlock, "Magical Thinking and Associated Psychological Reactions to Blindness," p.159.

217. Edward Bellamy, "The Blindman's World," pp.12–13.

3 Psychosocial Origins of Attitudes Toward Blindness and Blind People

1. Beatrice A. Wright, *Physical Disability: A Psychological Approach,* p.269.

2. Milton Rokeach, "Attitudes: The Nature of Attitudes," p.450.

3. Louis J. Thurstone and Ernest J. Chave, *Measurement of Attitudes: A Psychological Method and Some Experiments With a Scale for Measuring Attitudes Toward the Church,* pp.6–7.

4. Rokeach, pp.453–54, 456.

5. Ibid., p.456, citing Daniel L. Katz, "The Functional Approach to the Study of Attitudes," pp.163–204.

6. Ibid., p.457.

7. Gordon W. Allport, *The Nature of Prejudice,* pp.20–22.

8. George Herbert Mead, *Mind, Self, and Society,* pp.152–64.

9. Joseph S. Himes, "The Measurement of Social Distance in Social Relations with the Blind," p.54.

10. Erving Goffman, *Stigma: Notes on the Management of Spoiled Identity,* p.2.

11. Rokeach, p.450.

12. Anthony F. C. Wallace, "Cognitive Theory," p. 538.

13. M. Brewster Smith, "Attitude Change," pp.459–60, citing Donald T. Campbell, "Social Attitudes and Other Acquired Behavior Dispositions," pp.107–11.

14. H. A. Witkin et al., *Personality Through Perception: An Experimental and Clinical Study* pp.2, 467, and 491. See also, idem., p.503; Howard H. Kendler and Tracy S. Kendler, "Concept Formation," p. 206; Allport, p.324.

15. Solomon E. Asch, "Gestalt Theory," pp.165 and 165–66.

16. Renato Tagiuri, "Perception: Person Perception," pp.561 and 563.

17. Ibid.; Witkin et al., pp.501–2.

18. Allport, p.129; cf. S. E. Asch, "Forming Impressions of Personality," and G. Ichheiser, "Misunderstandings in Human Relations."

19. Allport, pp.131–32.

20. Ibid., p.131.

21. Tagiuri, p.565; Wright, pp.118–20.

22. Harold B. Gerard, "Social Psychology," p.463.

23. Rokeach, p.450.

24. Ibid., pp.451–52.

25. Ibid., p.453.

26. Allport, p.176.

27. Goffman, p.2; see also Joseph S. Himes, "Some Concepts of Blindness in American Culture," p.13.

28. Irving Faber Lukoff and Martin Whiteman, *Attitudes and Blindness: Components, Correlates, and Effects,* p.19 (hereafter cited as *Attitudes and Blindness*).

29. Vita Stein Sommers, *The Influence of Parental Attitudes and Social Environment on the Personality Development of the Adolescent Blind,* p.xi.

30. Charles G. Ritter, "Changing Attitudes Towards Blindness— From the View of 20/20," p.165.

31. Jerome Siller et al., *Attitudes of the Nondisabled Toward the Physically Disabled,* p.49.

32. Alan G. Gowman, *The War Blind in American Social Structure,* pp.198–99 (hereafter cited as *War Blind*).

33. Richard Slayton French, *From Homer to Helen Keller: A Social and Educational Study of the Blind,* p.20.

34. Goffman, p.129.

35. Roger G. Barker et al., *Adjustment to Physical Handicap and Illness: A Survey of the Social Psychology of Physique and Disability,* pp.76–77, citing H. Winkler, *Psychische Entwicklung und Krüppeltum.*

36. Jacob van Weelden, *On Being Blind: An Ontological Approach to the Problem of Blindness,* pp.96–99, citing W. J. J. Kooyman, "Het Houdings- en Bewegings-beeld van de Blinde Mens."

37. Alan G. Gowman, "Blindness and the Role of Companion," p.68.

38. M. Roberta Townsend, "Attitude of the Sighted Toward the Blind," p.58; Frank Nicholas Spindler, *The Sense of Sight,* p.5.

39. Louis Cholden, *A Psychiatrist Works With Blindness,* p.36.

40. Hector Chevigny and Sydell Braverman, *The Adjustment of the Blind,* p.69.

41. Siller et al., p.51.

42. Sadako Imamura, *A Critical Survey of the Literature on the Social Role of the Blind in the United States,* p.14.

43. Goffman, p.129; Weelden, pp.99–100.

44. Lee Meyerson, "Somatopsychological Aspects of Blindness," pp. 27–31; Ignacio de Satrustegui, "The Social Impact of Blindness on the Individual," p.106.

45. Meyerson, p.24.

46. Barker et al., p.278.

47. Meyerson, pp.30–31.

48. Goffman, pp.102–4.

49. Imamura, pp.11–12; cf. Himes, "The Measurement of Social Distance in Social Relations With the Blind," p.55.

50. Allport, p.178; cf. Himes, "Some Concepts of Blindness in American Culture," p.13.

51. Irving Faber Lukoff and Martin Whiteman, *The Social Sources of Adjustment to Blindness,* pp.158–59 (hereafter cited as *Social Sources*).

52. Robert A. Scott, *The Making of Blind Men: A Study of Adult Socialization,* p.3; cf. Irving Faber Lukoff, "A Sociological Appraisal of Blindness," p.23; Imamura, pp.30–33.

53. Scott, p.9; cf. Lukoff and Whiteman, *Social Sources,* pp.1, 244, 253–54.

54. Gowman, *War Blind,* p.4; Imamura, p.38.

55. Imamura, p.17.

56. Goffman, p.7.

57. Milton D. Graham and Leslie L. Clark, "The Social Management of Blindness," paragraph 40 (see Chapter 2, note 11, above); Barker et al., p.5.

58. Gowman, *War Blind,* p.4.

59. Allport, p.17.

60. Jacob Twersky, *Blindness in Literature: Examples of Depictions and Attitudes,* p.9.

61. Martin Whiteman, "A Psychological Appraisal of Blindness," p.45; Weelden, p.92.

62. Gowman, *War Blind,* p.4; Lukoff, p.21; Weelden, pp.92–93.

63. Lukoff, p.24; Himes, "Some Concepts of Blindness in American Culture," p.12.

64. John Harding, "Stereotypes," p.260.

65. Lukoff, pp.27–28; Harry E. Simmons, "The Attitudes of the Sighted Toward the Blind," pp.54–57.

66. Irving Faber Lukoff and Martin Whiteman, "Attitudes Toward Blindness—Some Preliminary Findings," p.43 (hereafter cited as "Attitudes Toward Blindness").

67. Meyerson, pp.13–14.

68. Imamura, pp.20–21; Joseph S. Himes, "Changing Attitudes Toward Blind People—From the Viewpoint of a Sociologist," p.161; W. E. Milton, "A Forward Movement in Worker-Community Relations," p.93.

69. Wright, pp.xvii and 71.

70. Townsend, p.58.

71. Gowman, *War Blind,* p.13.

72. Thomas J. Carroll, *Blindness: What It Is, What It Does, and How to Live With It,* p.5; Chevigny and Braverman, p.88; Alexander F. Handel, "Community Attitudes Influencing Psycho-Social Adjustment to Blindness," p.23.

73. Chevigny and Braverman, pp.vii and 87.

74. Wright, p.267.

75. Allport, p.179.

76. Berthold Lowenfeld, "The Social Impact of Blindness Upon the Individual," p.275; Allport, p.200.

77. Martin Whiteman and Irving Faber Lukoff, "Public Attitudes Toward Blindness," p.154.

78. Lukoff and Whiteman, *Attitudes and Blindness,* pp.59–60.

79. Frederick M. Jervis, "A Comparison of Self-Concepts of Blind and Sighted Children," p.24.

80. Goffman, p.49.

81. Gowman, *War Blind,* p.198.

82. Wright, pp.126–27.

83. F. Heider, *The Psychology of Interpersonal Relations.*

84. Wright, pp.262 and 263.

85. Ibid., p.73.

86. Ibid.

87. Fern Lowry, "Basic Assumptions Underlying Casework With Blind Persons," p.15.

88. Ibid., p.16.

89. Ibid., p.13; Barbara Bateman, "Sighted Children's Perceptions of Blind Children's Abilities," p.46. Marguerite O'Connor, John O'Connor, and Helen A. McNamara, *A Pilot Study for the Blind Students in Education, Who Plan to Teach Sighted Children,* p.18; Graham and Clark, paragraph 41.

90. Wright, p.73.

91. Allport, p.176.

92. Ibid., pp.24-25.

93. Gerard, p.462.

94. Ibid.

95. Henri Tajfel, "Perception: Social Perception," p.570.

96. Siller et al., p.6, citing Edith Steingisser, *The Influence of Set Upon Attitudes Toward the Blind As Related to Self-Concept.*

97. Siller et al., p.7, citing Norma Jabin, *Attitudes Toward the Physically Disabled As Related to Selected Personality Variables.*

98. Siller et al., pp.29-30.

99. Otto Klineberg, "Prejudice: The Concept," p.443.

100. Ibid.

101. Siller et al., p.80.

102. Klineberg, p.444.

103. Lukoff and Whiteman, *Attitudes and Blindness,* p.18.

104. Weelden, p.99; cf. Thomas D. Cutsforth, *The Blind in School and Society: A Psychological Study,* p.2; Berthold Lowenfeld, "Mental Hygiene of Blindness," pp.35 and 38.

105. Wright, pp.373-77.

106. Cutsforth, p.122; Barker et al., p.290.

107. Cutsforth, p.123.

108. Hector Chevigny, *My Eyes Have a Cold Nose,* p.176.

109. Jervis, p.25.

110. Helen Barshay, *Empathy: Touchstone of Self-Fulfillment: A Creative Approach to Self-Understanding,* pp.39-40.

111. Cutsforth, pp.124-25; Milton H. Klein, "Observations on the Attitudes of the Blind Toward the Sighted," p.61.

112. Sydell Braverman, "The Psychological Roots of Attitudes Toward the Blind," p.27; Gerhard Schauer, "Motivation of Attitudes Toward Blindness," p.6.

113. George Van N. Dearborn, Editorial Introduction to *The Sense of Sight*, p.xii; Spindler, p.1.

114. Bernard Seeman, *Your Sight: Folklore, Fact, and Common Sense*, p.4.

115. Arnold Gesell, Frances L. Ilg, and Glenna E. Bullis, *Vision: Its Development in Infant and Child*, p.3; cf. Spindler, p.3.

116. Gesell, Ilg, and Bullis, p.14; cf. Schauer, pp.8–9.

117. Cutsforth, p.4; Dearborn, p.vii.

118. Chevigny and Braverman, pp.52–53.

119. John Locke, "An Essay Concerning Human Understanding," Book II, Chap.IX, paragraph 8.

120. George Berkeley, "A New Theory of Vision," paragraph 41; see also paragraph 135.

121. R. L. Gregory, *Eye and Brain: The Psychology of Seeing*, pp. 193–98 and 215–18.

122. Chevigny and Braverman, p.54.

123. Berthold Lowenfeld, "A Psychological Approach to Blindness," p.5; Spindler, p.2.

124. Spindler, p.113.

125. Ibid., p.1.

126. Ibid., p.6; Gesell, Ilg, and Bullis, p.3.

127. Braverman, p.25; cf. Spindler, p.103.

128. Lowenfeld, "Mental Hygiene of Blindness," p.39.

129. Whiteman, p.47.

130. Gesell, Ilg, and Bullis, p.273.

131. Whiteman, p.47.

132. Humberto Nagera and Alice B. Colonna, "Aspects of the Contribution of Sight to Ego and Drive Development," p.283.

133. Anna Freud, "The Concept of Developmental Lines," pp.245–65.

134. Nagera and Colonna, p.283.

135. Whiteman, p.48.

136. Carroll, p.28.

137. Cholden, p.20; Graham and Clark, paragraphs 7, 11, 37; Weelden, p.84.

138. Graham and Clark, paragraph 38; Joseph F. Clunk, "Employer Attitudes and the Adjustment of the Blind," p.63.

139. Clunk, p.58.

140. Carroll, p.16; Gowman, *War Blind*, p.17; Weelden, p.91.

141. Wright, p.264, citing P. Schilder, *The Image and Appearance of the Human Body*; Barker et al., p.1.

142. Wright, pp.255–56.

143. M. Robert Barnett, "20 Centuries B.C. vs. 20 Centuries A.D.—So What Else Is New?" p.4; Gowman, *War Blind,* p.17.

144. Wright, p.264.

145. Barker et al., p.1; J. M. Heaton, *The Eye: Phenomenology and Psychology of Function and Disorder,* p.304.

146. Gowman, *War Blind,* p.10.

147. Wright, pp.118 and 149.

148. Cholden, pp.73–74.

149. Ibid., pp.75–76; cf. idem., p.18; Mary K. Bauman, "The Initial Psychological Reaction to Blindness," p.167; Carroll, pp.11 and 14.

150. Siller et al., p.50.

151. Ibid., p.80; Cholden, p.141.

152. Witkin et al., p.469.

153. Chevigny, p.141.

154. *The Random House Dictionary of the English Language,* awe, defs. 1, 2.

155. Wright, p.74.

156. Allport, p.176.

157. Meyerson, p.20.

158. J. Albert Asenjo, "Philosophy of Adjustment," p.15.

159. Sommers, pp.49–62.

160. Wright, pp.74 and 76.

161. Ibid., p.76; Gowman, *War Blind,* p.12.

162. Wright, pp. 242–43, 59, and 64.

163. Lauren G. Wispé, "Sympathy and Empathy," p.441.

164. Wright, pp.128–29, citing T. Dembo, G. L. Leviton, and B.A. Wright, "Adjustment to Misfortune—A Problem of Social Psychological Rehabilitation."

165. Wright, pp.78 and 82.

166. Lukoff and Whiteman, "Attitudes Toward Blindness," pp.41–42.

167. Lowenfeld, "Mental Hygiene of Blindness," p.40; Wright, pp. 269–70; see also J. W. M. Whiting and I. L. Child, *Child Training and Personality.*

168. Carroll, p.15; French, p.21; Lowenfeld, "A Psychological Approach to Blindness," p.6; Weelden, p. 87.

169. Weelden, p.87.

170. Wright, p.89; Lukoff and Whiteman, "Attitudes Toward Blindness," p.41.

171. Wright, p.96.

172. Ibid., p.86, citing Heider.

173. Ibid., pp.131–32, citing T. Dembo, "Devaluation of the Physically Handicapped Person."

174. Lowry, p.13.

175. Allport, p.23.

176. Wright, pp.13 and 7–8.

177. Lukoff and Whiteman, "Attitudes Toward Blindness," p.42.

178. Virginia Murray, "Parental Attitudes Affect Growth and Development of the Young Blind Child," p.9; Rachel F. Rawls, "Parental Reactions and Attitudes Toward the Blind Child," p.94.

179. Wright, p.13.

180. Allport, p.191.

181. Harding, p.259. Harding's discussion is largely based on a formulation first presented by Walter Lippmann in his book *Public Opinion*.

182. Weelden, p.85; Allport, p.192.

183. Allport, p.195.

184. Ibid., pp.189, 204, and 9.

185. Ibid., pp.14–15; cf. J. Milton Yinger, "Prejudice: Social Discrimination," p.449.

186. Yinger, p.450; cf. Wright, p.450.

187. Yinger, p.449.

188. Herbert Rusalem, "The Environmental Supports of Public Attitudes Toward Blindness," p.281; Lukoff and Whiteman, *Social Sources*, p.249.

189. Yinger, p.450.

190. Lowenfeld, "A Psychological Approach to Blindness," p.5; idem., "The Social Impact of Blindness Upon the Individual," p.273.

191. Emory L. Cowen, Rita P. Underberg, and Ronald T. Verrillo, "The Development and Testing of an Attitude to Blindness Scale," p. 304.

192. Lukoff and Whiteman, *Attitudes and Blindness*, p.146.

193. Lukoff and Whiteman, *Social Sources*, p.6; cf. idem., pp.249 and 252; Wright, pp.18–19; Klineberg, p.439.

194. Lukoff and Whiteman, *Attitudes and Blindness*, p.153b.

195. Sidney Jordan, "The Disadvantaged Group: A Concept Applicable to the Handicapped," p.314.

196. Goffman, p.5; cf. Barnett, p.4.

197. Goffman, pp.1–2 and 5.

198. Graham and Clark, paragraph 37.

199. Gowman, *War Blind*, p.3.

200. Wright, pp.251–53.

201. Ibid., p.258, citing Franz Alexander, "Remarks About the Relation of Inferiority Feelings to Guilt Feelings."

202. Wright, pp.256–61; cf. Graham and Clark, paragraph 11.

203. Goffman, p.5; Wright, p.77.

204. Barker et al., p.76, citing H. Meng, "Zur Sozialpsychologie der Körperbeschädigten: Ein Beitrag zum Problem der praktischen Psychohygiene."

205. Goffman, p.47; cf. idem., pp.18 and 111n.

206. Himes, "The Measurement of Social Distance in Social Relations With the Blind," pp.54–58.

207. Goffman, pp.119–25 and 122–23.

208. Weelden, p.110.

4 The Meaning of Blindness

1. Gerhard Schauer, "Motivation of Attitudes Toward Blindness," p.5.

2. Thomas J. Carroll, *Blindness: What It Is, What It Does, and How to Live With It*, p.69 (hereafter cited as *Blindness*).

3. Hector Chevigny and Sydell Braverman, *The Adjustment of the Blind*, pp.70–71.

4. Alan G. Gowman, *The War Blind in American Social Structure*, p.199.

5. C. G. Jung, "Approaching the Unconscious," pp. 95–96.

6. Edward C. Whitmont, *The Symbolic Quest: Basic Concepts of Analytical Psychology*, p.58. The term "complex" was coined by Jung and it should therefore be noted that the description cited here by Whitmont, who is a Jungian, varies somewhat from the meaning later adopted by Freud, one which is perhaps more commonly known.

7. Ibid., pp.58,59, and 60–63.

8. Ibid., p.62.

9. Ibid., p.66.

10. Ibid., p.68.

11. Chevigny and Braverman, p.71.

12. Whitmont, p.68.

13. Erich Neumann, *The Origins and History of Consciousness*, p.xv.

14. For a fuller explanation of the theory of the archetypes, the reader is referred to Jung's *Two Essays on Analytical Psychology* (Collected Works, vol.7) and *The Archetypes and the Collective Un-*

conscious (Collected Works, vol.9, pt.1). Both were published by the Princeton University Press, the former in 1953 (2d ed., 1966), the latter in 1959 (2d ed., 1968).

15. M.–L. von Franz, "Science and the Unconscious," p.377; cf. Jung, "Approaching the Unconscious," p.58.

16. Joseph Campbell, *The Flight of the Wild Gander: Explorations in the Mythological Dimension,* pp.33–34.

17. J. M. Heaton, *The Eye: Phenomenology and Psychology of Function and Disorder,* p.71.

18. M.–L. von Franz, "The Process of Individuation," p. 164; cf. John Freeman, Introduction to *Man and His Symbols,* edited by C. G. Jung, pp.13–14.

19. Jung, "Approaching the Unconscious," p.55.

20. The literature on the dreams of blind persons includes Blank (1958), Cason (1935), Deutsch (1928), Jastrow (1888), Johns (1885), Keller (1908), Kimmins (1920), McCartney (1913), Singer and Streiner (1966), and Wheeler (1920). Only Blank includes any interpretive treatment of imagery and reference to this will be made at the appropriate place later in this chapter. Most of the literature is concerned with the relationship of visual imagery in dreams to age at the onset of blindness and with the role of hearing, touch, smell, and taste in the dreams of blind people.

21. Joseph Campbell, *The Masks of God: Primitive Mythology,* pp. 57–58; cf. Chevigny and Braverman, p.43, and Heaton, p.71.

22. Neumann, p.109; cf. Heaton, p.74, and J. E. Cirlot, *A Dictionary of Symbols,* p.73.

23. Neumann, p.299; cf. C.G. Jung, *The Structure and Dynamics of the Psyche,* p.199, and Chevigny and Braverman, p.43.

24. Neumann, p.299; Whitmont, pp.136 and 276.

25. *The Random House Dictionary of the English Language,* light[1], defs. 17 and 18, and see, defs. 3, 4, 6, 8, 9, 21–24 (hereafter cited as *RHDict.*); cf. C. G. Jung, *Symbols of Transformation: An Analysis of the Prelude to a Case of Schizophrenia,* p.90; Heaton, p.73.

26. Cirlot, p.179; cf. Carroll, *Blindness,* p.32.

27. Thomas J. Carroll, "Developing Public Understanding About the Blind," p.58; Heaton, pp.72–73.

28. *RHDict.,* day, def. 8.

29. Ibid., white, defs. 17–20.

30. Cirlot, pp.55–56.

31. *RHDict.,* dark, defs. 7–13, 20.

32. Ibid., black, defs. 4, 6–11; Cirlot, p.55; Hector Chevigny, *My Eyes Have a Cold Nose*, p.151; Carroll, *Blindness*, p.32.

33. *RHDict.*, night, def. 4.

34. Cirlot, p.277.

35. Ibid., pp.55, 73, 218; cf. Heaton, p.74.

36. Heaton, p.72.

37. H. R. Ellis Davidson, *Scandinavian Mythology*, p.48.

38. Donald A. MacKenzie, *Teutonic Myth and Legend*, p.xxix; Peter Andreas Munch, *Norse Mythology: Legends of Gods and Heroes*, p.296.

39. *New Larousse Encyclopedia of Mythology*, p.276.

40. Heaton, p.75; Sadako Imamura, *A Critical Survey of the Literature on the Social Role of the Blind in the United States*, pp.12–13; *RHDict.*, eye, defs. 6, 11, 30, 39, 47.

41. Cirlot, p.95.

42. Arnold Gesell, Frances L. Ilg, and Glenna E. Bullis, *Vision: Its Development in Infant and Child*, p.3.

43. O. G. S. Crawford, *The Eye Goddess*.

44. Ibid., pp.27–28, citing M. E. L. Mallowan, "Excavations at Brak and Chagar Bazar."

45. Ibid., pp.25–27, citing Mrs. E. Douglas Van Buren, "Amulets, Symbols, or Idols?"; cf. Heaton, pp.75–76.

46. Bernard Seeman, *Your Sight: Folklore, Fact, and Common Sense*, pp.15 and 17.

47. Cirlot, p.95; Heaton, p.76.

48. H. G. Baynes, *Mythology of the Soul: A Research Into the Unconscious From Schizophrenic Dreams and Drawings*, p.335; cf. Cirlot, p.95.

49. Baynes, pp.334–35.

50. Stith Thompson, *Motif-Index of Folk-Literature*, motifs T541.7 and A1171.

51. Veronica Ions, *Egyptian Mythology*, p.27.

52. Ibid., p.41.

53. Thompson, motifs E780–E781.3.

54. Ions, pp.106 and 111.

55. Ibid., p.37.

56. Cirlot, pp.302–3; C. G. Jung, *Mysterium Coniunctionis: An Inquiry Into the Separation and Synthesis of Psychic Opposites in Alchemy*, p.53 (hereafter cited as *Mysterium Coniunctionis*); *New Larousse Encyclopedia of Mythology*, p.56.

57. Harold Bayley, *The Lost Language of Symbolism: An Inquiry Into the Origin of Certain Letters, Words, Names, Fairy-Tales, Folklore, and Mythologies,* vol.1, p.288.

58. Cirlot, p.95.

59. Ibid.; Bayley, vol.1, p.275.

60. Heaton, pp.77–78; Thompson, motif A123.3.

61. Heaton, p.77; Jung, *Mysterium Coniunctionis,* pp.51–53.

62. Cf. King James Version, Zechariah 3:9 and 4:10.

63. Jung, *Mysterium Coniunctionis,* p.51; Baynes, p.266.

64. Cirlot, pp.95–96.

65. Jung, *Mysterium Coniunctionis,* p.51.

66. Heaton, p.77.

67. Jung, *Mysterium Coniunctionis,* p.207.

68. Heaton, p.76.

69. Bayley, vol. 1, pp. 279–80, 287.

70. Heaton, p.78.

71. Ibid.; Baynes, pp.295, 333, 336–37, and 338.

72. Baynes, p.118n.

73. C. G. Jung, *Psychology and Alchemy,* p.250; A. R. Pope, "The Eros Aspect of the Eye: The Left Eye," p.34.

74. Jung, *Psychology and Alchemy,* p.322; cf. Chevigny and Braverman, pp.54–55.

75. Edward F. Edinger, "Christ as Paradigm of the Individuating Ego," p.7.

76. Thompson, motifs N111.2.1–111.2.3.

77. Chevigny and Braverman, pp.67–68.

78. Seeman, p.16.

79. Jung, *Mysterium Coniunctionis,* p.52.

80. T. F. Thiselton–Dyer, *Folklore of Women,* p.48.

81. Seeman, pp.16–17.

82. Jung, *Mysterium Coniunctionis,* p.97n37; cf. pp.53 and 207.

83. Carroll, *Blindness,* p.18; Heaton, p.76.

84. Heaton, p.76.

85. Ibid., p.77.

86. Ions, p.67; von Franz, "The Process of Individuation," p.200; Thompson, motif A714.1; Jung, *Mysterium Coniunctionis,* p.97n35; see also, Pope, pp.5–14.

87. Pope, pp.1–3.

88. Ibid., p.31.

89. For a further explication of the emergence of consciousness from the unconscious, see Neumann, pp.261–312, esp. pp.293–306.

90. Pope, pp.28–29.

91. Ibid., pp.15–17.

92. Ibid., pp.24–25.

93. Thiselton–Dyer, p.218; Thompson, motif D1812.5.2.1.

94. Pope, p.30.

95. Edward S. Gifford, Jr., "The Evil Eye in Medieval History," p.237.

96. Heaton, p.82.

97. Cirlot, p.95.

98. Ions, pp.27–32, 41, 47, 91, and 126; Seeman, p.16.

99. Gifford, p.237.

100. Heaton, pp.81–82; Thompson, motif D581.

101. Louis Ginzberg, *The Legends of the Jews*, vol.3, p.186; Thompson, motifs B12.2 and D2061.2.1.

102. Heaton, p.82; Thompson, motif D2071.

103. Heaton, p.82.

104. Gifford, p.239; Jerome Siller et al., *Attitudes of the Nondisabled Toward the Physically Disabled*, p.52.

105. The belief in the evil eye in the present day is found in the rural sections of England, Scotland, Ireland, Scandinavia, Greece, Italy, Spain, the Middle East, India, and the Far East, and in immigrant neighborhoods in American cities (Frederick Thomas Elworthy, *The Evil Eye: The Origins and Practices of Superstition*, p.3; Louis Barron, Introduction to *The Evil Eye* by Elworthy, p.ix; Chevigny and Braverman, pp.66–67).

106. Heaton, pp.83–84; cf. Schauer, p.6.

107. Gifford, p.237; cf. Elworthy, p.8.

108. Pope, p.30.

109. Ginzberg, vol.3, p.140.

110. Thiselton–Dyer, p.218.

111. Gifford, pp.238–39; Barron, p.x; Heaton, p.82; Elworthy, p.32.

112. Seeman, p.14; Gifford, p.237; William Graham Sumner, *Folkways: A Study of the Sociological Importance of Usages, Manners, Customs, Mores, and Morals*, pp.433–35.

113. Gifford, p.238; Heaton, p.82.

114. Heaton, p.82.

115. Ibid., p.83; Crawford, p.139.

116. Crawford, p.142.

117. Elworthy, p.9.

118. Baynes, p.324; Schauer, p.7; Heaton, pp.78–79.

119. Sophocles, *Oedipus the King*, lines 1261–64.

120. Heaton, pp.80–81.

121. Ginzberg, vol.3, p.479.

122. Thompson, motif E501.18.7.

123. Baynes, p.324.

124. Cirlot, p.303.

125. Ions, p.65.

126. Ibid., pp.67 and 75; Edward S. Gifford, Jr., "Patron Gods of Vision," p.901.

127. Davidson, p.48.

128. *New Larousse Encyclopedia of Mythology*, p. 257.

129. Baynes, pp.458 and 470.

130. Cited by Heaton, p.81.

131. Ibid., p.79; Thompson, motif T327.1.

132. James Kirsch, *Shakespeare's Royal Self*, p.199; see also pp.253–54 and 256.

133. Louis Cholden, *A Psychiatrist Works With Blindness*, pp.51–52 and 82.

134. Heaton, p.77.

135. Gowman, p.24.

136. Carroll, *Blindness*, pp.12–13.

137. Ibid., pp.13 and 365.

138. Ibid., p.366.

139. Schauer, pp.6 and 9; Milton D. Graham and Leslie L. Clark, "The Social Management of Blindness," paragraph 2 (see Chapter 2, note 11, above).

140. Thompson, motifs K621 and K1011.

141. Heaton, p.83.

142. Sydell Braverman, "The Psychological Roots of Attitudes Toward Blindness," p.27; cf. Carroll, *Blindness*, pp.17–18; Imamura, p.16.

143. Heaton, p.76. Other similar mythological motifs are found in Jung, *Symbols of Transformation*, pp.267–68, and Chevigny and Braverman, pp.61–62.

144. H. Robert Blank, "Dreams of the Blind," p.166; idem., "Psychoanalysis and Blindness," p.1; Fern Lowry, "The Implications of Blindness for the Social Caseworker in Practice—Implications for the Study Process," p.84; M. Robert Barnett, "20 Centuries B.C. vs. 20 Centuries A.D.—So What Else Is New?" p.3; Heaton, p.79.

145. Braverman, pp.30–31.

146. Chevigny and Braverman, pp.169–70.

147. Braverman, pp.29 and 30.

148. Sigmund Freud, "Three Contributions to the Theory of Sex," p.568.

149. Braverman, p.27; Chevigny and Braverman, p.57.

150. Freud, p.593.

151. Blank, "Psychoanalysis and Blindness," pp.1–2.

152. Sigmund Freud, "Psychogenic Visual Disturbance According to Psycho-analytical Conceptions," p.110.

153. Ibid., p.111; cf. Blank, "Psychoanalysis and Blindness," p.1, and Chevigny and Braverman, p.62.

154. Blank, "Psychoanalysis and Blindness," pp.1–2; Lowry, pp.84–85; cf. Siller et al., pp.52–53.

155. Blank, "Psychoanalysis and Blindness," p.11; Whitmont, pp.124 and 245–46; Carroll, *Blindness,* pp.11 and 18.

156. Neumann, pp.131–91.

157. Ibid., pp.293–97.

158. C. G. Jung, *The Archetypes and the Collective Unconscious,* p.39 (hereafter cited as *Archetypes*).

159. Ibid., pp.120–21; Neumann, pp.342–49.

160. Cirlot, pp.241–42.

161. C. G. Jung, *Aion: Researches into the Phenomenology of the Self,* p.39.

162. Cirlot, pp.6–8; C. A. Burland, *The Arts of the Alchemists,* pp. 70–72.

163. The fact that only the Shadow and the Stranger–Wise Old Man archetypes are discussed in this section is not meant to imply that these are the only archetypal patterns involved in relations between a sighted and a blind person. Since such an encounter is first and foremost one between two individuals, the psychodynamics of the situation could entail any one of many archetypal patterns. The Shadow and the Stranger–Wise Old Man are simply two that seem to relate specifically to the existence of blindness in one of the participants.

164. Jung, *Archetypes,* pp.8–10; Neumann, pp.351–53; Whitmont, pp.160–69.

165. Cirlot, p.301; cf. Gordon W. Allport, *The Nature of Prejudice,* p.130.

166. Jung, *Archetypes,* pp.216–30.

167. Aniela Jaffé, "Symbolism in the Visual Arts," p.267.

168. Jung, *Archetypes,* pp.216 and 222; Whitmont, pp.182 and 226.

169. Jung, *Archetypes,* pp.226–27.

170. Ibid., pp.120–21, 128–34, 207–42; Neumann, pp.409–18; Whitmont, pp.282–90.

5 Attitude Change

1. J. Albert Asenjo, "Philosophy of Adjustment," p.17; Joseph F. Clunk, "Employer Attitudes and the Adjustment of the Blind," p.64; Gerhard Schauer, "Motivation of Attitudes Toward Blindness," p.10; Harry E. Simmons, "The Attitudes of the Sighted Toward the Blind," p.54.

2. M. Brewster Smith, "Attitude Change," p.460.

3. Ibid., p.465; Otto Klineberg, "Prejudice: The Concept," p.445; cf. M. Brewster Smith, Jerome S. Bruner, and R. W. White, *Opinions and Personality.*

4. Sadako Imamura, *A Critical Survey of the Literature on the Social Role of the Blind in the United States,* pp.22–23.

5. Smith, p.466.

6. Klineberg, p.445.

7. Gordon W. Allport, *The Nature of Prejudice,* p.328.

8. Ibid., pp.12 and 13–14.

9. Imamura, p.13; Elizabeth Hutchinson, "The Visually Handicapped Person in His Own Community," p.38.

10. Klineberg, p.440; Simmons, p.54; Beatrice A. Wright, *Physical Disability: A Psychological Approach,* p.272.

11. Thomas J. Carroll, *Blindness: What It Is, What It Does, and How to Live With It,* pp.31–32 (hereafter cited as *Blindness*); idem., "Developing Public Understanding About the Blind," pp.58–59.

12. J. M. Heaton, *The Eye: Phenomenology and Psychology of Function and Disorder,* p.86; Jacob van Weelden, *On Being Blind: An Ontological Approach to the Problem of Blindness,* p.94; cf. Allport, pp.304–5, for a discussion of "power words" and of "linguistic precedence in learning."

13. Hector Chevigny and Sydell Braverman, *The Adjustment of the Blind,* p.39; Alan G. Gowman, *The War Blind in American Social Structure,* p.11; Imamura, pp.16–17.

14. M.–L. von Franz, "The Process of Individuation," p.172.

15. Carroll, *Blindness,* pp.14–15, 18, 21; Fern Lowry, "The Implications of Blindness for the Social Caseworker in Practice—Implications for the Study Process," p.85.

16. Edward C. Whitmont, *The Symbolic Quest: Basic Concepts of Analytical Psychology,* p.60.

17. Ibid., p.69.

18. Jolande Jacobi, *Complex/Archetype/Symbol in the Psychology of C. G. Jung*, pp.25–27.

19. Whitmont, p.51.

20. Ibid., p.68.

21. Carroll, *Blindness*, p.367 (emphasis added).

22. Ibid., p.5.

23. Josef Goldbrunner, *Holiness Is Wholeness*, pp.31–32.

24. Joseph Campbell, *The Masks of God: Creative Mythology*, pp. 4–6.

25. Allport, pp.280–81; Calvin W. Fenton, *A Study of Social Workers' Attitudes Toward Blindness*, p.38.

Index

"Action sequence," 87
Ainu (Japan), 24
Alchemy, 126–27, 144, 147
Allen, E. E., 16
Ambiguous psychological situations, 78
American Foundation for the Blind, 1
Anagnos, Michael, 41
Animals, blindness in, 63
Anormalization, 98, 100, 101, 108
Archetypal images, uses of, 114, 118, 158
Archetype, 117–18
Argus Panoptes, 126
Aristotle, 24
"Asset values," 99
Asylums, 54
Athens, 24
Attitudes: affective component, 71; cognitive component, 68–69; complexity of, 3; cross-cultural, 63; cultural origins, 22; and cultural values, 88; defined, 2–3, 67; depotentiation of, 152; effects of, 1–2, 14–15, 18–19; emotional component, 113; functions of, 67; heterogeneity of, 3, 19, 80; improving, 159; irrational component, 19–20, 113; learning new, 151; organization of beliefs, 72; overt vs. covert, 151; pattern of adjustment, 69; "primary," 14, 16; "secondary," 14–16; structure, 72; symbolic component, 113; unchanging, 24; unconscious

component 113; value-expressive function, 67
Authoritarian Personality, The, 88
Avoidance, 5, 53–55, 106, 108, 109

Balance theory of sentiments, 85
Balder, 123
Balmer, E., 59
Beggars, 8–9, 40–42
Behaviors: abilities denied, 101; acceptance, 97; admitting exceptions, 102; alteration of apparent reality, 85, 86–87, 88, 97; anormalization, 98, 100, 101, 108; avoidance, 5, 53–55, 106, 108, 109; coping devalued, 99; demand that blind person admit to misery, 98–99; denial, 97; disattending, 84; distortion, 87, 144; humanness denied, 106; manipulation of the object, 97; overprotectiveness, 97, 103, 116; positive actions sought, 87; positive values denied, 103; reactions to blind people, 74; rejection, 5–6, 13, 53–55, 88, 97, 103; response tendencies, 74; reversal of usual values, 98–99; self-righteous demands, 99; succumbing valued, 99
Bible, The, 22, 26, 28–29, 31, 33–34, 36–37, 39–40, 50–51, 52, 54, 60–61
Bissat, 128
Black, 122
Blind, the: actual limitations ignored, 4; ambiguous social role, 82; appearance, 75; as they really are,

89; attitudes of, 5, 9–10, 14; carriers of psychological projection, 145; coping aspects, role of, 86; covering and social management, 78–79; developmental retardation, 93; differentiated from blindness, 83–84, 153; disadvantaged group, 105–6; emotional adjustment, 89; employment, 43, 54; exemption from anti-mendicancy laws, 41; fear of, 113; "fellow humanity," 106, 110; homogeneous group, 12–13; "honorary" normalcy, 110; importance of face-to-face contact with, 158–59; interest in, 1, 2, 22–23, 24–25; mental faculties, 89; movements, 75; not a true group, 80–81; number of, 2; ordinary acts overvalued, 48; "phantom" normalcy and "phantom" acceptance, 109–10; physical deviance, 75; posture, 75; privacy invaded, 13; right to strong, honest expectation, 86; self-concept, 89; self-limiting behavior to decrease obtrusiveness, 110; sensory and motor activities, 89; stereotyped social role, learned, 79; successful adjustment reveals other's weakness, 96

—characterized as: abnormal, 13, 14; contemplative, 14; cruel and vicious, 16; dead, 20, 54; empathic, 18; envious of the sighted, 15; evil, 48–53, 56–58; "fascinating," 20; friendly, cheerful, 18; frustrated, 101; having additional or sixth sense, 17; having better hearing, 17; having fortitude, 6; having inner vision, 129; having special gifts, 17–18; helpless, 8, 33–35, 101; hiding sorrow, 6; hypersensitive, 15; immoral, 16, 48–53, 56–58, 116; inferior, 12, 101; inner-directed, 14; living in an inner world of imagination, 20; magical, 19–20, 113; maladjusted, 15, 55, 89; miserable, 6, 27–31, 98–99; musical, 18; mysterious, 19–20, 59–62, 113; psychologically warped, 15; religious, 18; self-pitying, 15; spiritual, 18; suffering from physical and intellectual lassitude, 15–16; unable to function, 13; unfriendly and aloof, 15; unhappy, 6; useful, 10, 25, 42–46; useless, 8, 39–40, 101; yearning for sight, 15

Blind, connotations of, 83

Blinding, 29, 52, 135–42

"Blindisms," 75

"Blind man": as an image, 83; as a devaluation, 102–3

"Blindman's World, The," 64–65

Blindness: adjustment to, 154, 157; as a blessing, 18; castration, equated with, 140, 142, 143; death, compared with, 29, 52, 96; differentiated from blind person, 83–84, 153; evil, 108; guilt, shame, disgrace, 11–12; loss of consciousness, 140; loss of control, 142; loss of creative power, 140, 142; loss of general ability to function, 13; loss of identity, 143; loss of "magic," 139; loss of power, 139–40, 142; loss of self, 96; magical causes of, 62; and miracles, 60–61; other handicaps, compared with, 2, 4–6, 28–29, 30, 143; and possession, 108; punishment, 11, 48–53, 100, 109; reactions to, 95–96; sacrifice, 143; sign of inferiority, 107; sin, 100; supernatural causes, 98; symbolic death, 136–37, 138–39; and the unconscious, 146; unique position of, 2

Blind persons, historical and fictional: Anysis, 42; Bertha, 38; Billy Blind, 58; Bridgman, Laura, 32; Dea, 30, 32–33, 35, 52, 59, 62; Demodocus, 46; Eli, 34; Elymas, 51; Fortuna (Justice), 129; Gervais, 42; Gloucester, Earl of, 37–38, 51, 138; Hanawa, Hokiichi, 43; Heldar, Dick, 30–31, 35, 38, 55; Höd, 36, 123; Indrabodhi, 130–31; Isaac, 36; Jackson, Edward, 52; Lamech, 35–36; Larsen, Wolf, 45, 47–48, 57; Mackiegh,